BY GEOFF AYLING

WITH JENNY AYLING, KERRI AYLING AND JEFF AYLING

RAPID RESPONSE
ADVERTISING

AUSTRALIAN EDITION

Business & Professional Publishing

Business & Professional Publishing Pty Limited

Unit 7/5 Vuko Place
Warriewood NSW 2102
Australia

Email: info@woodslane.com.au

Copyright © 1998 Geoff Ayling,
Jenny Ayling, Kerri Ayling and Jeff Ayling.

First published in 1998

National Library of Australia
Cataloguing-in-Publication entry

    Rapid response advertising.

    ISBN 1 875680 57 8.

    1. Advertising – Australia. I. Ayling, Geoff.

  659.1

Designed by Ranya Langenfelds
Printed in Australia by Star Printery

Distributed in Australia and New Zealand by Woodslane Pty Limited. Business & Professional Publishing publications are available through booksellers and other resellers. For further information contact Woodslane Australia on +61 2 9970 5111 or Woodslane Ltd, New Zealand on +64 6 347 6543, or email info@woodslane.com.au

ABOUT THE AUTHORS

In 1967, Jenny and Geoff Ayling started a small production company with a focus on brand awareness in advertising. Today, the WAM Communications Group has turned around more than ten thousand projects for every conceivable type of business. Jenny and Geoff have been involved in over $4 billion of mainstream advertising, and have put the magic into many of the products and brands which have become household names throughout Australia and South East Asia.

If you have ever bought a loaf of Tip Top bread, been on a P & O cruise, bought a TDK cassette, or visited Strathfield Car Radio, the chances are that you have been influenced by WAM's work, and the ground-breaking ideas and concepts outlined in this book.

The WAM Communications Group is a specialist advertising agency, with a focus on results advertising. Unique in the industry, the WAM team has established a reputation for developing a clearcut, genuine competitive advantage for companies and brands of all sizes through its business development clinics.

This book is very much a collaborative effort. The original ideas and concepts it contains have been developed over time through countless hours of brainstorming and practical application as a family group. Jenny Ayling is CEO of the WAM Communications Group. Geoff Ayling, an advertising response specialist, is Executive Creative Director. Kerri is Creative Director and Jeff is Marketing Director.

WHAT AUSTRALIAN BUSINESS MANAGERS HAVE TO SAY ABOUT THIS BOOK

• 'Wow' >> Sam Linz, Chairman, Barbecues Galore • 'A complex subject made brilliantly simple with an entertaining style.' >> Jeff Grover, Managing Director, Dick Smith Electronics • 'With laser-like precision, this new technique shows how to develop crystal-clear campaign concepts that work every time.' >> John McCallum, Advertising & Promotions Manager, Countrylink • 'Timely, thought-provoking and a measurable approach to advertising and brand-building in tomorrow's world. A must read.' >> Jan Pawley, Chief Executive Officer, Ella Baché Cosmetics • 'One of the best marketing publications I have ever encountered. Outstanding!' >> Van Lucas, Marketing Manager, Melitta House of Coffee • 'This simple but remarkably fresh approach to marketing and advertising has had a significant impact on the Lite n' Easy business.' >> Graham Mitchell, Managing Director, Mitchells Quality Foods • 'At last. A practical "how to" book that brings advertising into the twenty-first century.' >> George Kafataris, Retail Operations Manager, Civic Video • 'A fascinating and thought-provoking book guaranteed to make business managers rethink their approach to advertising and marketing.' >> Patricia Field, CEO, Noble Beverages • 'A fresh, exciting and innovative approach to response advertising and brand-building for a new millenium.' >> Tom Eklot, Business Development Manager, Elna Australia • 'Written in a way that is simple to follow and easy to understand, clearing away the mystery and challenge in obtaining better results from advertising.' >> Kristina Sullivan, National Marketing Manager, Tourism Council Australia • 'The information contained is informative and demonstrates the principles of well-formulated campaigns.' >> Glenn Houston, Managing Director, Rola Roof Racks • 'Makes very clear, in an easily understood style, the basics and content of successful advertising. It will form the basis of all our future advertising and promotional expenditure.' >> Mark Hill, Managing Director, Grace Courier Systems•

ACKNOWLEDGEMENTS

We will always owe a debt of gratitude to the team at Woodslane: to Tim for believing in this project and making it happen, Kate for her marketing expertise, Jane for her seamless editing, Ranya for her innovative design work, and Anke for pulling it all together.

A special thanks to Louise Hogarth, Chris Martin-Murphy and Brian Sher for their input.

CONTENTS

INTRODUCTION

This book is directed at those chief executives, advertising managers, marketing managers, business managers, product managers and brand managers who find themselves under increasing pressure to produce better results from their advertising, but who are nevertheless operating on tight budgets. For these people, finding ways to make one advertising dollar do the work of three or four has become a number one priority.

This raises the question: 'How effective is advertising really?' According to the most up-to-date national survey of chief executives, not nearly effective enough. The survey, commissioned by The Executive Connection, an international organisation of chief executives, revealed the disturbing fact that chief executives rated advertising as providing the least value for money, behind financial planning, market research, accounting, legal services, marketing, public relations, human resources and software systems. This was despite the fact that nearly two-thirds of companies surveyed employed the services of advertising agencies.

Things don't appear to be any brighter from the public's point of view. In Grey Advertising's latest *Eye on Australia* research study (1996), a national survey of consumer attitudes, people were less than enthusiastic about the advertising which plays such a dominant part in their daily lives. Ninety per cent of people surveyed said that some advertising is so bad that it puts them off buying the product or service, 80 per cent felt that most advertising treats consumers like idiots, 64 per cent said that advertising is out of touch with everyday life, 75 per cent said that advertising bombards them with useless information and 71 per cent saw advertising as boring and repetitious. What's going on here? How can the advertising industry produce such abysmal results, from both sides of the fence?

To gain an insight into the nature and extent of the problem, try this experiment: Take a magazine, any magazine, and begin browsing through it. As you turn the pages, you'll notice that certain pieces of information hit your eyes as 'packets' of meaning which create instant comprehension. In the space of a split second, without any effort at all on your part, you understand exactly what the advertisement or article is about. In a single glance, an idea has been cleanly and accurately downloaded from one mind to another via the media. You turn a page, and *Zap!* – a packet of meaning hits you between the eyes:

Earthquakes rock LA

There is instant comprehension. You may not have any detail yet, but you understand the point of the article. You've got the plot. Then you turn the page, and *Zap!* – another packet of meaning:

World backlash against paparazzi

Again, there is instant comprehension. For most people in the civilised world, there is no doubt whatever as to what that means, particularly given the circumstances surrounding Diana's sad and untimely death in September 1997.

The alarming thing is that those packets of meaning that create instant comprehension are much more likely to come from the editorial sections than the advertising. In fact, as you turn the pages, the chances are that 90 per cent or more of the advertisements will fail to convey their key idea or proposition in an instantly clear and cogent way, if indeed they have a key proposition at all. Many advertisements are quite ambiguous, or obscure, and require you to stop and concentrate in order to figure out what they're all about. Clouded by ambiguity, some advertisements seem to challenge you to understand them. Unfortunately, many readers are not prepared to make the effort, and simply turn the page.

When you advertise, you normally have only a tiny window of opportunity of one, two or maybe three seconds in which to grab your prospect's attention, and download a stream of information. The failure of advertising to achieve this level of instant communication is the basis of its widespread ineffectiveness.

If you look analytically at the advertising you see around you, you'll come to realise that most of the problem is centred on the almost universal emphasis and value the advertising industry places on 'clever', but irrelevant, creativity. Self-indulgent creativity has become an end in itself, an ego trip that has become a status symbol among many agency creative writers and art directors. Many industry awards encourage this warped, inefficient approach to advertising. As computer graphics technology has become increasingly more sophisticated and accessible, communication has given way to aesthetics at an alarming rate.

This attitude has become so deeply entrenched, it has created a widespread phenomenon I have come to call the Lemming Effect. The Lemming Effect is a paradox, whereby otherwise astute business managers become inexplicably blind to the fact that their advertising does not actually promote their product or brand, but merely their product or brand *category*, rendering it largely ineffective. It is this peculiar inability to see what is really happening that causes far too many companies to follow each other blindly down the path to mass financial suicide.

A typical manifestation of the Lemming Effect is an advertisement for Qantas, which was on the back page of the *Good Weekend* magazine in the *Sydney Morning Herald*. It showed a man in a business suit, lying back and relaxing in business class. On his tie was a picture of himself lying back and relaxing. That creative concept doesn't promote Qantas. It promotes the generic idea of travelling business class. This is light years away from actually inspiring a prospect to choose Qantas business class above all others by creating a sense of competitive uniqueness about the airline in the public mind.

A campaign for the Peugeot 406 featured the following headline statement:

Pace and quiet

What does that mean? That it's fast and it's quiet? That description would apply to just about any modern car. If it is actually significantly faster or quieter than other comparable cars, there are much more credible ways to articulate those attributes than with a glib statement like

'Pace and quiet'. Would a top salesperson use 'Pace and quiet' as a key selling tool to entice a customer to buy a new Peugeot 406 from the showroom floor? If those words wouldn't inspire a customer at the point of sale, why would they work in an advertisement?

The profound implications of the Lemming Effect really swing into focus when you see it in high-end television commercials that cost hundreds of thousands of dollars to produce, and consume multi-million dollar media budgets. Many of these commercials have little or no ability to produce a tangible consumer response. At best, they produce a level of brand awareness which could have been achieved in a much more cost-effective way.

As the great TV physics professor Julius Sumner Miller used to ask repeatedly: 'Why is it so?' If your outcome is to produce a high level of consumer response, why in the world would you want to complicate or compromise your advertising with ambiguity, or worse, anonymity?

In his foreword to *Tested Advertising Methods* by John Caples, David Ogilvy wrote:

> Experience has convinced me that the factors that work in mail-order advertising work in *all* advertising. But the vast majority of people who work in agencies, and almost all their clients, have never heard of these factors. That is why they skid helplessly about on the greasy surface of irrelevant brilliance. They waste millions on bad advertising, when good advertising could be selling nineteen and a half times as much.

Advertising is an investment, just like any other investment, in which you outlay money in the hope of an equitable return. In normal circumstances, an investor will do everything possible to minimise risk before committing funds to an investment. But let the investment be advertising, and people who should know better take the most extraordinary risks. Every day of the week, untold millions of dollars are placed in the hands of people, many of them barely out of school, who have never sold anything in their lives, but who have exhibited a flair for creativity.

Rampant creativity has a lot to do with the consumer disenchantment with advertising as outlined above. In fact, there are two distinctly different types of creativity in advertising. There is 'creative creativity', and there is 'strategic creativity'. The first tends to be self-indulgent and largely irrelevant, while the second is the kind of creativity that draws attention, gets down to business, and influences consumer buying decisions.

Whoever came up with the line 'There's more than one way to skin a cat' could well have written those words with advertising in mind, because there are certainly many ways to produce a response from an advertisement. One way is to take any idea at all and throw enough money at it over an extended period of time. It will work – no question about it. You see it happening in the media all the time, particularly with some of the major brands. However, in the real world, the world of bread-and-butter advertising where predictable consumer response and account-ability are important issues, things are not always that easy. Many people who create advertising have stumbled upon techniques that work, simply by trial and error. Typically, these techniques tend to produce advertising that works reasonably well some, but not all, of the time. Coming up with a winning combination is generally a hit-and-miss affair, and not at all reliable.

On the client side, the responsibility for accepting an advertise-ment or a campaign submitted by an advertising agency very often falls upon business managers with the wrong skills for the task. For exam-ple, a high percentage of chief executives and general managers come from accounting backgrounds. These people are usually the first to admit that accounting, administrative, and even entrepreneurial skills do not automatically give a person an understanding of how advertising works, or the ability to recognise a good advertisement if he or she sees one. It's testimony to these people's competence that they are able to keep their companies afloat and in profit *despite* the generally poor perform-ance of their advertising.

Many of the people we at the WAM Communications Group deal with on a day-to-day basis have a degree in marketing. Marketing graduates, like accountants, are masters of measurement. They can measure the performance of an advertising campaign down to the last cent, com-plete with graphs and detailed analyses of what happened, relative to a wide range of criteria.

The problem is that advertising is an exercise in consequences, in cause and effect. Marketing graduates are taught everything there is to know about the 'effect' side of the equation, but very little of value about the side that really counts: the 'cause' side. It's not difficult to figure out why this is so. All you have to do is to look at their teachers – often the very same agency people who are responsible for the dismal results in the research studies above.

Because so much advertising is ineffective, it stands to reason that if you want to produce extraordinary results, you have to do things that most advertisers don't do. If you model your advertising on other advertising that doesn't work, then your advertising probably won't work either. Obvious as this may seem, it nevertheless happens all the time. In the following chapters, you'll be introduced to a technology, a methodology, that will revolutionise the way in which you approach your advertising.

Most of the advertising in the world today is based on ideas and concepts which are more than half a century out of date. They were formulated when consumers were naive about advertising to an extent that's difficult to imagine today. Back then there was much less competition in the marketplace, and much less competition for the consumer's attention in the media.

Today, as we approach a new millennium, we have a whole new ball game on our hands. We're facing a consumer who's smarter, more cynical, better informed and more hard-nosed than ever before. The inescapable fact is that yesterday's thinking was never designed to cope with today's problems. You'll find this book a source of many new and exciting solutions to these issues.

In Chapter 5, you'll learn how to hit the marketplace with a full-blown, ethical, genuine competitive advantage for your company or brand, even if you don't appear to be unique in any way. The WAM Rapid Response System, which is at the heart of this book, will show you how to create massive cut-through by driving that point of difference into the public mind in a way that causes people to want to buy from you.

Why does one advertisement work better than another? How can two advertisers, using the same media, with the same budget, advertising basically the same thing, produce such wildly different results? One captures the public's imagination and takes off, while the other sinks quietly into the mush and disappears. Why do some ideas, concepts and advertising campaigns seem to be quite contagious, while others are not? These intriguing questions are the subject of this book. Their answers will open up a whole new range of possibilities, and catapult you to a new level of consumer response to your advertising and marketing.

We live in an age in which competition for the consumer's attention in the media has reached flashpoint. Everywhere we look, we're deluged with advertising messages. One study suggested that the average person in a large city is subjected to something in the order of two thousand advertising impressions every twenty-four hours, but has difficulty recalling even one or two of them the following day. We passed the point of sensory overload long ago, and for the most part, advertising simply rolls off us like water from a duck's back.

This already difficult situation is exacerbated by the fact that, as time goes by, the consumer is being presented with more and more buying options. Choices abound, competition is tough right across the board, and it can only get tougher. If you want to improve the performance of your advertising, the answer is not to throw yet more money at it, but to work much smarter.

The advertising methods that worked so well fifty or more years ago don't seem to work any more. When you advertise, you're operating in an already glutted environment of media wallpaper. Under these conditions, you need to find a reliable way to consistently cause your advertisements to leap off the printed page, from the TV or the radio, if you're to break through the clutter and move ahead.

Since its origins in ancient times, advertising has grown into a quasi-science. Today there is an almost unbelievable accumulation of technical expertise, with any number of courses, seminars, books, tapes and videos available for anybody willing to study them. Yet despite this wealth of knowledge and experience, there is no doubt that the vast majority of advertising in the world today is based almost exclusively on guesswork, and the big missing element is control.

The idea that advertising is largely ineffective is not new. This was whimsically articulated by William Wrigley Jr, the great chewing gum magnate, at a time when he already dominated his industry with a clear market leadership. At that time, he was one of the biggest advertisers in America, spending vast amounts of money. This gave him access to the best advertising brains that money could buy. But in the face of all that expertise, and all that financial clout, he made the most extraordinary statement:

> I know that half of my advertising is wasted, but I do not know which half.

Does that sound familiar to you? Does it ring any bells? Is this something you can relate to? At our company, the WAM Communications Group, we found ourselves wondering whether that statement was simply a figure of speech, or whether it could possibly be something more widespread; something endemic throughout the business community. To find out for ourselves, we decided to conduct an informal research study over several years. During that time, we asked every new client, business associate and seminar audience an interesting question:

With the benefit of hindsight, how much of your last year's advertising expenditure do you feel was utterly wasted?

Across the board, regardless of the industry, their replies ranged from *40 per cent to 90 per cent!*

When you extrapolate this across a thirteen billion dollar advertising industry, you begin to see the enormity of the problem.

But then William Wrigley went on to say another interesting thing, this time in response to a question (and I'm paraphrasing here). Somebody said: 'Mr Wrigley, why do you still need to advertise to the extent you do? You're the market leader. You're so far ahead of the competition that it doesn't matter. But still we see you on television every day, and in magazines and on billboards right across America. Why do you need to do that?' He replied:

If you were racing across the desert in a train at eighty miles an hour, why would you want to unhook the engine?

And with those two insights, William Wrigley put his finger on the great dilemma that continues to haunt business managers throughout the world today. Although they know that much of their advertising is ineffective, they feel they can't stop, because advertising of one kind or another is their only real lifeline to the marketplace – their source of new customers. This attitude was reflected in the survey of chief executives referred to earlier. Even though they saw advertising as being poor value for money, 67 per cent said that they would be outsourcing advertising services over the following two years. It reflects a widespread attitude of 'damned if you do, and damned if you don't'.

The purpose of this book is to provide you with some new and exciting tools and techniques that will enable you to see advertising in a new way. By the time you're through, you'll have the insights to allow you to predict the effectiveness of any print, radio or television advertisement, or any direct mail piece, with a high degree of accuracy. You'll be able to apply this knowledge to your own advertising and marketing to produce results well beyond your present expectations.

In my professional role as a marketing troubleshooter, I find it fascinating to work with all kinds of people, ranging from university-trained marketing directors and chief executives of huge corporations to medium- and small-business managers. Ultimately they're all trying to do the same thing: to achieve a better response from their advertising expenditure.

They know exactly what they want the outcome to be but, with some notable exceptions, a glance at their past five years' advertising makes it clear that neither these clients nor their advertising agencies has a clue about how to accomplish it.

The irony is that their advertising is invariably formulated in a way that *precludes* any likelihood of success. The point of the advertisement is hidden behind a mask of cryptic or 'clever' creativity. When this happens, the advertisement is practically guaranteed to fail. There is no place for ambiguity in advertising.

Think about it. If you're flying an aeroplane, you're bound by certain immutable laws of physics, and you break any of them at your peril. This is why airline pilots all over the world follow identical procedures and conventions. The same applies to advertising. If you're trying to create a successful advertisement, you're bound by certain immutable laws of *psychology*, and if you break even one of them, your outcome will suffer to that extent. The problem is that very few people who create advertising know about these laws, or how to deal with them.

If your desired outcome is to create consistently successful advertising, you need to take every opportunity to hit your prospect between the eyes with those instant packets of meaning. You must be able to frame each key idea in a way that creates instant comprehension. The secret to accomplishing this lies in an exciting new technology.

Everybody is aware that when water is cooled beyond a certain point, its physical characteristics change radically, and it transforms into something quite different, that is, ice.

However, very few people are aware that in the same way, when an idea or concept is *simplified* beyond a certain point, its character radically changes, and it transforms into something quite different, called a 'meme' (pronounced *meem*). In this new form, it takes on many of the key characteristics of a virus. It becomes contagious, with the ability to spread rapidly from one mind to another with frightening agility.

We've always been aware of the importance of simplicity in advertising. This has given rise to admonitions like the KISS principle (Keep It Simple, Stupid). The message of this book is that it is not only possible, but imperative, to raise simplicity in advertising to an art form, and in the process, produce a dramatic increase in your level of advertising response. The key to achieving this lies in the new science of meme technology, which will be discussed in detail in the following chapters. You'll learn how to use memes to make your advertisements leap off the printed page, from the television or radio, from billboards – in fact, from any media at all.

Once you have an understanding of memes, and you begin to see their profound effect, you'll find yourself looking at advertising from a very different perspective. You'll experience a new level of control, and the advertising process will become greatly simplified and demystified.

There's an old maxim: 'If you do what you've always done, you'll get what you've always got.' Instead of doing the same old things the same old way, and getting the same old results, you're about to shift your advertising into an exciting world of memes, Hot Zones and Activators.

You're about to discover a wealth of brand-new information, and a whole new approach to advertising that puts the meme concept into the context of an integrated system that will lift your consumer response to a new level of effectiveness. Through this new cutting-edge technology, you'll learn how to blitz your competition, and in the process, explode your bottom line profits.

Good luck. Hang on and enjoy the ride.

Geoff Ayling
Greenwich

CHAPTER 1

THE MAGIC OF THE MEME

If the consumer has to stop and figure out what you're trying to say, forget it. It probably isn't going to work.

Through his work in genetics, Oxford biologist Richard Dawkins discovered a hitherto unnoticed aspect of human evolution. In 1976 he coined the word 'meme' in his book, *The Selfish Gene*. Through this discovery, Richard Dawkins identified the mind mechanism that drives cultural development through the propagation of ideas. This breakthrough has spawned a whole new branch of science called 'memetics'.

Although the meme has been the subject of scientific discussion by many eminent and distinguished people, it has remained more or less confined to the scientific community, isolated from the industry that perhaps could most benefit from it: the advertising industry.

The meme is the missing piece to the advertising puzzle. It's the missing link that pulls it all together in a way that finally begins to make sense.

So what is a meme? Among other things, it has been called a mind virus because of its contagious nature. Richard Dawkins' definition of the meme is 'a basic unit of cultural transmission or imitation'. This definition, accurate though it may be, is not particularly helpful in establishing an understanding of the concept.

A good place to start is through an analogy. In algebra, you can nominate anything at all, and abbreviate it by calling it X, which then symbolises that idea within a calculation. The simple X carries an identical meaning to the more complex idea it embodies. It is compressed information.

Memes work in exactly the same way, but with an important distinction. The symbolic meaning of X in a calculation is always *predetermined*, while the symbolic meaning of a meme in a communication is always *self-explanatory*.

Meme technology is simple. Imagine being able to routinely take any idea or concept you wanted to communicate to the public through your advertising, and chunk it down until you were left with the essence of the idea expressed as a symbol, with the functional simplicity of X. Because of both its extreme simplicity and its self-explanatory nature, a meme is able to slip into the mind very easily and create instant understanding. This is why memes have such a natural affinity with advertising.

This book introduces the meme concept to the world of advertising, where companies and brands live or die on their ability to communicate key concepts quickly and efficiently to a marketplace already suffering from information overload.

COMMUNICATING IDEAS

We communicate with each other by symbolising our thoughts through words, pictures, sounds, actions or imagery. A meme can be any of these things. Our inner thoughts are represented by external symbols. The simplicity of these symbols, known as memes, makes rapid transmission of ideas and concepts possible.

•

>> **A meme is a self-explanatory symbol representing a complete idea.**

•

Memes are those packets of compressed information that create instant comprehension. People look at a page, see the symbol (a meme) and, in a split second, understand the larger concept. Through the astute use of memes, a deceptively simple advertisement can convey a deep level of meaning to the consumer.

People invariably find the meme concept tricky to grasp at first, because it is so unfamiliar. As you discover for yourself what it can do, however, you'll begin to understand why the meme is unquestionably the most powerful and exciting concept to hit the advertising industry since positioning.

There is much more to memes than meets the eye. As we develop the concept, the following may prove helpful:

1   A meme is a self-explanatory symbol representing a complete idea.
2   A meme is the 'lowest common denominator' of an idea or concept; a basic unit of communication.
3   We communicate our thoughts by externally symbolising them as words, pictures, sounds, actions and imagery. A meme can be any of these things.
4   A defining characteristic of the meme is its extraordinary ability to dictate and orchestrate patterns of behaviour.
5   A meme is a replicator, and leaves copies of itself as it spreads from mind to mind.
6   A meme is contagious to the extent that it is laced with emotion.

Imagine the following scenario:

A caveman is standing in a stream catching fish. He comes from a tribe in which the only known way to catch a fish is to pluck it out of the water by hand. A little later, he discovers a cave with a rock painting on the wall. The painting depicts a man standing on the bank of a stream spearing a fish on the end of a sharp stick.

In the space of a split second, he understands. In an instant, a totally new technology takes root in his mind. Excited, he races back to his tribe to tell them about his discovery. The idea then spreads like wildfire until it has replicated itself in the mind of every person in that community. The cave painting, in its extreme simplicity, constitutes a visual meme; an icon representing a complex idea which is able to be transmitted and replicated in a moment.

Ultimately, the most relevant aspect of the meme, at least from the perspective of advertising and marketing, is its unique ability to influence consumer buying decisions.

A meme orchestrates human behaviour in the same way that your PC's printer driver software orchestrates your printer's behaviour.

>> **Memes are the mental software drivers that dictate and orchestrate human behaviour.**

In the above example, the man began with the belief that the only way he could catch a fish was with his bare hands. Then he was exposed to the meme, which downloaded into his mental database at lightning speed. Based on the proposition embodied in the meme (he could catch a fish on the end of a sharp stick), his perceptions altered. A new belief formed. He took the meme at face value, and responded predictably. His new mental driver software (the new meme) orchestrated a sequence of behaviour not only in him, but in everybody subsequently affected by it. These people can be said to have 'caught' a contagious meme in the way that they might have caught a cold. As a direct result of this, they can now be observed standing along the riverbank spearing fish on the ends of sharp sticks. Memes are the architects and the blueprints of human behaviour.

A WORKING DEFINITION OF THE MEME IN THE CONTEXT OF ADVERTISING

Since Richard Dawkins coined the term, scientists have given the meme various definitions, depending upon their particular discipline. However, this practical definition puts it in a nutshell:

> In the context of advertising, a meme is an idea or concept that has been refined, distilled, stripped down to its bare essentials and then super-simplified in such a way that anybody can grasp its meaning *instantly* and effortlessly.

Memes can consist of words, pictures, sounds, symbols or actions, individually or in combination. Because a meme is self-explanatory, no effort is required to comprehend or grasp its meaning. Consequently, because of its extreme simplicity, a meme has the ability to enter the mind without our conscious awareness, and plant a thought in there.

To be effective in an advertisement, a meme must strike a strong emotional chord in the consumer. Imagine a motorist driving along a highway, just rounding a bend. Suddenly a large billboard comes into view, showing a mutilated child, an ambulance, paramedics, flashing lights, weeping parents and a grim police officer. The bold caption consists of two words:

Speed kills.

The combined effect of the photograph and the caption constitutes a visual meme which instantly, effortlessly and lucidly transmits an entire complex concept into a human mind in a single involuntary glance. If you happened to be exceeding the speed limit and came across that sign, there is every chance you would find yourself modifying your speed without even thinking about it at the rational level.

•

>> **Memes have an enormous impact on our lives. Being instantaneous transmitters of information, they invade our minds without either our knowledge or our permission, and initiate a chain reaction. Acting both above and below the cognitive threshold of awareness, memes create an involuntary shift in perception. This creates a shift in attitude, which creates a shift in behaviour, which is the ultimate goal of all advertising.**

•

Returning to our example, you can see that there would be many other ways to execute that 'don't speed' concept which would not cause it to leap off the poster in the same way. A meme's power to influence lies in its extreme simplicity. Unfortunately, many millions of dollars are wasted every year on advertising that is either 'clever' to the point of being cryptic, or just bland and meaningless. For all the effect such advertising has, it might as well be invisible. This applies equally to television, print, radio, outdoor advertising and direct mail.

•

>> **As a general rule, you have only a second or two in which to grab your prospect's attention, and download a stream of information. When you consider that within those two seconds you have to convey a feeling of who you are and why somebody should buy from you rather than one of your competitors,**

trigger an emotional response, and generate a desire for whatever it is you're trying to sell, the value of memes immediately becomes apparent.

•

The secret to achieving spectacular results from your advertising is the new technology of effective meme management. If your prospect has to stop and figure out what you're trying to say, forget it: it's probably not going to work. This is the problem with advertising that is based on tricky turns of phrase and 'creative' ideas. These kinds of advertisements often win industry awards and satisfy the egos of the people who created them, but they have very little power to produce a measurable, positive consumer response.

When advertising fails, it fails at the strategic level. Whenever you're creating advertising, you're in the psychology business, whether you like it or not. The message of this book is that creativity should always be executed within the framework of a cogent strategy. It should make immediate and logical sense to the consumer.

Conventional thinking separates advertising into two main categories. First there is institutional or brand advertising. This is specifically designed to create a brand personality, a market positioning and a general feeling for the product or brand. It is not normally intended to produce immediate and measurable results in terms of sales. Institutional advertising tends to blur reality by presenting the product or brand in a fantasy setting that often bears little or no relationship to the way things actually are. This is where creativity tends to run amok.

Then there is the poor cousin, retail advertising, which is designed to produce sales. The sad thing about the majority of the retail advertising you see around you is that it is focused almost exclusively on price. Much of it is rendered impotent by outmoded ideas and concepts, and created by either directly stealing, or bouncing ideas and concepts from competitors' advertising. Unfortunately, this is nearly always a case of the blind leading the blind, and explains why so much retail advertising looks so similar.

As you begin to get a grasp on the concepts outlined in this book, you will see clearly that it is essential to find a way to run both types of advertising *simultaneously*, if your objective is to optimise your advertising and marketing dollars.

•

>> Memes are the mental software drivers that dictate which products and services a consumer will or will not buy.

MEME TECHNOLOGY

Without question, the most effective advertisements are those which say what they have to say in an instant. Even though there may be many details contained within the advertisement, the core message leaps off the page, or from the TV screen or the radio, and is instantly understood. Creating advertising that does this, however, is easier said than done. The secret lies in the astute use of memes. With memes, the pattern of consumer response to advertising can be accelerated.

There is more to memes than meets the eye. The aim in this section is not to present a detailed scientific or philosophical discussion, but to give you a basic intuitive feel for the concept of memes, an understanding of their awesome power to affect consumer attitudes and their practical application to the specific area of advertising and marketing.

Just as you don't need to have a degree in computing sciences to operate your PC, you don't need to be a biology professor to incorporate the meme concept into your next advertisement. Before you can effectively import them into the world of advertising, you need to take a close look at exactly what memes are, and what they are not, and how and why they work the way they do. To do this you need to take a step back, and look at the meme in its broader context, and gain an understanding of its integral role in the development of human culture.

THE ORIGIN
AND NATURE OF MEMES

Perhaps the best way to approach the subject is to take our cue from Richard Dawkins. In *The Selfish Gene*, Dawkins draws definitive parallels between memes and genes. He points out that for the past three thousand million years or so, genes have ruled the earth. If you were talking about replicators, the gene was the only show in town. Through the process of self-replication, the gene mechanism is responsible for the bewildering diversity of life forms we see around us, as well as those which have become extinct along the way. In order to be successful replicators, genes had to have three essential characteristics:

1   longevity – the ability to stand the test of time
2   fecundity – fertility and the ability to replicate abundantly
3   copying fidelity – the ability to create accurate self-copies over an extended period of time.

It occurred to Dawkins that at some point in human evolution, for the first time, a new replicator had entered the picture. The medium for its development was not biological, but the evolution of human culture. Its incubator was the human mind. The new replicator was, basically, cultural imitation: the idea of copying ideas. To quote from *The Selfish Gene*:

> Geoffrey Chaucer could not hold a conversation with a modern Englishman, even though they are linked to each other by an unbroken chain of some twenty generations of Englishmen, each of whom could speak to his immediate neighbours in the chain as a son speaks to his father. Language seems to 'evolve' by non-genetic means, and at a rate which is orders of magnitude faster than genetic evolution ...
>
> ... I think a new kind of replicator has recently emerged on this very planet. It is staring us in the face. It is still in its infancy, still drifting clumsily about in its primeval soup, but already is achieving evolutionary change at a rate that leaves the old gene panting far behind.
>
> The new soup is the soup of human culture. We need a name for the new replicator, a noun that conveys the idea of cultural transmission, or a unit of imitation. 'Mimeme' comes from a suitable Greek root, but I want a monosyllable that sounds a bit like 'gene'. I hope my classicist friends will forgive me if I abbreviate mimeme to 'meme'.

Like a gene, in order to be a successful replicator, a meme must have the same three essential qualities: longevity, fecundity and copying fidelity.

As you know by now, a meme can be many things: a word, a group of words, a sound, a visual image, a ceremony, a mannerism, a design, a symbol, or any number of ways of instantly transmitting a complex thought or an idea. As Daniel C. Dennett points out in his book *Consciousness Explained*:

> A wagon with spoked wheels carries not only grain or freight from place to place; it carries the brilliant idea of a wagon with spoked wheels from mind to mind.

We see the contagious effects of memes about us all the time, particularly with fashion, fads, music and design. One day everything's normal, the next day an idea seems to have caught on everywhere. We saw this phenomenon in action very vividly with the global explosion of ideas like the hula hoop, skateboarding, rollerblading, the miniskirt, Beatle haircuts … the list is endless. Concepts like these seem to race through the community like a brush fire.

A meme operates through the process of chunking a complex concept or idea down into a simple, easily communicable unit. Imagine this scenario:

At some point in human evolution, a number of people had a hazy notion of some kind of spiritual entity which exerted an unpredictable and sometimes malevolent influence on their lives. Then some individual coined the word 'God', or one of its variations. Suddenly there was a way to chunk the idea down into a single word (a meme), which represented the entire concept. Then the idea was free to leap from mind to mind, uncluttered by the burden of detail. Once the concept became installed via the meme, the detail could come later. You have only to travel around the towns and cities of Europe to see the effect of the 'God' meme. Without exception, the centrepiece of each city and town is some kind of imposing church, many of which have stood for centuries.

The meme is the mechanism which allows us to mentally import concepts such as 'Honesty', 'Compassion' or 'Children should be seen and not heard'. Once imbedded in our minds, often in childhood, these memes form the bedrock of our social conditioning and direct every aspect of our behaviour.

MEME EVOLUTION

The meme concept can be awkward to grasp at first, because it does not fit comfortably within people's conventional mode of thinking. Technically, a meme can be said to be anything which has been learned, because in order for learning to occur, a concept must be transferred from one mind to another.

This is where things become confusing. For example, all of the words used to describe the world around us are memes. Now you might jump in and say: 'Hang on a minute! That means that *everything* is a meme. How can that possibly be useful as a concept?' In fact, there is much, much more to the meme concept than first meets the eye. This is why science has become so preoccupied with it.

Consider this scenario:

The clock has been wound back a few million years. There are three nomadic tribes living on a large continent and separated by vast distances. All these tribes have become aware of a type of small green creature with protruding eyes. These creatures hop about and inhabit creeks and ponds. The leader of tribe A, hearing the distinctive sound of this creature, decides to call it a 'ribbit'. He gathers the tribe together and passes on this information. Soon everybody in the tribe knows what a ribbit is, and it becomes a part of that tribe's vernacular. The word 'ribbit', within this insular group, is an identity meme. It is a verbal representation of a concept. 'Hey Dad! I'm going out to catch some ribbits' has a definitive meaning to people within this culture.

Meanwhile, a similar story is unfolding within tribe B. The difference here is that the leader, also hearing the distinctive sound of the creature, decides to call it a 'ne-deep'. She goes back to her tribe, passes on this information, and now everybody in tribe B knows what a ne-deep is. It becomes part of that tribe's vernacular.

While all this is happening, the leader of tribe C, observing how the creature moves about, decides to call it a 'hop'. In tribe C 'hop' now becomes the accepted term for that creature.

These three isolated communities can live quite happily with their three separate memes. The problems begin when the tribes eventually connect and try to communicate with each other. Arguments then ensue as to which is the correct meme for the creature. At some point, when these three tribes agree to join forces and merge, the three memes will find themselves locked in a battle to the death, along the lines of Darwin's theory of natural selection. A meme can be successful within an insular group, but a failure within the wider community. The newly assimilated tribe must decide on one meme for the creature, and the other two will simply wither and die through lack of general acceptance.

Then, several million years later, someone comes along and coins the term 'frog'. For whatever reason, the 'frog' meme hit the jackpot. It gained universal acceptance. All other memes for the creature went the way of the dinosaur and the dodo. Today, every person in the English-speaking world has a copy of the 'frog' meme permanently installed in his or her mind.

Interestingly, this identical process has occurred in cultures throughout the world. Every French-speaking person knows what a grenouille is. Every German-speaking person knows what a frosch is, and every Hungarian-speaking person knows what a béca is. These 'frog' memes have taken on all comers and emerged the clear winners in each culture. The familiar, everyday words we use to describe the world have all been through a similar process of natural selection.

For many years, lawyers around the world have been able to obtain lenient judgements for their clients on the basis of 'temporary insanity'. 'Temporary insanity' is a justification meme and, in the hands of a capable lawyer, can lead to the acquittal of even violent and malicious people.

At present a new meme, 'road rage', is finding its way into the contemporary lexicon. Historically, driving in a menacing and dangerous way, regardless of provocation, was regarded as a self-indulgent, antisocial crime of violence, and carried harsh penalties. Recently, however, this idea of 'road rage' has gained momentum. Suddenly, there is a new potential source of blame. Like temporary insanity, 'I was a victim of road rage' is a defence we will hear more frequently as this new meme becomes integrated into our culture. It is quite sobering to reflect on the power that a meme like this has, not only on our judicial system, but upon the way people are able to sidestep responsibility and justify actions which would otherwise be seen as indefensible.

A fascinating battle for meme supremacy occurred in the late 1960s, when Australia changed over from the British imperial system to decimal currency. Being a dedicated royalist, the then Prime Minister, Bob Menzies, announced with complete conviction that Australia's new unit of currency would be the 'royal'. The newspapers of the day were full of it, and people were horrified. Lobbying for the 'dollar' began in earnest. The more the public began to protest, the more the Prime Minister declared his immovable stance on the issue. He was determined to implant the 'royal' meme into the Australian culture, no matter what. And Australians didn't want a bar of it.

Anti-royal graffiti began to appear on buildings throughout Australia. 'Out royal, in dollar', it said. Gradually the media began to pick up on the issue. Finally the Prime Minister was forced to cave in to public opinion, and the 'royal' went to that great meme graveyard in the sky, along with 'ribbit', 'ne-deep' and 'hop'. The 'dollar' meme won the day and, as they say, the rest is history.

A distinguishing characteristic of a meme is its universal, or at least widespread, general acceptance throughout an entire cultural group. The point here is that each of the words we habitually use and take for granted today is the clear winner of a life and death struggle for survival. As we learn each new word, we simply accept it, never comprehending its true memetic nature.

TRANSFER
OF INFORMATION

In order to make maximum use of available resources, technologies such as the Internet and satellite transmission use a method of transferring data from one place to another that involves breaking information down into 'packets', which are transmitted very quickly in short bursts, and then automatically collated and decoded at the other end.

Memes work in exactly the same way, but with an added feature. They have the ability to enter our minds without our knowledge, our awareness, or our permission.

Once they have become imbedded in our minds and integrated into our cognitive reality, memes have a profound effect upon the way we perceive the world and, consequently, upon our belief patterns and our subsequent behaviour.

THE POWER OF THE MEME

In Australia during the mid-1970s, the Liberal Government was un-ceremoniously dumped after an unprecedentedly long term in office by a simple, two-word meme:

It's time.

These two words became the battle cry of the Labor Party, the linchpin of the devastating advertising campaign that swept it to power. People who had been quite happy with the status quo began to speculate that perhaps the Libs had been in office a bit too long, and that maybe a change in government was well overdue.

The power of the 'It's time' meme lies in the fact that it is far more than meets the eye. It is not merely two words on a page. It's a complex idea chunked down to two rapid-fire words which carry a clear subtext. That meme contains a depth of meaning and innuendo that belie its simplicity. It is essentially an icon which represents and instantly trans-mits a message with a deeper meaning, a more complex idea. A meme is basically a type of cognitive shorthand.

It is essential here to make the distinction between a meme and a slogan. A meme can certainly be used as a slogan, but most slogans do not qualify as memes. More often than not, the slogans that many companies and brands adopt are really just glib statements that represent nothing more than wishful thinking.

Memes, however, accurately capture the essence of a concept, and rapidly spread through the community, essentially by stealth. More often than not, people have no idea they have taken a meme on board. As the result of a casual glance, a meme can take root in the mind and begin to modify attitudes and behaviour at the pre-cognitive level.

Memes put the magic into advertising. Often a meme will take the form of an exceptionally clear and lucid statement like 'Strong pain, powerful Panadene'. A meme like that can and does work very well on its own. The addition of a dynamic, emotive photograph or illustration that people can easily relate to can produce a deceptively simple communication that leaps off a billboard or the page of a magazine and instantly modifies the way people think and behave.

THE COMPUTER ANALOGY

In order to understand the meme mechanism better, it is useful to return to the computer analogy. When you download a file from the Internet, it arrives down the telephone line as a compressed packet of information. Before you can access the information contained in the file, it has to be decompressed by a program such as Zipit™ or Stuffit Expander™, which restores the file to its original form.

On a billboard, a meme is just a meme. The eyes see the words 'It's time' (a compressed packet of information), which you voluntarily or involuntarily 'download' from a newspaper banner or an advertisement into your mental database in an instant, often without even knowing it. From there the chain reaction begins, as the words are 'decompressed' into various layers and levels of meaning by your unconscious cognitive processing and assimilated into your personal reality. The mind operates as a kind of 'meme incubator', altering and modifying your attitudes in a way that causes you to see things in a different way, as though through a distorted lens.

From that point, repeated exposure to that meme over time serves to compound the perception and reinforce the concept. Not only did the 'It's time' meme transmit from the various forms of media to individual minds, but by means of social conversation, discussion and debate, the concept quite literally leapt from mind to mind until it swept through the community like a virus. The rest is history. That is the power of the meme.

A CLOSER LOOK AT MEMES

When you are beginning to understand the nature of memes, there is a tendency to conclude that a meme is simply a belief. This is not so. A meme is the precursor to a belief, the proposition upon which a belief is formed. Let's look at some of the things memes are, and some of the things they are not:

- A belief is a feeling of certainty about what something means. A meme is the source of information which created that feeling of certainty.
- A belief is an effect. A meme is a cause.
- A belief is an attitude which springs from an idea. A meme is a simplified representation of an idea.
- A belief is a feeling, a mental disposition or inclination. A meme is essentially an icon with an implied subtext.
- A belief is internal. A meme is external until it replicates. The copy then becomes internalised, and develops into a belief.
- A belief can last a lifetime. A meme can invade the mind in an instant.
- A belief is an expanded attitude to life. A meme is a compressed and highly transmissible packet of information.
- A meme is the quickest and most effective way to transmit and receive complex concepts from one mind to another.
- Conscious consideration takes time. A meme is transmitted in a moment.
- A meme can be consciously questioned and overridden, rendering it impotent.

Once a meme has created a duplicate of itself in a mind, it can quickly and easily develop into a contagious, communicable belief, which perpetuates its growth as it spreads through the community. In order for a meme to become contagious, there are three prerequisites:

1	extreme simplicity (in terms of the core message)
2	emotional impact (the stronger the better)
3	critical mass (enough people must be exposed to it).

Advertising, by its very nature, is able to consistently deliver these three factors very easily. This is what makes it the ideal medium to capitalise on the explosive power of meme technology. If you take a step back and analyse some of the most effective advertising campaigns of all time, you'll find that these three elements are absolutely funda-mental to their success.

The other side of this coin, however, is that if a meme is able to be intercepted and 'locked out' of the mind by conscious appraisal and rejection, it is effectively neutralised. In fact, we do this all the time. We see advertisements that are so blatantly manipulative or patronising that we instantly dismiss them as irrelevant. We see right through them, and ignore them. It is the covert memes that are the most successful.

As Richard Dawkins points out, when we talk about memes 'invading the mind', or people being 'infected by a mind virus', we understand that nobody is suggesting that either genes or memes are alive or aware, or that they operate from a position of consciousness. Turns of phrase like these are strictly metaphorical. Both genes and memes are simply very effective data processors. They are both merely bundles of information. However, in order to work effectively with either entity, it is useful to regard them as though they were alive, because they certainly behave as though they were.

The meme concept is inclined to be ambiguous and rather slippery. In trying to understand memes, it is not difficult to conclude that a meme is just an idea. But the distinction is that although a meme is an idea, an idea is not necessarily a meme.

Even if an idea has the potential, it does not become a successful meme, a potent replicator, until it is distilled, compressed, simplified and focused, laced with emotion, and then held out in a way that can be instantly communicated through a variety of media. The main considerations when dealing with memes are compressed information, extreme simplicity, emotional impact, and the attitudes and predispositions of the recipient.

MEMES ARE THE BASIS OF HUMAN CULTURE

A meme is not just a subversive, manipulative device dreamed up by some advertising agency. Rather, a meme is a by-product of our evolutionary psychology, a part of nature and, as such, a crucial part of our survival mechanism. Having evolved in tandem with human culture, memes have been around for a long time, and in fact are the very basis for our perception of the world as we see it today. It is only recently that they have been isolated and identified, and that we have begun to study them and reveal their true nature, and understand their implications.

Complex concepts are effectively compressed and loaded into simple memetic expressions. Ideas such as religion, faith, God, life after death, heaven, hell, superstition, marriage, linear time, space, geographic boundaries, right and left, right and wrong, capitalism, democracy, racism, discrimination, astrology, cults, shaking hands, monogamy, celibacy, promiscuity, ceremonies, hygiene, protocols, fashion, dancing, music, skiing, currency, games, social status, politics, design and sport are just a few of the memes which have made our world what it is today.

There is nothing about human culture today that existed in pre-history. As individuals dreamt up various ideas and concepts, the memes that represented those ideas and concepts went through a process identical to that of genetic selection: the survival of the fittest. Memes either 'lived' or 'died', depending upon their ability to replicate themselves in the minds of many.

Science has shown us that memes are the agents that quite literally sculpt our neural circuitry and set the direction of our lives. The mind of a baby is 'neutral' at birth. The memes which are imbedded from that point on dictate that person's future life experience. Muslim memes are going to create a radically different life experience from, say, Christian memes, agnostic memes, atheistic memes or Taoist memes. As each successful meme was instilled into the minds of more people, a vast and intricate cultural infrastructure began to develop. The world we see around us today is nothing but the sum total of the fittest memes that have withstood the test of time.

From the time we are born and take our place in the world, we accept the status quo, quite oblivious to the true nature of the accumulated memetic environment in which we live. This is why neither language nor culture remain static. They grow in response to a constant input of new, better and more successful memes.

Like genes, memes are passed on through countless generations of people. For example, the ubiquitous children's game, 'Ring a Ring of Roses', is a memetic encapsulation of the infamous Black Plague which swept through most of Europe in the Middle Ages. The 'ring of roses' refers to the circular sores which erupted on the skin of those infected. A 'pocket full of posies' refers to the small package of highly scented flowers that people would carry about in their pockets to disguise the cloying smell of sickness in the air. 'A-tishoo', is, of course, the sound of people sneezing as the virus went about its wretched business, and 'we all fall down' relates to those who succumbed to the disease and lay where they fell.

Once imbedded, memes colour our perceptions, shape our attitudes and modify our belief patterns, and therefore our behaviour. 'A woman's place is in the home' is a meme which has had a devastating effect on women's quality of life and place in society for longer than any of us cares to think. Relatively recently a more empowering meme, 'Equality for all' has transformed life for many women throughout the western world.

MEMES IN ADVERTISING

The idea of memes in advertising raises some interesting questions. For instance, if memes are indeed the building blocks of successful advertising, and the meme concept was not even identified until 1976, why was there so much effective advertising before then? The simple answer is that just as some people have a natural affinity with things like music, art and mechanics, some people also have an affinity with memes.

The fact that famous musicians such as John Lennon and Paul McCartney had no formal musical education did not stop them writing some of the most loved music in the world. In the same way, certain advertising writers have become legendary because of their ability to consistently produce highly effective advertising, David Ogilvy of Ogilvy and Mather fame being a prime example. However, when you take the time to analyse the work of these people, it becomes immediately apparent that their advertisements are loaded to the teeth with highly potent and contagious memes.

You may also find yourself asking why, if the concept of memes is as powerful as it seems to be, has the advertising industry not latched onto it before now? The answer to that is both simple and profound. Because the 'meme' meme (the complex idea which the word represents) is quite new, its meaning has not yet spread to any extent beyond the scientific community and students of popular psychology. Until recently, the only people to have become aware of the 'meme' meme are scholars, who have been more interested in considering the social and cultural ramifications of memetics than the more mercenary purpose of advertising. We hope this book will help to change that situation by making the meme more user-friendly, and bringing the meme concept into popular usage. There is no doubt that once a critical mass of people who advertise come to grasp its implications, it will spread like wildfire. Recently Don Beck and Christopher Cowan published *Spiral Dynamics*, a book which takes the meme concept into uncharted waters with a revolutionary concept they call ^VMEMEs. *Spiral Dynamics* is a report of a deep and complex study which reveals the hidden codes that shape human nature, create global diversities and drive evolutionary change.

As Dawkins points out, unlike the sleepy gene, meme evolution is exploding at an exponential rate. In an incredibly short space of time, meme awareness has gone from obscurity to the point where an Internet search will reveal ever-increasing masses of information. The term 'meme' is now in common usage in computer programming terminology. It is only a matter of time before it breaks through into the world of mainstream advertising, and it is up to us to be there at the cutting edge to take full advantage of the benefits and insights it offers.

THE SUBLIMINAL NATURE OF THE MEME

A classic advertising teaching device is to imagine each member of the public as having an antenna sticking out from the top of his or her head. These antennas are tuned into a radio station called WIIFM (an acronym for 'What's in it for me?'). And that's exactly how it is. Our minds are fitted with a kind of 'opportunity scanner' that operates constantly, pulling in any information which seems to be of interest right now, or which may be worth filing away for future use. Everything else is filtered from our consciousness by a mind mechanism called the Reticular Activating System.

And it is here, from an advertising viewpoint, that memes come into their own. Whereas a conscious discussion, for example with a sales person, can be rationally considered and then be either accepted or rejected, a meme enters the mind with impunity at the pre-cognitive level as an impression. This impression registers unconsciously as a feeling. This feeling is entered in our mental database as a biochemical marker, which is then programmed to spring to top of mind in response to an appropriate stimulus or need. If there is more than one marker, then we produce a menu of options. These biochemical markers are used to recall the appropriate memes on cue in response to specific needs or wants.

We tend to recall memes rather than long information files because the simplicity of the meme offers the mind the path of least resistance. Once the meme has been consciously validated, we can then access more detailed information from our mental database at our leisure. When we have to think quickly, it's easier for the mind to juggle memes than to sort through masses of detailed information. It is through this process that memes have become an integral part of our survival mechanism, providing as they do a quick, simple and reliable way of acting in our own best interests. This is, after all, the object of genetic evolution.

MEMES ARE EMOTIONAL BUTTON-PUSHERS

The most potent memes are those that push the right emotional hot buttons. Imagine yourself as having a kind of internal control panel. It would put the control panel of a commercial airliner to shame. It would be bristling with buttons of all kinds. There would be three big buttons in the middle, labelled 'Fear', 'Food' and 'Sex'. Being primal and basic to our survival, these have always been the 'big three', and advertisements which can find a way of pushing any or all of them invariably emerge the big winners.

There are as many kinds of memes as there are hot buttons. There are *aspirational* memes, *dream* memes (a new home), *greed* memes, *scarcity* memes, *authority* memes, *reciprocation* memes, *attraction* (liking) memes, *success* memes, *escape* memes, *gambling* memes (low risk, high potential payoff), *popularity* memes, *pride* memes, *career* memes, *association* memes, *compulsion* memes, *achievement* memes, *distinction* memes, *sticky* memes (memes which stick easily in the mind), *solution* memes, *curiosity* memes, *status* memes, *guilt* memes, *strategy* memes, *sex* memes, *consensus* memes, *romance* memes, *maternal* and *paternal* memes, *paradigm* memes, *consistency* memes, *contrast* memes, *love* memes, *romance* memes, *family* memes, *travel* memes, *fashion* memes, *thrill* memes, *excitement* memes, *responsibility* memes, *security* memes, *health* memes, *youth* memes, *fun* memes ... the list is endless. Being the emotional creatures that we are, we all have emotional hot buttons, and the most successful memes are the ultimate button-pushers.

It is here that we need to make some distinctions. A meme is an *active transmitter of specific information*, not merely a glib statement. For example, the legendary meme used by Avis, 'We're no. 2 because we try harder', was the launching pad that revolutionised Avis' position in the marketplace. Avis was actually number three, behind National, but by pre-empting the number two spot in the public mind, it was able to perform a perceptual leap-frog act, and position itself next to the number one car rental company, Hertz.

People around the world were exposed to that meme, saw Avis in a different light and reacted accordingly. Nothing else changed. Just adding a contagious meme to the equation performed the magic. Of course, if you claim to do something like try harder, there had better be some evidence of that when people come to do business with you, or it can very quickly come back and bite you.

PRODUCT AND BRAND NAMES

Once you have a working knowledge of the meme concept, you'll find you have gained many valuable new insights that will influence the way in which you approach your business. For example, let's suppose you're about to launch a new company, product or brand. At some point, you're going to have to dream up a name for it. If you can create a name which is also a meme, then you've just given your new venture a massive boost.

Whipper-Snipper, Flymo, Alfoil, Kreepy Krauly, Lean Cuisine and Rare Spares are all memes. They are verbal symbols that have the ability to capture the public's imagination and, more importantly, to make it extremely simple for people to understand what the names mean. The takeout is that these companies and brands are able to extract more value from their advertising dollars because they don't need to waste money on educating the public about what they are. The names alone tell the story. The lesson from this is that you should frame your company, product or brand name as a meme. But before you do this, you need to be very certain that the meme you're about to unleash on the public is always going to serve you well. Could things change in the future so that your company, product or brand name becomes a liability?

This happens to companies all the time. Why would you go to Barbecues Galore? To buy a barbecue, of course. 'Barbecues Galore' is a classic meme, which has been pivotal in producing by far the highest brand recall of any barbecue retailer in Australia. The problem is that, since its inception, Barbecues Galore expanded to include home heating and camping equipment, neither of which is implicit in the name 'Barbeques Galore'. In order to boost public awareness of the camping goods aspect of the company, The Galore Group initiated a program designed to reposition the company as 'Your outdoor cooking and camping store'.

But because it is so strong, no matter how much money is spent, the 'Barbecues Galore' meme will always mean 'lots of barbecues', and will continue to function brilliantly as a perceptual filter in the marketplace.

In the same way, there is no doubt that a new meme on the scene, 'Camping Galore', would create a new level of meaning and awareness in the public mind, resulting in a far greater share of the camping goods market.

Why would you go to Ultratune? To have your car engine tuned? That was the original concept when the company began many years ago. 'Ultratune' is an identity meme, which encapsulates that idea. Today, however, things are very different. The company now consists of a network of hi-tech service centres providing a complete factory service on your car to the manufacturer's specifications. It also provides a comprehensive tyre, suspension, steering and brake service. Ultratune's regular customers understand this, because they've had the experience. But how about the general public?

If you needed tyres, would you think to call Ultratune? If you needed your suspension, steering or brakes repaired, would Ultratune spring to mind? Possibly, but the chances are that the 'Ultratune' meme would mislead you into believing that the company is still as it was many years ago – a tune-up service. Once again, the company could save itself vast amounts of money, while still keeping the distinctive company logo basically intact, through the simple expedient of revamping the 'Ultratune' meme in a way that retained the old recall, but carried an enhanced meaning to the marketplace – perhaps something along the lines of 'Ultra Car Care Centre'.

Why might you want to visit Jax Tyres? To buy tyres? That was certainly the original idea. However, today Jax Tyres would like you to think of them when you need repairs to your suspension and brakes as well. But why would you? In its present context, the word 'tyres' is extremely counter-productive. The company would be well advised to re-look at its name from a memetic perspective. There are all kinds of ways in which it could retain the word 'Jax', and at the same time clarify its vision and purpose in the public mind. This simple expedient has the potential to quadruple its sales, simply by targeting more people with the right kinds of problems.

Perhaps one of the most expensive brand names you can own is one that is expressed as an abbreviation. With very few exceptions, this is about as far away from a meme as you can get. There are thousands of companies out there with three-, four-, five- and even six-letter names. Companies such as ABC, FAI, AGC, BHP, CML, DHL, EAC, HCF, IMB, NRMA, RACV, RACQ, MBF and M.U.I.O..O.F have spent uncounted millions of dollars over the years, in an effort to educate the public about what their names mean.

The name 'ABC' could work well as a meme for a company that provides educational material for children, because of its 'kiddy' classroom connotation. The same name for a courier company or a mobile phone company would be meaningless.

When your objective is to squeeze the most out of your advertising and marketing dollars, setting up your new company, product or brand name as a meme can save you a lot of money, time and effort. You can hit the ground running, as it were. Instead of wasting precious resources educating people about what the name means, you can focus on influencing people to want to buy it.

THE NEED FOR A MEME MENTALITY IN ADVERTISING

Many advertising agency writers seem to believe that if they come up with a tricky creative idea and simply include a logo somewhere in the ad, then people will somehow magically associate the two and remember the brand being advertised. In the real world, it doesn't work like that. Research has shown that many of those anonymous advertisements come across as generic rather than brand-specific, and therefore represent a complete waste of time, money and effort.

Lacking an understanding of memetics, the majority of agency writers use 'clever' creativity as their default strategy. As a result of this hit-and-miss approach, they may sometimes stumble upon a great meme. It is much more likely, however, that they will simply come up with a tricky idea or turn of phrase which is either ambiguous, misleading, or something that amounts to nothing more than vapid, corporate fluff. The point is that, without a grasp of memetics, these people don't have the distinctions to know the difference.

REVERSE MEMES

At the time of writing, a campaign is being run to promote Hamilton Island. It features the headline:

Hamilton. The island that's spoiling Australia.

While this statement is most definitely a meme, it is the wrong kind of meme. It's a reverse meme, sending a negative message. Who wants Australia spoilt? To most people, the word 'spoil' means 'ruin', or 'damage', as any dictionary will tell you. Certainly it has a secondary connotation of indulgence, and the body copy of the print ads support this idea. However, all the enticing body copy in the world is useless if people are turned off by the key proposition, and don't read any further.

Not all people will see this headline as a negative statement, but many will. If the campaign works at all, it will work in spite of its ambiguous campaign hook, not because of it. Presumably the campaign is trying to say something like 'Spoil yourself rotten at Hamilton Island', which would have conveyed a far more cogent meaning to the consumer.

The difference between these two approaches, from a memetic perspective, is the emotional implications of each. If at any level you interpret the first as a literal statement, then it will leave you with a bad feeling about Hamilton Island. The real damage occurs when people are not aware that they have downloaded a meme like this. It can happen quite unconsciously in an instant as a person drives past a billboard, or flips through a magazine. Many people may now feel ambivalent towards Hamilton Island without quite knowing why.

One advertisement in this campaign featured a photograph of a crocodile in attack mode, with its jaws wide open, together with the headline:

If you like we can take care of the kids.

At the bottom of the poster was:

Free kids club on Hamilton. The island that's spoiling Australia.

Okay, maybe it was intended to be humorous, but is there any truth in it at all? Are there crocodiles on Hamilton Island? If so, might you run into one of them on a bushwalk? Apart from anything else, a ferocious crocodile is probably not the ideal meme if the aim is to persuade people that their children will be in safe hands on their next holiday.

GENERIC MEMES

One of the most common advertising mistakes is to waste precious resources running advertisements which promote a generic product, rather than the product or brand featured in the advertisement.

A typical example of this was a billboard featuring an illustration of a Jeep Wrangler on a deserted beach. Beside the vehicle was a parking sign that read:

Park wherever you damn well please.

Unfortunately, on a billboard, a Jeep Wrangler looks pretty much like any other four-wheel drive vehicle. The eye takes in the combined effect of the four-wheel drive, the deserted beach and the parking sign; a compound meme that says: 'If you want to escape the traffic and hassle, get a four-wheel drive.' To passing motorists, that billboard could just as easily have been an ad for Toyota Landcruiser, because the brand name was not locked in as an integral part of the meme. It was simply an add-on.

The function of a meme is to symbolise an idea. Before an advertisement is created, there must first be an idea, which you then chunk down until it becomes a self-explanatory meme. So far so good. The problems arise when there *is* no big idea, no real reason to choose a particular product or brand. Lacking something solid to work with, creative writers routinely produce 'clever' generic advertisements which actually promote a category, rather than a specific product or brand.

The purpose of this book is to show you that there is another way. You don't have to waste your precious resources promoting other people's products by default. We invite you to become an avid student of meme technology, and to learn how to fire your advertising messages straight at the hearts and minds of your customers and prospects.

NON-MEMES

Often something that looks like a meme is not a meme at all. We see certain advertisements that effectively communicate a particular concept, but are so poorly identified that the public hasn't any idea which particular brand is being advertised.

A billboard at a busy London intersection featured an illustration of a small car, and a bold headline:

It thinks there's a permanent petrol drought.

In the lower right-hand corner was a tiny logo, and to this day we have no idea which car was being advertised. This could not have happened had the creative team been proficient in meme technology.

Another example of obscure advertising appeared on a Sydney billboard, featuring the headline statement:

Do your do.

The advertisement depicted a stylish woman reclining on a chair, sporting a slinky hat which completely covered her hair. At the bottom right-hand corner of the advertisement was a picture of a container of hair product called Works, adjacent to a positioning statement that read:

Haircare that does.

But what is the point to this advertisement? Why would anybody respond? There was no apparent product benefit, no meaning, no enticement of any kind. 'Haircare that does' is not a meme. It is ambiguous and requires the reader to figure out what it means. 'Haircare that works' is a meme with an implied benefit, a link to the product name, and would have carried at least some level of meaning to the public. Maybe this campaign somehow managed to produce a satisfactory response, but to invest precious dollars in this type of cryptic advertising is extremely risky, and not something we would recommend.

By way of contrast, a simple sign outside the duty-free store at Singapore airport seduced passers-by with the following meme:

We absorb your GST.

For passengers from countries with a goods and services tax, that attraction meme has a special appeal, and the management folk at that duty-free store tell us that it has been extremely effective in generating business.

OUTDOOR ADVERTISING

Two good places to study advertising memes are buses and billboards. The restricted space available demands simplicity and clarity if the message is to be communicated in the short space of time available: the time it takes for a vehicle to whiz by. Sometimes these advertisements are so 'clever' or obscure that their meaning is completely lost on their target audience, those people who will be exposed to them for perhaps only a second or two before they move on in a busy city environment. The most effective memes are those which download their essential message in a split second.

•

>> **Memes can be qualified, quantified, calibrated, counted, layered, stacked, bundled and engineered to provide a level of control and predictability unprecedented in the world of advertising.**

QUALIFYING MEMES

Whenever you're creating an advertisement, be certain that your focal point is actually a meme. Understand that before you can have a meme, you must first have an idea, which is then transformed into a meme by the process of extreme simplification. To determine whether or not you actually have a viable meme, ask yourself these questions:

- Is it an arrangement of words/pictures/sounds/actions that effortlessly communicates an idea or concept in an instant?
- Is it a self-explanatory symbol representing a complete idea?
- Is it a compressed packet of information with an implied subtext?
- Does it really qualify as a basic unit of communication; the 'lowest common denominator' of an idea?
- Is it laced with emotion?
- Which specific emotional button or buttons has it been designed to push?
- Would it qualify as an active transmitter of specific information designed to engage consumer interest, or is it simply a glib statement?

QUANTIFYING MEMES

A good system for analysing and quantifying memes is to grade them in order of potency. This gives you a basis for assessing the potential of your own memes, as well as those contained in the advertising you see around you. You may find the following classification system useful.

• A - m e m e s •

These are memes which are of particular interest to large numbers of people, and are serious button-pushers. Examples are:

- Coke – the real thing.
- Join the Pepsi generation.
- Nike – just do it!
- TAB, the adrenalin bet.
- This goes with that at Sussan.
- Lose weight for life with Lite n' Easy.
- Absolutely, positively overnight. (Federal Express)

All of these statements spearhead an engaging concept.

• B - m e m e s •

These may be simply poorly articulated A-memes, or memes of only moderate interest to a smaller number of people, and medium button-pushers. B-memes can usually be upgraded to A-memes with a little thought and effort. Examples are:

- Two for the price of one.
- Buy one and get one free.
- We guarantee to match any advertised offer.
- Satisfaction guaranteed.
- The right advice.

These have all become basic consumer expectations.

• C l i c h é s •

These are glib phrases, 'clever' turns of phrase, and memes which have forfeited their appeal by becoming passé. A vast amount of advertising agency creative output falls into this category. Examples are:

- NIB – health cover for every body. (with illustrations of various types of bodies)
- ANZ – best by all accounts.
- Samsung. Leadership through products.
- Budget. All the difference in the world.
- Macquarie University. The INFORMED choice.
- You know where you stand with St George.

• F l u f f •

This is boring media clutter, advertising 'wallpaper'. Examples are:

- Network Vodafone. Oh yeah!
- We're the good guys in hi-fi.
- Striving for excellence.
- We will not be undersold.
- Committed to value and service.

- We aim for quality above all else.
- We give great service.
- Rapid-fire product and price commercials, and 'buy from me' advertising in general.

Much of the content of the advertising we see around us qualifies as fluff.

CALIBRATING MEMES

Calibrating memes means numerically rating them in order to assess their likely degree of effectiveness. There are basically two ways to calibrate memes. The first and most accurate is to rate them by their performance in terms of advertising results. We suggest keeping a meme book of some kind so that you can keep track of results, and refer back to memes which have performed well in the past. These can then be re-engineered, modified and adapted to perform well in another context.

The second way to calibrate memes is subjective, and therefore less accurate, but nevertheless useful. During the creative stage of your advertisement, try to formulate as many alternative memes as you can, and then have people give them rating points out of ten for intelligibility and emotional impact. This will at least give you a basis for assessing your options.

COUNTING MEMES

How many memes are there in your advertisement? Can you differentiate between memes, clichés and fluff? It is a useful discipline to go through each new advertisement with a fine-tooth comb, and qualify and quantify your material until you're sure you know exactly how many memes there are, what kind they are, exactly which buttons they're designed to push, and what level of potency you estimate them to have. This simple analytical process will give you real power.

LAYERING MEMES

Layering memes is the process of arranging different kinds of memes in a pattern or sequence to create an overall synergy . We often see good examples of meme layering on billboards. There may be a romance meme expressed as a photograph, a solution meme expressed as the key proposition in a word or short statement, and an association meme, locking the illustration into the brand name or logo. Executed correctly, layered memes combine to produce a compound meme. A single glance tells the whole story. One meme builds on the power of another until the sum of the parts becomes greater than the whole.

When layering memes, a good strategy is to try to arrange them so that they push different buttons. That way, if you miss a prospect with one button, you may just pick him or her up with another. Layering can be a devastatingly powerful technique.

STACKING MEMES

Stacking memes is possibly the most powerful technique of all. Stacking means placing different kinds of memes on *top* of each other to create a compound meme. 'We're Woolworths the fresh food people' is a classic example of a stacked compound meme:

1   It functions both as an identity meme and an attraction meme, instantly transmitting a differentiating and engaging idea.

2   The word 'fresh' is in itself an attraction meme with a strong emotional appeal, and carries an implied subtext.

3   The name 'Woolworths' permanently and indelibly integrated into the concept creates a powerful association meme – think of fresh, think of Woolworths. (For Victorians this becomes Safeway, for Tasmanians, Purity and Roelf Vos.)

4   The verbal sequence of words forms a sticky meme, containing two sets of alliterative words: the two Ws in 'We're Woolworths', and the two Fs in 'fresh food'. These word groupings combine to make the meme extremely memorable. The fact that identical copies of this meme reside in the minds of many Australians provides compelling evidence of its success as a replicator.

5   A sticky musical phrase was created to contain an already sticky verbal meme. The simple act of seeing a Woolworths or Safeway delivery van go by can be enough to trigger the musical meme.

The combined effect of these separate but symmetrically stacked memes is to create a new single entity; a compound mega-meme with the ability to influence the behavioural patterns of millions of people.

It's an interesting exercise to compare the memetic structure of Woolworths' advertising with that of Coles. There is no comparison. It should come as no surprise to note that Woolworths is the market leader.

BUNDLING MEMES

Bundling involves creating an extremely attractive meme which appears to be completely innocent, and imbedding the real meme within it – a Trojan Horse, in fact. You will see examples of this all the time. You're invited to enter a competition for a trip for two to Disneyland. This is articulated as a gambling meme, pushing the 'low risk, high potential payout' button. Having committed to the competition, you're asked to do something like write a short sentence singing the praises of a leading breakfast cereal. The catch here is that once you have written those words, you have put yourself under the influence of the Law of Consistency. You will feel a pressure to act in a way that is consistent with your stated position. As a result, there is every chance that, even if it is not your regular brand, you may decide to try the breakfast cereal out of curiosity, and perhaps recommend it to others.

Examples of bundling are seen in advertisements for record clubs, book clubs, mobile phones, cable TV and Internet service providers. You are tempted with some irresistible offer that seems just too good to pass up. As a consequence, you find yourself locked into an organisation with some kind of ongoing financial commitment. This is not to say that bundling is a bad thing. People all over the world are more than happy to belong to organisations such as Reader's Digest, American Express and the World Record Club, all of which prosper through the simple expedient of bundling memes.

The dark side of bundling memes is that it is also the method used to seduce people into joining various religions and cults. An advertisement promising friendship and acceptance for lonely people may turn out to be an introduction to a cult or quasi-religion.

ENGINEERING MEMES

This is where you can really spread your wings and take control of your advertising and marketing. Many people have great difficulty with the creative process, particularly when it comes to making creative decisions which may dictate the success or failure of an important ad campaign. How do you go about creating a potent meme from scratch?

Please commit the following meme to memory, because it can save you a lot of time and effort if you use it correctly:

•

>> **When you need a meme,
just call in the TEAM.**

•

TEAM is an acronym which can save you a lot of time and effort. TEAM stands for Transplant, Enhance, Adapt and Modify.

TRANSPLANT

To transplant a meme is simply to import an existing meme and take ownership of it. There are many ways to do this. You may find the meme overseas or interstate, in an unrelated industry, or from some other remote source. If the source is sufficiently obscure, simply replacing the original advertiser's name with your own may be all you need to do. Often you come across the basis for a fabulous meme in the most unusual places, for example the classifieds in a regional newspaper.

What if the meme happens to 'belong' to a major advertiser and is widely known to the public? No problem – just transplant it anyway and then re-engineer it by working your way through the TEAM acronym, and nobody will ever recognise it. It's called 'creative licence', or 'inspiration', and it's quite ethical because the end result bears no resemblance to the original.

ENHANCE

To enhance an existing meme simply means to upgrade it by making it even better than the original, by using some of the techniques you have already learned. Could you improve it by flipping it around and simplifying it even further? Could you re-calibrate it by targeting a more potent emotional hot button? Could you create a Trojan Horse situation and bundle the meme along with another?

A good way to enhance, or upgrade an existing meme is to:

1   Identify the button the meme was designed to press (for example convenience).
2   Look for another button with higher emotional leverage (for example taste).
3   Look for the ultimate way to press that button. 'Brand X makes your tastebuds tingle!' (As long as it's true.)

ADAPT

To adapt a meme is to take it out of its original context, re-engineer it, and apply it to your own situation. If the original meme related to food, you could very easily adapt it to relate to, say, cosmetics or fashion. A good place to start is to begin with an existing meme, and then look for ways to relate it to your particular situation without compromising its memetic integrity.

Suppose you're the marketing manager for Sony, and you're trying to develop a powerful corporate statement for the brand. You begin looking through old books and magazines for a suitable meme to adapt. You come across an old advertisement for Coca Cola featuring the meme 'Coke – the real thing'.

You feel that this expresses exactly the sentiment you want to project for Sony. It pushes the 'exclusivity' button, creating an aura of authenticity, authority and brand leadership.

The next step is to 'massage' the meme; to re-articulate it in such a way that it loses nothing in the translation. Perhaps something like 'There's only one Coca Cola'.

Then you'd replace 'Coca Cola' with 'Sony', and arrive at the line: 'There's only one Sony'.

Then you might want to work on it a little more, and perhaps come up with 'The one and only Sony' or 'Sony. The one and only'.

The interesting thing is that, in the context of Sony, the adapted meme has not lost anything at all in the translation. It carries an identical subtext to the original. Looking at this final articulation, it would be impossible to trace the evolution of the meme.

This is purely a hypothetical example, but you can see what a powerful, useful and ethical technique it is. To try to carry this kind of exercise off without first having a clear understanding of meme technology would be very difficult indeed.

If you do a good job of adaptation and follow the TEAM process, there is every chance that the meme you produce will be even more potent than the original.

MODIFY

Modifying an existing meme means taking a simple meme and turning it into a compound meme. Returning to the Coke example, you could first transplant and adapt it, and then begin layering or stacking complementary memes to enhance it. You could then create an association meme by linking it to an emotive illustration, re-verbalise it to create a sticky meme, and perhaps lock in an attraction meme in the form of a testimonial.

Think of a meme as being like a key frame from a movie sequence which is then used to promote the movie. This analogy is very useful when you're trying to get your head around the meme concept. The 'It's time' meme discussed earlier is like a key frame in the political drama which was unfolding at the time. It hit the nail on the head, so to speak. Millions of Australians saw it, understood, and once again, a meme could be observed dictating and orchestrating patterns of human behaviour at polling booths all around the country.

SPOT THE MEME

By now you should have enough information to begin looking at the media in a new way, and play a game called 'Spot the Meme'. When playing 'Spot the Meme', one of the first things you're likely to notice is that there are not too many contagious advertising memes around to spot. This is why most advertising is ignored. A headline statement in any advertisement, whether it be in print, or on TV or radio, should be a meme showcase. All too often, however, headlines consist of clichés, fluff, or both, and simply go unnoticed.

Sydney people will remember classic memes such as 'Up the Windsor Road' for Tony Packard. After all these years, most people can still complete the phrase 'You come and see me, Tony Packard, up the Windsor Road from Baulkham Hills, and let *me* do it right for *you!*' Like all successful memes, it has demonstrated an ability to transcend the passage of time. The same is true for the word 'Update', which, for many Sydney people, immediately evokes the name Ron Hodgson Motors. Viewed from a memetic perspective, you can see that there is more to that word 'Update' than first meets the eye. In its original context of 'Update with Ron Hodgson Motors', it is actually a highly sophisticated compound meme, created by stacking four separate memes: a solution meme (update your old car), an association meme (Ron Hodgson is the 'update' specialist), a sticky verbal meme ('Update with Ron Hodgson Motors') and a sticky musical meme (articulated in a popular radio and TV jingle). No wonder so many people remember it.

'It's Mac time now at McDonald's', 'Nike – just do it!', 'Coke – the real thing', 'Take me away, P & O', 'Meadow Lea, you ought to be con-gratulated', 'Holler for a Marshall', 'Drive in and jive away at Strathfield Car Radio today', and 'TDK does amazing things to my system' are just some of those contagious, super-successful memes which have brought tremendous brand acceptance and market share to the companies concerned. You will spot many more throughout the course of this book.

Of course a meme disseminated via a national TV campaign is much more likely to spread through the community than a meme with less exposure. It goes without saying that people are affected by a meme only to the extent that they have been exposed to it.

A recent local meme-spotting expedition produced the following collection of memes:

- The crave crushers

  This provocative meme, which appears on the pack of Arnotts Shapes, was supported by a major TV campaign. 'The crave crushers' is a compulsion meme that pushes the primal 'Food' button in a big way, and will certainly have a positive impact on people who like their munchies.

- Sex Diet Health

  New Woman magazine featured this devastating compound meme on an outdoor banner. This is a good example of the technique of layering memes to create an enormous incentive for large numbers of people to rush in and buy a product. It hits all three primal buttons simultaneously. Whether the magazine actually lived up to the memetic promise is beside the point. The leverage, the motivation to buy, lay in the potency of the meme and its ability to download itself instantly into the mind of anybody of the right predisposition who happened to glance in that general direction.

- Windscreens O'Brien

  This definitive communication gem from Australia's leading windscreen specialist appeared on a tiny sign placed at a public carpark exit. Anything more would have been superfluous:

WINDSCREENS O'BRIEN

ANY CAR　ANY GLASS　ANYWHERE

13 16 16

- Jordache Jeans

  A billboard depicted a semi-erotic photograph of an attractive young couple embracing, wearing nothing but their jeans. The Jordache name is strongly integrated into the photograph to form a potent compound meme which will certainly have influenced public perception of the product. The interesting thing is that the product itself may or may not be any better in either fit or quality than a less expensive brand. Fashion, food and cosmetics advertisers often use these kinds of association memes as a means of instantly identifying with their target market.

•

>> **To create a compound meme, you must find a way to indelibly link the brand name to the image. Very few advertisers do this successfully. If you fail to get this right, you've just consigned a large chunk of your media expenditure to the scrap heap.**

•

• Hand made beer
Together with a simple graphic of a red bottle-top carrying the Coopers logo, these three words appeared on a large outdoor poster. This is another good example of an association meme layered with an identity meme to create an advertisement with the ability to create a very specific market positioning for a product or brand. After even one exposure to that meme, it's next to impossible to perceive Coopers to be a down-market beer for the masses.
This compound meme instantly gives Coopers a feeling of sophistication, of being special. You can practically see the Coopers master brewer at work in a small boutique brewery, creating a fine, exclusive beverage. The two layered memes were featured on an outdoor poster at a major intersection, and their combined effect was powerfully transmitted in a single glance.

• Wheels car of the year
This outdoor poster for the Honda Odyssey was extremely simple, providing an instant transmission of information to anybody who might have been in the market for a new car around that time. The stamp of approval by *Wheels Magazine* made it especially noteworthy to people in the right target audience. Positioned at a major intersection, it was virtually impossible to miss. Even people who were not in the market for a car would have had a modified impression of the Honda Odyssey as a result of involuntary exposure to that pattern of layered memes. Together with a photograph of the car, the entire poster became a giant compound meme which was cleanly transmitted in a single glance.

• Macquarie challenges Oxford
A twenty-four sheet poster carrying only these three words and the

Macquarie University logo was placed strategically along a main traffic artery on Sydney's North Shore. This three-word association meme may well have a positive effect for a number of reasons. Firstly, it is a classic example of the distinction between a rational and a subliminal proposition. At the rational level, nobody in their right mind would seriously consider Macquarie University, as good as it may be, to be the equal of the legendary Oxford, steeped as it is in history and tradition. But seen from the memetic perspective, Macquarie is placed at a perceptual level of comparison which it might not otherwise enjoy.

Those three words, when taken in at the subconscious level as simply part of the urban scenery, support an implied subtext which makes a bold statement about the quality and status of the university. The real pay-off from this potent meme lies in the comparison which people might now make between Macquarie and other local universities.

There is a second spin-off from this association meme; the dictionary wars. Many people might now see the Macquarie Dictionary in a different light, perhaps imagining that somehow it has gained some kind of superiority or advantage over the traditional authority of the English language, the Concise Oxford Dictionary.

Unfortunately, Macquarie University's follow-up advertisement on the same billboard lacked the same level of insight. It proclaimed:

Macquarie University. The INFORMED choice.

What does that mean? It could mean anything at all, and is unlikely to inspire anybody to do anything.

- Workbrutes

This was the brand name of a pair of otherwise ordinary-looking boots in a store window. That name has a direct effect on the way people perceive the product. They seem tougher than they otherwise might, and are therefore more desirable. The name carries an implied subtext, a hidden agenda. Shakespeare said:

What's in a name? that which we call a rose by any other name would smell as sweet.

Had Shakespeare been in the business of selecting product names, he might have discovered the hard way that the name alone can quite literally make or break a product or a brand.

- Zoomerang
  This was the brand name of a small cardboard glider being demonstrated by kids outside a toy store. The glider would fly in a wide circle, and with uncanny precision, come gently to rest in the hand of the person throwing it. The implied subtext of the name Zoomerang creates an expectation that makes the product more believable and far more desirable than if it were called 'The Acme glider'. The long queue of people waiting at the cash register told the story.

- Strong pain, powerful Panadene
  Interposed with a dynamic illustration depicting a Panadene tablet breaking through shattering glass, this powerfully stacked compound meme could be seen on the sides of buses as they threaded their way through city traffic. Without doubt, it would have had a profound effect on consumer buying decisions.

- Hold your breath – Stallone – Daylight ...
  This example of layering memes to create an enhanced effect was seen on the side of a bus. Expressed as simply as it is, this compound meme says it all; any additional text to promote the movie would have been superfluous.

Meme-spotting is an excellent way to become aware of what is happening in the world of advertising both at home and overseas. Invariably, whenever you come across an advertisement which has proved to be extremely effective, you'll find a big fat meme, right there in the centre of the action.

YOUR ULTIMATE PROSPECT

As we noted earlier, on a billboard, or anywhere else for that matter, a meme is just a meme. To become active and begin its incubation process it requires a human mind. For that reason, we're about to involve the other half of the equation: your prospect.

Most of the advertising in the world today is based almost exclusively on guesswork. The missing element is control. Our purpose here is to give you that control, and to do that, we'd like to introduce you to a key character in your advertising and marketing program.

At this point in our business development seminars, we produce a small, odd-looking, but somehow appropriate doll – Stanley, your Central Demographic Model.

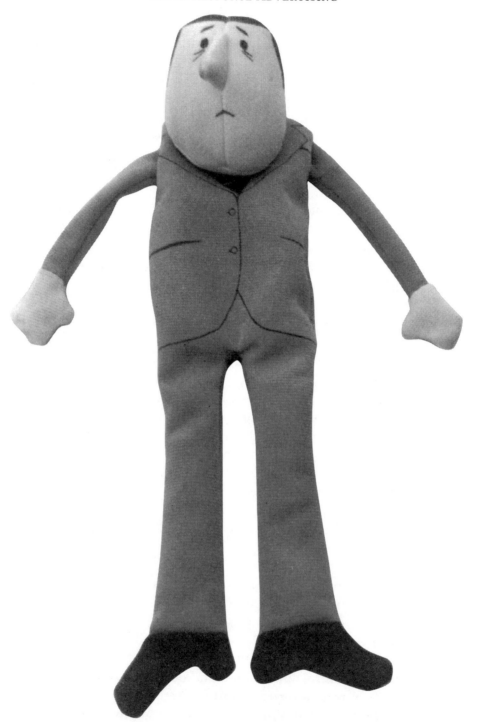

**STANLEY – YOUR CENTRAL
DEMOGRAPHIC MODEL**

Stanley is absolutely ideal for you. He's the very person you're trying to attract right now through your advertising and marketing. He has the right demographic profile, the right psychographic profile, he's from the right socio-economic group, he's ready to buy whatever it is you sell, and he's exactly the kind of person you'd like to acquire as a repeat customer. That's the good news.

The bad news is that Stanley has no intention of ever buying from you. The reason for that is that he doesn't need you. He's quite happy doing what he's doing now – buying from your competitors. It's not that he's hostile towards you or your company or brand; he's just *indifferent*.

Given that, by definition, Stanley is the very person you want to target most of all, the question becomes: What would have to happen in order to move Stanley from the point of indifference, to the point where he'd be receptive to the idea of buying from you on a continuing basis?

Initially at least, there are two things:

1   You would have to get inside his head and connect with him, which is easier said than done.
2   You would then have to create a shift in perception, which creates a shift in attitude, which creates a shift in behaviour, which, as we pointed out earlier, is the ultimate goal of all advertising.

What is involved in getting inside Stanley's head? It's right here that you bump up against two major issues: sensory overload and the Inner Circle.

SENSORY OVERLOAD

There was a time when advertising was something of a novelty, and people used to take notice and believe what they were told. Those days are long gone, and today Stanley, like the rest of us, is swamped with advertising. It's screaming at him from all directions twenty-four hours a day. It's on television; it's on the radio; it's in newspapers, magazines, the movies; it's on bus sides, taxi backs and outdoor posters. He goes out to his letterbox and it's full of junk mail, and, quite frankly, it's enough to drive Stanley, and us, up the wall.

There's simply no way that we can possibly process all of that information, so to insulate ourselves against it, we use the only real defence we have. We simply tune it out. We switch off. What might have been useful information becomes relegated to media wallpaper. And when we do that, when we don't take it in any more, we become basically immune to advertising. Of course we're never completely immune – there are always things of particular interest that will get through. But once we've tuned out and switched off, for all practical purposes we become immune.

INNER CIRCLE

The second major issue is either a blessing or a curse, depending on whether or not you're in it. It's called the Inner Circle, and we look at it in detail in the next chapter. You are about to immerse yourself in a new technology consisting of memes, Hot Zones and Activators, that will really get your advertising humming.

THE MAIN POINTS

•

1 >> THE PARALLELS BETWEEN MEMES AND GENES
•

In order for memes to be successful, they had to demonstrate the genetic qualities of longevity (the ability to stand the test of time), fecundity (fertility and the ability to replicate abundantly), and copying fidelity (the ability to create accurate self-copies over time). The memes used by thousands of companies have complied with those three prerequisites, and have played a major role in gaining market share as a result.

•

2 >> THE CONTAGIOUS NATURE OF MEMES
•

The story of the rock painting depicting the caveman spearing the fish, illustrates the way in which memes 'use' people to spread rapidly from mind to mind. It is the extreme simplicity of the meme, combined with its ability to push emotional buttons, that allows it to perform its magic. One child sees another child spinning a hula hoop, and the idea spreads throughout the community, the nation, and across the world in an incredibly short space of time.

•

3 >> HOW A MEME OVERTHREW A GOVERNMENT
•

The 'It's time' campaign which swept the Australian Labor Party to power in the mid-1970s is a classic example of the sheer power of the meme to influence public opinion.

•

4 >> THE COMPUTER ANALOGY

•

Computer files can be compressed, so that a large amount of information is able to be squeezed into a small space. In many ways, these compressed files are like memes, in that they can then be expanded to their original size. The 'It's time' meme is like one of these compressed computer files. It carried an enormous depth of meaning and innuendo as a subtext. Once a meme has been downloaded into a human mind, it begins its covert work at the pre-cognitive level of altering perceptions, attitudes, beliefs and, finally, behaviour.

•

5 >> MEMES AND THE EVOLUTION OF CULTURE

•

There is nothing about human culture that existed in pre-history. As individuals dreamed up each new idea, custom, ritual or concept, these things had to be simple enough and at the same time emotionally relevant enough to be easily grasped by other people if they were to catch on and replicate. They then swept from mind to mind as memes, the simplest and most contagious being the most successful. The world in which we find ourselves today is nothing more than the sum total of the successful memes that have stood the test of time.

•

6 >> MEMES IN ADVERTISING

•

The meme concept grew out of the study of human culture, and until very recently has remained more or less confined to the scientific community, isolated from the very industry that perhaps could most benefit from it – the advertising industry. The extreme simplicity of the meme allows advertisers to chunk a complex idea down into a highly communicable unit of information: a memetic symbol with the power to influence the attitudes and buying habits of millions of people, often without their conscious awareness.

•

7 >> THE SUBLIMINAL NATURE OF THE MEME

•

A discussion with a sales person can be rationally considered, and then be either accepted, rejected or negotiated. A meme can enter the mind with impunity at the pre-cognitive level as a feeling or impression, which then filters through the various layers of consciousness to alter the way we think. Because of their covert nature, we usually have no idea that we have taken a meme on board. Consequently, we are unaware of the real reasons for many of our preferences and behavioural patterns.

•

8 >> MEMES AS EMOTIONAL BUTTON-PUSHERS

•

Humans are emotional creatures, and the ideas and concepts that we adopt are invariably those which tend to either bring the most pleasure, or avoid the most pain. For this reason, the most successful memes target one or more of the emotional triggers which we call 'hot buttons'. When people have experienced the pleasant emotional pay-off of one of these memes, they feel a desire to pass it on to other people, thereby ensuring its propagation throughout the community. The most successful memes are the ones which trigger the strongest emotions.

•

9 >> OUTDOOR ADVERTISING PRESENTS
•   GOOD OPPORTUNITIES TO STUDY MEMES

The restricted space of outdoor advertising makes the use of memes quite essential. There are times when a person may have as little as half a second during a break in traffic in which to grasp the message on the side of a bus. A meme is the only possible way to achieve this. For that reason, certain creative teams have learned to develop an affinity with memes without ever being aware of their existence as a technology. Unfortunately, a great deal of outdoor advertising is so obscure, or 'clever', that it fails to communicate effectively, and represents a complete waste of time and money.

•

10 >> MEME MANAGEMENT

•

Memes can be qualified, quantified, calibrated, layered, stacked and engineered to provide a level of control and predictability unprecedented in the world of advertising.

•

11 >> ENGINEERING MEMES

•

When you need a meme, just call in the TEAM. To Transplant is to take ownership of an existing meme. To Enhance is to upgrade a meme using the various techniques covered in this chapter. To Adapt is to take a meme out of its original context and apply it to your own situation, as in the hypothetical Sony example. To Modify is to take a simple meme and turn it into a compound meme, thereby increasing its power enormously.

•

12 >> SPOT THE MEME
•

When you're out and about, keep your eyes open and sharpen your awareness of the use of memes in the marketplace. To become skilled in meme management, you need to distinguish between memes, clichés and fluff. Meme-spotting is an excellent way to do this. Keep a meme notebook handy, and before long you'll find yourself becoming very aware, and skilled, in the recognition and creation of effective memes.

•

13 >> YOUR CENTRAL DEMOGRAPHIC MODEL
•

For the purpose of discussion we use Stanley to represent this key character in your advertising and marketing program. Consider locating a photograph which approximates your ultimate prospect, and keep it somewhere in your office where you can see it at all times. You can then look at your creative concept, look at the photograph, and you'll know when it's right. A photograph like this can also simplify the communication process when you're briefing creative people on an advertisement or a campaign.

•

14 >> SENSORY OVERLOAD
•

When you look at the vast amount of advertising out there, it's not hard to accept that the average person is subjected to around two thousand advertising impressions every day. Because there is simply no way that we could cope with trying to process all that information, most of it irrelevant at the time, we simply filter it out of our consciousness. For this reason, it's not difficult to believe the research that tells us that most advertising is ignored. Sensory overload is arguably the biggest single barrier to the advertising process. This book is about the art, craft and science of breaking through this formidable barrier to communication.

CHAPTER 2

THE INNER CIRCLE

We enter into a very special relationship with certain products,

services and brands; a long-term relationship built on familiarity

and trust.

Billions of dollars annually are being spent, and for the most part wasted, attempting to solve an age-old, universal problem: how to persuade significant numbers of people who normally use a competitor's product to switch and use your product on an ongoing basis. In order to grow and prosper, companies and brands around the world find themselves in a struggle to win more and more market share. Competition is the great leveller, and the business manager who is able to consistently outmanoeuvre the opposition is going to win the day.

Companies tend to be run by accountants, who have their eyes glued to the bottom line and who are constantly looking for ways and means to cut costs and increase overall efficiency. Invariably these people are so myopic, so focused on the little things, that they completely miss one of the greatest areas of financial waste in the business community today: the cost of acquiring a new customer through advertising and marketing.

Ultimately, the most effective long-term strategy for any product, service or brand is one which is designed to attract new customers, and then to lock them into a buying cycle. This introduces the dynamic of 'marginal net worth', or the lifetime value of a customer. When you get this working for you, you drastically reduce the unit cost of acquiring a customer, because you don't have that first crippling acquisition cost attached to each subsequent purchase by that customer.

To carry this off effectively, you need to approach advertising in a very different way from the way most companies and brands do. You have to take a consumer who has never bought from you, and systematically turn that person into not just a regular customer, but a vocal advocate. Imagine an individual out there in the marketplace who for some reason is, for all practical purposes, oblivious to your product, service or brand. For our clients at the WAM Communications Group, we set about moving these cold prospects through a process which we call the WAM Customer Acquisition Sequence.

1 **Brand recognition**

Brand recognition is a low-grade consciousness of your product, service or brand in the public mind. Your advertising has made some impression, but not enough to be effective. This is as far as many advertisers ever get, because of poor communication, or inadequate media penetration, or both.

2 **Brand awareness**

Brand awareness happens when your brand name becomes familiar to large numbers of people within your target market. In a research situation, a person may say something like: 'Yes, I'm aware of Brand A. I've never bought it, but I'm aware of it.' Brand awareness is crucial to the success of any advertising strategy, but on its own, it is still not enough. You need to progress to the next stage.

3 **Brand recall**

Brand recall occurs when, at the moment of a buying decision, a consumer is able to produce a menu of buying options from top of mind. A person who suddenly needs to buy a mobile phone might instantly produce a shortlist like:

WAM CUSTOMER
ACQUISITION SEQUENCE

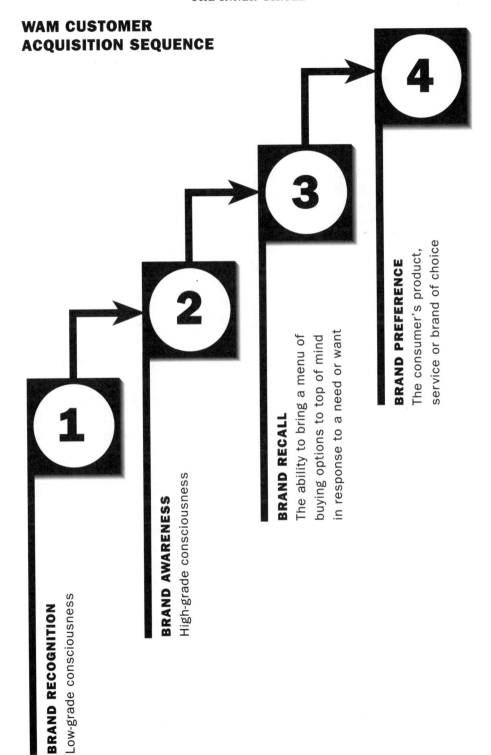

BRAND RECOGNITION
Low-grade consciousness

BRAND AWARENESS
High-grade consciousness

BRAND RECALL
The ability to bring a menu of
buying options to top of mind
in response to a need or want

BRAND PREFERENCE
The consumer's product,
service or brand of choice

i   Strathfield Car Radio
ii   Ryda
iii   The Com Store
iv   Century 21 Telecommunications

The chances are that this person will buy from one of those four suppliers, rather than go to the trouble of locating more buying options. The moral here is that if you're not on that shortlist, you're not in the game. Brand recall is as far as most advertisers go. But to achieve that ongoing buying cycle mentioned earlier, you need to move on to the fourth and final stage.

4   Brand preference

Brand preference happens when a consumer says: 'I can recall Brand X, Brand Y and Brand Z, but I choose Brand X because ...' Making this happen is the object of this book. Everything you will read from this point on is designed to bring about this intriguing and tantalising outcome. The secret is to use your existing advertising budget to move people further along the Customer Acquisition Sequence than would normally be possible, simply by working smarter.

An interesting way to approach this whole topic is to take your mind back to your last visit to the supermarket. As you look around the store, in your mind's eye you become aware that every single product in that store falls either inside, or outside a threshold we call the 'Inner Circle'. The Inner Circle is something everyone has, each is unique in its own way, and it plays a major role in the customer acquisition process.

Think of the Inner Circle as an imaginary circle that contains everything that constitutes your personal and private world. It contains your family, your special friends, your favourite brand of toothpaste, your favourite breakfast cereal, tea, coffee – in fact all of those special products, services and brands you've adopted as your own. And you've developed an intimate relationship with those products and services and brands in your Inner Circle. You've bonded with them in a very special way. They've become like family, and it's a long-term relationship built on familiarity and trust. They are not just casual purchases; they play a pivotal role in your life support system.

There are three things to understand about the Inner Circle if you're to come even close to optimising your advertising and marketing expenditure:

1   The Inner Circle is the basis of all repeat business.
2   You can't gatecrash the Inner Circle.
3   You're not in it, and your competitors are.

THE INNER CIRCLE IS THE BASIS OF ALL REPEAT BUSINESS

Think about those products, services and brands inside your own Inner Circle. Isn't it true that these are the very things that you buy again and again? Occasionally you may be seduced into buying a competitive brand because of some special deal, or maybe because your favourite brand is out of stock, but you always come back, because the things in your Inner Circle are special.

This is another way of saying that if you want repeat business, then you'd better figure out a way to get into your prospect's Inner Circle. Ultimately, because of the repeat business factor, the Inner Circle is the name of the game. The Inner Circle is where the action is, and because it takes into account the accumulated lifetime value of a customer, it's also where the long-term profits are.

YOU CAN'T GATECRASH THE INNER CIRCLE

This is because admission to the Inner Circle is by *invitation only*. You see, as consumers, it's our Inner Circle, and we get to decide what goes in there and what doesn't. This is one reason why so many people find those aggressive hard-sell retail commercials so abrasive and patronising. An Inner Circle relationship is a lot like a romantic relationship in that it's based on attraction, not coercion. And herein lies one of the great lessons not only of advertising and marketing, but of life itself:

> >> **Attraction happens *when we become attractive*, not when we come on strong.**

YOU'RE NOT IN IT, AND YOUR COMPETITORS ARE

With this in mind, understand that whenever you run an advertisement, what you're actually saying to your version of Stanley and all of those thousands of other Stanleys out there in the marketplace is: 'Hey! Don't buy that product in your Inner Circle, the one where you have this great relationship built on familiarity and trust. Buy from us instead, this bunch of complete strangers.' It's not until you see things in that light, you begin to appreciate the absolute futility of so much of the advertising you see around you, and come to understand why so much of it is ignored.

This is an inconvenient situation to say the least. Here you are trying to connect with a prospect who doesn't want to know about you, a prospect who has tuned you out, and is for all practical purposes immune to advertising, and you're trying to get inside an Inner Circle that can't be gatecrashed. However, because long-term profits occur as a direct result of repeat sales, you must find a way to enter the Inner Circle of this person if you're to continue to prosper and grow as a company or brand.

If you agree that the Inner Circle is the name of the game, that the Inner Circle is where all the action is and where the long-term profits are, then the sixty-four thousand dollar question becomes: How do you get inside the Inner Circle?

> **It goes without saying that your product, service or brand must first be *worthy* of being in your prospect's Inner Circle. It must stack up favourably with your competition in terms of both excellence and value.**

For all its impregnability, there is a way inside the Inner Circle, but this requires that you do certain things in a certain way, every single time. In other words, you need a system. At the WAM Communications Group, in order to achieve this outcome consistently for our own clients, over many years we developed an extraordinary technology that we call the WAM Rapid Response System. The system approaches advertising in an unorthodox way, and certainly produces unorthodox results for our clients.

There are two quite separate issues with the Inner Circle. First you have to get on the inside, and then you have to figure out how to stay there. The Rapid Response System is the key to influencing people to want to buy from you, but from that point, it's up to you to do whatever it takes to turn them into not just customers, but advocates. One of the most effective ways to do this is to build a culture within your organisation which values and consistently delivers the highest levels of customer service.

Research has shown that the major reason for people dropping out and changing brands is perceived indifference. Customers need to believe that you care about them. It goes without saying that you must never, ever, fail to deliver on your promise. To lose a one-time customer is bad enough, but to lose a regular customer is a tragedy.

THE WAM RAPID RESPONSE SYSTEM IN A NUTSHELL

Standing between you and the Inner Circle are five Hot Zones: very specific and very sensitive areas of resistance in your prospect. In order to break down these areas of resistance and create a connection, you'll need to use a special set of marketing tools called Activators. You'll engage these Activators by systematically loading them with memes, and then use them as building blocks for all of your future advertising. This means that you'll have a solid base to work from, rather than starting from scratch each time you run an advertisement or a campaign.

The five Hot Zones stem from the fact that despite the many differences that exist between individuals, there are certain key characteristics of the human psyche which cross all boundaries. They are cross-cultural and common to all age groups, socio-economic groups, religious groups and nationalities. They also have a profound effect on the marketing process, and constitute formidable barriers to the Inner Circle.

Although there are many of these universal human traits, we have identified the five which most impact upon your ability to connect with people through your marketing and advertising. These barriers, or Hot Zones, are so fundamental that they can be regarded as universal laws of nature.

1   **Identity**
    To make sense of a complex world, people have a fundamental need to pigeon-hole and classify everything in order to understand what things mean, and how to relate to them. Your product or brand name must convey a definitive meaning beyond that of simply an industry participant.

2   **Emotion**
    The most important thing in people's lives at any given moment is the way they feel. You must connect with them at the emotional level.

3   **Self-interest**
    The number one motivator of human behaviour is self-interest. You must clearly indicate how and why your prospect's sense of self-interest will be best served by buying from you rather than a competitor.

4　**Recall**

People's short-term memory is extremely volatile, and evaporates very quickly. You must provide a way to help people to remember your product or brand name at the moment they're ready to make a buying decision.

5　**Resentment**

People tend to have an underlying resentment towards advertising and see it as an intrusion, an invasion of their privacy. Consequently they tend to ignore it. You must find a way to break through this growing tide of resentment and connect with people in a way that they find both appealing and engaging.

To have any hope of success, advertising must find a way to align itself with these human traits or propensities, in a way that causes the ripple of attraction to flow from the consumer to the product, rather than the other way around. It is the failure to do this that causes people to shy away from advertising, particularly if they feel they are being patronised or deceived in some way. In the chapters which follow, we will be discussing each of these human traits in depth, and exactly how to turn them to your advantage.

•

>> **Any time an advertisement works, it works only because it has managed to break through at least one of the five barriers. However, very few people who create advertising have even the foggiest notion of the existence of these barriers, much less a strategy for routinely dealing with them in order to create a favourable consumer response.**

•

During our diagnostic consultations, we find that business managers are very seldom clear about why some commercials or campaigns were more successful than others. When you analyse them in terms of the above five areas of resistance, however, things very quickly swing into focus. The act of removing just one of these barriers, whether by accident or design, makes it just that much more likely that a consumer will respond favourably to an advertising message.

Remove two or more of these barriers and you greatly increase your chances of success. The Rapid Response System has been designed to take the guesswork out of advertising by routinely removing all five of these barriers, and in the process creating an environment of attraction, not coercion.

•

>> **Just as the martial arts employ the principle of channelling your opponent's strength to work to your advantage, the Rapid Response System is designed to channel the five areas of resistance and redirect them so that they work for you, rather than against you.**

•

THE CREATIVE CHALLENGE

The secret to creating effective advertising revolves around identifying and executing all of the ideas which must be conveyed in an advertisement so that a consumer feels comfortable, or indeed motivated, to respond. It is a widely held maxim that an advertisement should be built around one single idea, and this is quite true. The problem you have, however, is that unless and until people can somehow intuit answers to those issues embodied in the five Hot Zones, your advertising is unlikely to prove effective in the long term. This raises the issue of foreground and background information.

FOREGROUND INFORMATION

Foreground information relates to your key proposition. People must be able to comprehend instantly what the advertisement is all about. Foreground information usually works best when it is executed as a headline statement embodying some kind of engaging proposition. Foreground information fulfils two main functions:

1   To flag down targeted consumers and create interest.
2   To buy precious time. Once you have your prospect's attention, he or she is much more likely to take the time to examine your advertisement more fully.

BACKGROUND INFORMATION

Background information relates to those elusive but essential ideas which defuse and neutralise the five Hot Zones. If these ideas are not evident in your advertisement, you're operating under a very serious handicap. The following chapters provide a wealth of information and techniques to help you to get these ideas across in ways that don't impinge upon your core message. Background information usually takes the form of layered or stacked memes of various kinds, which clearly express those key ideas without getting in the way of your key proposition.

PREPARING YOUR CREATIVE BRIEF

After you have done all your homework, when you're very clear on exactly what you want to say in your advertisement, break it all down into a series of separate ideas and put it all in a list. Express each idea in as few words as it takes to encapsulate the thought. The headings for your list might look something like:

Idea 1   This is my key proposition or offer: …

Idea 2   This is how I want people to pigeon-hole us: …

Idea 3   This is the emotional takeout for the consumer: …

Idea 4   This is why the consumer's sense of self-interest is best served in buying from us rather than from a competitor: …

Idea 5   This is how I intend to make it easy for people to remember our name when they're ready to make a buying decision: …

Idea 6   This is how I intend to break through the media clutter and connect with my prospect: …

The next step in the creative challenge is to ask yourself the question: Which of these ideas is *really* my key proposition? You may think that it's your promotional offer but in fact it may be, for example, that first of all people have to trust you. This would mean creatively articulating the 'trust' idea as an engaging, cogent security meme. If you can find a way to make this meme function as *background* information, you will then have more space available in your advertisement to say what you really want to say.

This was executed to perfection in the old Norman Ross television commercials which featured the Reverend Barrie Howard, whose closing words were always:

These offers are genuine, otherwise I wouldn't be doing this commercial.

How can you argue with the messenger of God? The good Reverend himself became a security meme that is about as good as it gets. Using this brilliant marketing strategy, Norman Ross was able to very quickly build up enormous credibility with the buying public without ever needing to come right out and say: 'Trust us'. Reassured by the ultimate security meme, people were free to focus on the promotional offer. There was no need for the advertiser to waste valuable media space in the commercial establishing credibility. It all happened *concurrently*.

Your next question then becomes: How can I simplify each of the remaining ideas, and lace them with emotion, so that they become not just ideas, but memes?

If you put some time into studying the chapter on memes, you'll begin to see all kinds of ways in which you might accomplish this. In all likelihood, you'll find that layering and stacking are the two techniques you will use most often to execute this concept of foreground and background information.

After you have gone through this process a few times, you'll find that these background issues can be standardised into a working template format, and integrated into your advertisements in a way that gives them continuity. When you do this consistently, people come to recognise your advertising, regardless of the medium. They come to know and trust you, and understand how you fit into their world, regardless of what your present promotional offer happens to be.

The object of the exercise is to use the power of memes to transmit these background ideas to your prospect without that person realising exactly what is happening. Ideally, your prospect should be consciously aware of your key proposition, but quite unaware that his or her five Hot Zones are being systematically neutralised.

The following five chapters are devoted to the five Activators, which resonate and harmonise with these five Hot Zones. The secret to success with the Rapid Response System lies in engaging all five Activators on a consistent basis. When you become familiar with the system, you'll recognise that certain advertisers use some of them some of the time. But use all five Activators all of the time, and you won't believe the results that are possible.

You'll find that they don't simply add together, but rather they interact *exponentially* to produce explosive results.

THE MAIN POINTS

-

1 >> EVERYBODY HAS AN INNER CIRCLE

-

Every product, service or brand in the marketplace falls either outside or inside a threshold called the Inner Circle, and it's different for each individual. We have a very special relationship with these products, services and brands, a relationship built over time and based on familiarity and trust. That's why we keep coming back.

-

2 >> THE THREE THINGS TO UNDERSTAND
ABOUT THE INNER CIRCLE

There are three things to understand about the Inner Circle:

i   Because it contains only those products, services and brands that people buy over and over again, the Inner Circle is the basis of all repeat business.

ii   You can't gatecrash the Inner Circle, because admission is by invitation only.

iii You're not in it, and your competitors are.

-

3 >> THE INNER CIRCLE IS THE NAME OF THE GAME

-

For most companies, the only kind of customer really worth having is a repeat customer. A one-shot sale is all well and good, but at the end of the day, it's the repeat business that makes the difference. For that reason, the Inner Circle is the name of the game. It's where the action is, and where the long-term profits are.

-

4 >> THE FIVE HOT ZONES

-

Within the human psyche, there are five cross-cultural traits or characteristics which constitute formidable barriers to the advertising process. In broad category terms, these barriers relate to Identity, Emotion, Self-interest, Recall and Resentment. Just as the martial arts employ the principle of channelling your opponent's strength to work to your advantage, the WAM Rapid Response System is designed to channel these five areas of resistance and redirect them so that they work for you, rather than against you.

5 >> FOREGROUND AND BACKGROUND INFORMATION

Foreground information relates to your key proposition or offer. It should be designed to attract attention and buy enough time for your prospect to become interested enough to look for more information. Background information is designed to neutralise the barriers embodied in the five Hot Zones. In an ideal world, these background issues should operate almost at a subliminal level.

The secret to success lies in your ability to turn these ideas into contagious memes. You must then arrive at a creative solution in which you juxtapose your key memes in a way that keeps the foreground information in the foreground, and the background information in the background. When you do this correctly, your advertisement comes across as being very simple and clear, but at the same time neutralises the barriers implicit in the five Hot Zones.

Now that you have a working knowledge of the meme concept and the five Hot Zones, it's time to start turning things to your advantage. Take a look at Activator One ...

CHAPTER 3

IDENTITY

'Who are you?'

For a brand to take off and fly, it must first deliberately and single-mindedly set about acquiring and owning a little piece of the minds of millions of people.

Activator One is about your identity in your industry, and specifically about your focus as a company.

We all have a fundamental need to make sense of the world around us. We do this by pigeon-holing and classifying everything, so that we understand what it means, and how to relate to it. We do this with people, and with products, services and brands. If you want to buy an expensive, sophisticated gift for someone special, certain suppliers spring to mind because you have them mentally categorised in that way. If you happen to be looking for things like convenience, or the lowest price in town, other suppliers will spring to mind. You know exactly what to expect when you get there, you understand how to relate to them, and you can be reasonably certain there will be no surprises.

Understand that people are going to pigeon-hole your product, service or brand whether you like it or not, and it's up to you to tell people exactly what you want to be pigeon-holed *as*, because if you don't, they're going to give you a default definition of their own, and you probably won't like what you hear; something like 'Just another one of *those*', or even worse, 'I don't know and I don't care'.

So many companies and brands make the fatal mistake of trying to be all things to all people. They believe this will expand their customer base, thereby increasing their profit potential. But that's not how it works.

> **>> In trying to become all things to all people, you end up becoming nothing to anybody, and basically render yourself invisible in the marketplace.**

The secret is to have your product or brand name become synonymous with something special to your customers and prospects. When you become widely known for something special, you give people a reason to find you interesting, intriguing and attractive, where before there was nothing special; and in the process, you'll find you've just knocked over the first major barrier to the Inner Circle.

'WHO ARE YOU?'

This is one of the most simple, yet profound questions you could ever be called upon to answer. Why? Because from a business perspective, your identity, or lack thereof, is one of the main determining factors that control the level of success or otherwise that your company, product or brand is capable of reaching in the long term.

Before a customer can be expected to make an intelligent and informed decision to buy from you, that person must have a clear perception of how and where you fit into their world. Your name must somehow convey a secondary meaning, a deeper, defining meaning beyond that of an industry participant. People operate from a mental hierarchy of suppliers, and to qualify as a viable option, you must first occupy a position on their hierarchical ladder.

Success in business is all about making critical distinctions. The following key distinction is not generally recognised or understood, which places you in a position of power when you take advantage of it:

●

>> **There is a world of difference between a prospect knowing your product or brand name, and understanding what it *means*.**

●

It is quite possible for people to be very familiar with your brand name, but not to consider buying from you because it has no defining meaning for them, no sense of identity.

What does your product or company name mean? If you could look it up in a dictionary what would it say? Imagine you're at a social function and an overseas visitor comes up and says something like: 'Hi, which company are you with?'

You tell them, and they reply 'Oh really, what's that?'

What are you going to say in reply to that question that expresses exactly the right sentiment and creates understanding, something that evokes the unspoken response, 'Oh, right. I get it.'

It may come as a surprise to learn that very few people in business can come up with a lucid short statement that describes their product or brand in a simple and concise way. We're not talking about slogans. Statements like 'Committed to excellence', or 'Number one for quality and service' amount to nothing more than corporate fluff. They come across as glib, superficial phrases which serve no useful purpose at all, except perhaps to stroke the corporate ego.

The answer is to develop an identity meme, a clear and cogent identity statement that creates instant understanding. Depending upon your individual circumstances, you may or may not want this identity statement also to provide a reason for people to favour your company or brand in the marketplace. We'll be exploring this possibility in Chapter 5.

Developing an identity meme means aligning your strategic thinking with people's basic need to categorise. Before they can make you a part of their world, their reality, they need to mentally pigeon-hole you in a way that defines your relative position in the marketplace.

You know what Smiths means. It means potato chips: 'the original and the best'. It says so, right there on the pack. You know what Evian is: 'natural spring water from the French Alps'. It's on the label of every bottle, right alongside the logo. Stolychnaya is 'genuine Russian vodka'. Again, that short, descriptive statement appears as part of the logo, effectively distinguishing Stoli from its many non-Russian competitors. This idea of an identity statement applies to all companies and brands, from the biggest to the smallest. Very few, however, get it right.

At our business development clinics we ask each of the participants, people from top management through to front-line personnel, to write down the answer to that simple question: Who are you? These people are amazed at the extent of the differences of opinion between members of the group. Seldom, if ever, is there a solid consensus. Each person seems to have his or her own personal concept of what their company or product name means. If *management* is not clear about exactly who you are, then it should come as no surprise to learn that the public hasn't a clue who you are either.

•

>> **Consumers identify with specialists, not generalists. For this reason, people need to comprehend your market niche before they can relate to you and make intelligent buying decisions.**

•

The very mention of your product or brand name should evoke a specific feeling, in the way that we respond to people's names with specific feelings. This feeling then becomes an integral part of your product or brand's personality.

BRAND PERSONALITY

In his book *Ogilvy on Advertising*, David Ogilvy makes some interesting comments on brand image, or brand personality:

> Products, like people, have personalities, and they can make or break them in the marketplace. The personality of a product is an amalgam of many things – its name, its packaging, its price, the style of its advertising, and, above all, the nature of the product itself.
>
> ... When you choose a brand of whisky, you are choosing an image. Jack Daniel's projects an image of homespun honesty and thereby persuades you that Jack Daniel's is worth its premium price.

Jack Daniel's advertising plays the meme game for all it's worth. Whenever you see advertising depicting those laid-back old Tennessee boys with all the time in the world, just sitting back waiting for that whisky to mature, you're taking a powerful mind virus, an identity meme, on board. Having downloaded into the consumer's mind, that meme works away silently but efficiently beneath the surface, systematically shifting perceptions, and shaping consumer beliefs about the product.

Ogilvy is right. People aren't buying the whisky at all. They're buying an image, a feeling about the way they believe the product to be. Even though a person may now buy the product for its taste, the original motivation to buy will have been related in some way to the personality of the brand.

Brand personality has the ability to obscure reality, and in the process, determine a product or brand's degree of success or failure in the marketplace. For this reason, brand personality should be a major consideration when you are working on positioning your company, product or brand.

THE LEMMING EFFECT

In the introduction to this book we spoke of a paradox called the Lemming Effect, whereby otherwise astute business managers inexplicably become blind to the fact that their advertising does not actually promote their product or brand, but merely their product or brand *category*, rendering it largely ineffective. At first glance this apparent inconsistency can be a complete mystery, until you look at it from the perspective of memes. You will remember that one of the defining characteristics of the meme is its ability to drive human behaviour. The key to understanding the uncharacteristic behaviour implicit in the Lemming Effect lies in a meme whose meaning has become corrupted over time. That meme is the word 'positioning'.

Try this test for yourself. Ask a number of advertising or marketing people to define the term 'positioning'. The chances are that every one of them will give you an answer along the lines of: 'Targeting a product or brand to consumers within a specific demographic and/or psychographic grouping.'

As it happens, that is not what positioning is about. Positioning is not just about targeting. It is about a product or brand *owning an idea* in the minds of consumers within a specific demographic and/or psychographic grouping – a very different concept. Over time, the original meaning has become seriously corrupted, but the corrupted meme has nevertheless continued to spread from mind to mind throughout the advertising and marketing community, resulting in a widespread misconception of the original idea. Unfortunately, in the process, the original meme has lost much of its potency.

Consequently, instead of using advertising to create a sense of competitive uniqueness about a product or brand in the public mind, which was the original concept, the advertising industry and its clients are pouring money into creating brand awareness, a much weaker proposition than the concept of competitive uniqueness implicit in the original idea of positioning.

As a result of this misconception, advertising has become much less efficient than it would otherwise be. It's like using a sumo wrestler to move a boulder, when all it requires is a kid with a crowbar. Companies with massive advertising budgets have the luxury of brute strength at their disposal. They are able to meet their advertising and marketing objectives, albeit with gross inefficiency. If you don't have those kinds of resources to throw around, it's worth taking a step back and revisiting the original concept of positioning from the people who developed the idea.

POSITIONING

In 1971, American marketing consultant Jack Trout wrote an article in *Industrial Marketing* magazine entitled 'Positioning is a game people play in today's me-too marketplace'. Ten years later, Jack Trout and his business partner Al Ries published a now-classic marketing book entitled *Positioning: The Battle for Your Mind.* The term 'positioning' has now become firmly established as part of the advertising and marketing vernacular.

To use their own words:

> According to Positioning theory, the human mind contains slots or positions which a company attempts to fill. This is easy to do if the position is empty, but difficult to do if the position is owned by a competitor. In the latter case a company must 'reposition its competition' if it wants to get into the mind.

The final sentence in Jack Trout's book *The New Positioning* really pulls the whole positioning concept together with the quintessential statement:

If you don't have a simple, differentiating idea to drive your company or brand, you'd better have a great price.

Who *are* you? Are you the experts? Are you the fun people to do business with? Do you make shopping easy? Are you the industry specialists? Do you have the longest guarantee? Are you the biggest in the country? Like Joy perfume, are you the most expensive? Or like Nordstroms, or Stu Leonard's grocery stores in New York, are you renowned for your legendary customer service? Are you the freshest, the cheapest, the trendiest, the most convenient? Are you always on time? Who are you?

Take mints for example. What differentiates one mint from another? The taste? The packaging? The shape? Certainly these things play a part, but the inclination to prefer one brand over another has little to do with the commodity itself, and everything to do with perception, positioning, and brand personality.

In a marketplace already crowded with mints of all kinds, a product called SMINT has positioned itself as the mint for lovers. Its positioning statement is a good example of how to use the super-simplicity of an identity meme to get your point across in an instant:

NO SMINT. NO KISS.

Rendered in a graffiti script, the headline for a print advertisement for SMINT in *Who Weekly* read:

The difference between a good night kiss and a good morning kiss.

The reality is that any mint at all would probably work just as well as another. However, positioning SMINT as the mint for lovers is a strategy which will undoubtedly have a positive effect on that market segment and, as a result, win market share that it might not have otherwise won.

It is the same with soy drinks. When WAM was appointed to the Vitasoy account, the brand had been declining in market share, having lost its second place in the category to So Natural. Because of the nature of the market forces inherent in brand leadership, the number three slot is not an attractive place to be.

By implementing a strategy whereby Vitasoy rapidly and decisively took ownership and control of the 'organic' segment of the soy drink market, and by implementing the system outlined in this book, we were able to recapture the number two market position for the brand. In the following twelve-month period, Vitasoy experienced a 96 per cent volume increase, and became one of the fastest growing packaged goods brands in Woolworths: a convincing demonstration of the power of owning an engaging idea in the mind of the consumer.

There was a time when, although it was an excellent product at a premium price, Vitasoy was just another soy drink, just another face in the crowd. Today, Vitasoy is the *organic* soy drink, and that distinction has made all the difference in the world.

So what is it about your product or brand that defines your position in the marketplace? What is the one distinguishing characteristic, or area of focus, that will make it easy for people to tag your name mentally and understand exactly what to expect when they come to do business with you?

Identity is something you absolutely must define and control, because if you don't, the public will do it for you and, as has already been pointed out, you're probably not going to like what you hear. It can be a humbling experience to discover that, in spite of your achievements, your innovations, your policies, your systems, your expensive advertising campaigns, your staff training and everything else that has been a source of pride to you, to most people your product or brand name means nothing at all.

DEVELOPING A CONGRUENT IDENTITY

So how do you go about creating a clear and powerful identity for your product or brand?

Firstly, understand that although you may think of your identity as being something straightforward and simple, you actually have to contend with four identities:

1   **Your Cognitive Identity**
    This is the identity you think you have.

2   **Your Projected Identity**
    This is the identity you're actually sending out into the marketplace. Depending on your ability to keep a check on things like quality control and staff attitudes, your projected identity may bear no resemblance whatsoever to your cognitive identity.

3   **Your Perceived Identity**
    This is the way the marketplace actually sees you. It takes into account

things like packaging, product consistency, customer service, the attitude of your sales people, the look and fitout of your premises compared with that of your competitors.

4   Your Optimal Identity

This is the congruent identity you need to develop and project into the marketplace if you are to achieve your desired outcome in business. Ideally, all four identities should be the same, but rarely ever are. McDonald's is a good example of a company with a totally congruent identity.

CREATING A POSITIONING STATEMENT

You identify and claim your place in the public mind by developing a lucid and well-considered positioning statement and articulating it as a meme. Remember our working definition of a meme? It's a self-explanatory symbol; an idea or concept that has been refined, distilled, stripped down to its bare essentials and then super-simplified in such a way that anybody can grasp its meaning instantly and effortlessly.

A positioning statement is a crisp, simple sentence or phrase (a meme), which defines your chosen market niche, using as few words as it takes to convey the meaning. It needs to convey something beyond 'We're in the computer industry'.

Compaq and Dell Computers have very different modes of operation, which certainly have a bearing on the way in which they attract customers. Compaq markets its range of products through retail outlets, and maintains warehouse stock.

Dell, on the other hand, does not have a warehouse at all. Nor does it carry any stock. Dell computers are custom-made, shipped direct to customers from overseas, and are not available from retailers anywhere. They're sold direct. This is achieved by giving customers a hands-on experience of the product by means of a free thirty-day trial, an attractive proposition in anybody's language. Try getting that from a Dell competitor.

However, it's unlikely that the average person about to buy a computer would have any idea of these fundamental differences between the two companies, because of the lack of a defining positioning statement from either of them. Compaq's 'Quality and performance without compromise' slogan certainly doesn't give us any real idea of what the brand is all about, nor does it describe Compaq's market niche. We would hope that any computer at all would have those attributes. Dell's corporate slogan, 'Your very personal computer company', carries more meaning, but is not a meme.

Ideally, your positioning statement should appear in all of your communications with the marketplace in a way that's consistently visible and permanently integrated into or around your logo.

In an industry characterised by look-alike alternatives, the whitegoods manufacturer Fisher & Paykel leaves the consumer in no doubt as to its niche in the marketplace. Right there as an integral part of its logo are two magic words:

The innovators.

One look at any Fisher & Paykel product confirms that corporate stance in a way that is at once appealing and credible. The products even *look* hi-tech, with soft touch switches, imaginative styling, and many product features simply not available in competitive products. Customers who want the latest technology are left in no doubt as to which brand to buy, because of F & P's stated market positioning. Its products deliver what it promises: innovation.

•

>> **The words 'The innovators' constitute an identity meme; a textbook model of a well-crafted positioning statement.**

•

To begin the positioning process for your company, product or brand, you need to first identify, and then lay claim to some perceptual high ground. Take a good hard look at your competitors and see if any of them has a clearly articulated positioning statement, or a clearly defined market niche from the customer's perspective. Are any of them widely known for some specific attribute?

•

>> **The key to spectacular success is to have your company, product, or brand name become synonymous with something your customers and prospects value highly.**

•

AN EXERCISE IN POSITIONING

Imagine for a moment that you were given the task of developing a market positioning for the women's cosmetics brand, Ella Baché. Your desired outcome is to have the Ella Baché name become synonymous with an engaging idea; something highly desirable and attractive to a large slice of your target market. To achieve this, you would need to bring together three sets of criteria:

1   the wants, needs and attitudes of the marketplace
2   the philosophy and corporate vision of the company
3   the market positions already owned in the public mind by competitive brands.

To begin the positioning process, you would have to carry out some market research in order to get an understanding of the wants, needs and attitudes of your target market. For the sake of argument, let's suppose your research revealed that the four most important attributes of a cosmetics brand to your target market were:

At this point, according to your market research, you could move in any of four different directions, and expect a positive result.

Now suppose the company has a corporate philosophy that values healthy skin much more highly than the other three options. The next question is: Do any competitors already own that market niche? Fortunately for Ella Baché, the answer is no. This makes things relatively easy.

The most effective way to have the Ella Baché brand name become synonymous with the idea of healthy skin is to express it as an identity meme, and then expose it to the marketplace.

In the event, the company, with its advertising agency, did an excellent job of executing that meme. It now appears along with the logo wherever the brand is sold:

Ella Baché Skin fitness

Anybody seeing that four-word identity meme, even just glancing at it casually, would be in no doubt as to what the brand is all about. This simple but definitive positioning statement carries a clear subtext which indelibly links the Ella Baché brand with a health mindset, which is highly desirable to women who value healthy skin as opposed to 'skin camouflage'. The 'Skin fitness' identity meme is so lucid that you could almost write a descriptive essay on the Ella Baché brand based on those two words alone.

FINDING YOUR NICHE

You have now reached a fork in the road. Before you begin the task of developing a positioning statement for your company or brand, you have to decide which of two directions you want to take. In setting up your pigeon-holing communication with the marketplace, you must decide whether to define your company, product or brand name literally, or perceptually.

When you look closely at the positioning statements companies and brands use to describe themselves, you'll find that they fall into three main categories:

1   **Slogans**
    These are lofty statements, like Budget's 'All the difference in the world', and Compaq's 'Quality and performance without compromise'. Statements such as these offer little credibility or value in a cynical marketplace.

2   **Literal descriptions**
    These are short descriptive phrases that tell you what a product or brand *is*. Examples of this are Evian's 'natural spring water from the French Alps', and Stolichnaya's 'genuine Russian vodka'. There is no doubt that a literal description is light years ahead of a meaningless slogan. The downside, however, is that if you have a number of serious competitors with exactly the same kind of literal description, it can sink you in the murky waters of anonymity.

3 Perceptual descriptions

These are short descriptive phrases, or even single words, which in-dicate how and where products and brands fit into people's lives. For example, Ella Baché, Fisher & Paykel and Woolworths do not offer literal descriptions of their brands. Their positioning statements each describe a finely targeted niche within their industry.

>> **To stand out from the pack, you need to take on the persona and the aura of a specialist. Your positioning statement should reflect that area of specialisation, rather than simply describe you in a way that makes you appear to be just like your competition.**

Assume for a moment you have discovered that three of your com-petitors have good, clearly articulated positioning statements. Your next task is to locate a niche, a powerful area of focus which has not been claimed by your competitors, and which you would feel comfortable in filling.

Even though each of you may be doing exactly the same thing, you must appear to specialise in some specific area. Your chosen niche should appeal to one specific market segment above all others, if you are to move ahead and gain market share.

It's called polarity. If one of your competitors is focusing on range, another is focusing on convenience and another is focusing on price, then you need to focus on an equivalent but opposite attribute. Maybe something like outstanding customer service.

The wonderful thing about positioning is that it has the effect of segmenting the market for you. If you are not interested in getting into a competitive price spiral, if range and convenience are not your strong points, then positioning yourself as the people who give legendary customer service will serve to filter out the kinds of people you don't really want, and attract the very people you do.

The process of articulating a positioning statement normally requires a great deal of thought and collaborative effort. Invariably your first attempts seem to come close, but don't quite make it. They don't feel quite right, or something is missing. Usually they're too long, wordy or complicated. Your best attempt needs to be systematically reverbalised, stripped down and polished until it sparkles with clarity. You'll recognise it as soon as you see it, because it will feel just right.

Our suggestion is that you first collect all the relevant information you can find that relates to what your competitors are doing in the marketplace. This includes TV commercials, radio spots, press clippings, mailers, anything at all. Then you analyse it and identify exactly which market segment, if any, each of them addresses *and owns* in the public mind.

If a competitor does not yet actually *own* a niche or position, if they have not yet driven it into people's minds to the point that it is generally recognised throughout the marketplace, then it's fair game. Go for it!

You then get together with your key people and go through the process of identifying and selecting the point of focus you all agree feels right for your company, making sure that it is not already owned by one of your competitors. In its final form, to qualify as an identity meme, it must of necessity be short, sweet and lucid. It must be a model of simplicity.

PRE-EMPTIVE MARKETING

Provided you are not being blocked by a competitor, you can always take the initiative and adopt an ideal and obvious positioning which any of them could have claimed, but as yet have not. This is called 'pre-emptive marketing', and it's one of the single most powerful concepts available to you. Drive an identity meme into the public mind quickly and efficiently, and you own it.

However, when you choose your niche, be very certain it is something you can (or could) deliver consistently, and to a high degree of excellence, or people will not believe you. It's the combination of the promise, and then going over the top on the delivery of that promise, that brings the marketplace to life and gets people excited.

A brilliant example of pre-emptive marketing in action was the Heinz Peak Nutrition Process®. Heinz baby foods, like most other baby foods, were sealed and then cooked in the container, which locked in the goodness. The decision to take ownership of this simple generic idea in the minds of consumers by refining it and registering it as the Heinz Peak Nutrition Process was a marketing master-stroke. The 'Heinz Peak Nutrition Process' name is a highly potent attraction meme, which indelibly locks the brand into the concept. The name says it all. But the real zinger lies in the emotional connection. What more could any mother ask for in her baby's food than peak nutrition? It doesn't get any better than that.

'We're Woolworths the fresh food people' is a classic example of pre-emptive marketing in action. Are Woolworths' products any fresher than those of its competitors? Maybe, and maybe not. But if you ask a random group of people what word they associate with Woolworths, 'fresh' will come up somewhere close to 100 per cent of the time.

In getting that positioning statement out into the marketplace first, Woolworths has effectively blocked any competitor from using the same hook. This is not only because the risk of confusion would be out of line with the possible rewards, but because people tend to see advertisers who blatantly copy as somehow lacking in integrity.

The only real threat to the Woolworths positioning on the horizon at the time of writing appears to come from Franklins 'Big Fresh', a food chain based on the famous Stu Leonard stores in New York. It will be interesting to see if and how this affects Woolworths' market position in relation to the concept of 'fresh'.

It makes no difference at all if each of your competitors is doing exactly the same thing, and providing exactly the same services. It's a very simple matter to take one specific service niche, one that the consumer finds relevant and desirable, and to become widely known for it; to specialise in it. Whoever is first into the minds of your customers and prospects with a concept owns it, lock, stock and barrel.

POSITIONING AND BRAND EQUITY

There is an important issue to be considered regarding corporate positioning. To be effective in the long term, each advertisement must have a residual effect. It must leave a lingering trace in the mind of the consumer. Every time you advertise, another layer of perceptual veneer is laid over the marketplace. Eventually, you reach the stage where you own a little piece of the minds of millions of people.

Many companies fail to comprehend the value of the intellectual property which has been installed in people's minds. The residual brand awareness and brand recall that has been built over time is extremely valuable. It could very easily have a negotiable value of many millions of dollars.

For this reason, you should think long and hard before you finally adopt a corporate positioning, and be quite certain it is going to remain viable for many years into the foreseeable future and beyond.

If, for example, Big Fresh were to step up its advertising to the point where 'the fresh food people' positioning for Woolworths ceased to have credibility in the public mind, Woolworths could well find itself being forced to consider an alternative positioning stance.

Should something like this happen, and sooner or later it probably will, the dollar loss in accrued brand equity would be incalculable. It would simply vanish overnight. Then the next problem would be to make the Woolworths name mean something else, something quite different; an exercise which would take a lot of time and untold millions of dollars to accomplish.

A less painful strategy for Woolworths might be to take the initiative and dramatise its 'fresh food people' statement, and to give it a new level of credibility; to give it a spectacular presence by developing a corporate policy designed to recapture the imagination of the buying public.

THE FIVE WORD TECHNIQUE

A very effective method you can use to determine your ideal market position is the Five Word Technique. The idea is to survey random members of the public and ask them for five words which they feel describe your product or brand, and five words for each of your main competitors.

Be prepared for a shock when you discover the words that people use to describe you. Unless you already have a strongly established market position, you may not like what you hear.

Recently, we went through this exercise with one of our new clients, who was in serious need of positioning. When we asked people for five words that best described his main competitor, the most frequent answers were:

1   conservative
2   old-fashioned
3   reliable
4   Australian
5   helpful

This gave us a clear direction in formulating an alternative positioning for our client. Working together, we arrived at a new set of five words that represented an opposite polarity from that of his main competitor:

1   young
2   innovative

3   trendy
4   international
5   fashionable

This client now has a clear direction and an image to shoot for, and realises that he must now do whatever it takes to make his business reflect these feelings. Once his brand develops to the point where it matches the new image, we can begin to salt these words throughout the body copy of his advertisements. In the process, we'll gradually create a market position very different from that of his main competitor. We will also have laid the groundwork necessary to develop a formal, cohesive positioning statement. This will then be articulated as an identity meme. In that way, even people who are not in the market will find that they have an understanding of this client's niche in the marketplace.

THE POWER OF A SINGLE WORD TO CREATE A FEELING

It is also possible that just *one* word could be the very thing you need to help you create that special feeling that will identify you, and position you in the minds of your prospects.

The Australian brewer Tooheys has effectively utilised a single word to create a specific feeling:

Tooheys Old – the quiet ale.

The *quiet* ale. How fascinating. They could have just as easily called it 'The raging party animal ale' and it would have been the same product, but with a very different brand image. But as it stands, that positioning statement constitutes an identity meme which is cleanly transmitted in a single glance. It creates a specific feeling about the brand which otherwise would not exist. You can just visualise some guy coming home after a hard day's work, and all he wants to do is just sit down, relax and have … a quiet ale. Which one is he likely to go for?

Is this something that you could apply to your particular product or brand? If one single word could generate the very feeling you would like to convey to your prospects through your advertising and marketing, what would that word be?

Never underestimate the power of a single word to transform the way people perceive your product or service. To quote Ries and Trout:

The most powerful concept in marketing is to own a word in the mind of the consumer.

Real estate people understand this, and play it for all it's worth. Take a glance through the real estate section of any newspaper or magazine, and you'll see this phenomenon in action. More often than not there will be a word or short phrase, usually some kind of superlative, tied in some way to a photograph of the property. Examples of this in a recent magazine were: 'A piece of paradise', 'Entertainer's delight', 'Golden oldie – Circa 1903', 'Art Deco charmer', 'Renovator's dream'. Hackneyed phrases though they may seem, they really do act as a perceptual filter, and colour our perceptions.

Having been set up by one of those descriptive phrases, there is a distinct pressure to see the property in a particular way – one which tends to validate the phrase. Viewed through such a descriptive lens, the reader is subtly manipulated towards a pre-defined interpretation. 'Renovator's dream' might otherwise have been perceived as 'Dump'.

This concept is both subtle and powerful. The words we use to describe something directly influence our focus, and we involuntarily tend to filter out those aspects which do not relate, and to see those that do. Having seen it in this way, it then can be quite difficult to alter our perception and see it any other way.

THE CONCEPT OF REPOSITIONING

Sometimes it turns out that you already have an established market position which for some reason has become non-viable. Maybe technology has changed and now you're perceived to be old-fashioned or out of date. Maybe times have changed to the extent that your company name no longer adequately reflects what you do, or is downright confusing. Is there anything you can do about it? Absolutely. It's called repositioning. It's not easy to do, but it can be done.

With repositioning you take people through a two-step process:

1   You ask them to forget an existing idea.
2   You ask them to learn a new one.

The problem with asking people to forget an idea, concept or perception, is that, in the process of formulating it, a physical connection of molecules called neuro-peptides was created in the brain to support it. This thread of molecules is able to be located, tracked and mapped, and is as real as a strand of fibre optic cable. We have all become in effect hardwired, and the more the concept is reinforced through repetition, the more molecules are added until the original thread becomes a highway.

If you visit someone and a dog rushes out and bites you, a neurological link is created which 'wires' that event into memory. No amount of subsequent friendly behaviour from that dog is ever likely to erase the inevitable twinge of apprehension precipitated by the original event.

When repositioning a brand, a product or a company, it is futile to attempt to erase the existing chain of molecules. It's not possible, because those molecules are as real as the nose on your face. They're there to stay, although they do tend to fade over time.

You begin by laying another thread of molecules; one which does not conflict with the original strand, but which expresses a different and, hopefully, more compelling idea. Then you lay another thread, then another, and another. Through repetition, this new thread develops until it becomes another highway.

In their book *The 22 Immutable Laws of Marketing*, Ries and Trout highlight this idea with their marketing law number two, 'The Law of Category', which states:

> If you can't be first in a category, set up a new category you can be first in.

To put this idea into practice, you have first to decide what your new market niche is going to be, based on where your competitors are at this point in time.

What you don't do is to simply run advertisements that say: 'We've changed! Just come and look at us now.' You have to begin by making both cosmetic and fundamental changes to your organisation that reflect what is in effect a new market category.

For example, maybe you were just another shoe retailer, but now you're repositioning yourself as a specialist in children's footwear. By segmenting the market in this way, you become a bigger fish in a smaller pond. If you're smart, you can create a new market segment or category, and then proceed to dominate it. There's nothing more powerful in business than market leadership, and repositioning is one way of achieving just that.

For many years in the United States, popcorn was just popcorn. In the supermarkets, one brand was pretty much the same as another. Then along came Orville Redenbacher. He had the foresight to adopt this powerful positioning strategy, and created Orville Redenbacher's Gourmet Popping Corn®, complete with his picture on the pack. Suddenly, there was a brand-new category, which Orville Redenbacher's proceeded to dominate.

If your new positioning is high-tech, then you had better look and feel high-tech when people come to do business with you, or you're sure to create an effect called 'cognitive dissonance' in the minds of your prospects. They'll never believe anything you tell them in the future, and they'll never come back because they won't trust you.

Having made the necessary cosmetic and organisational changes to your operation first, you then begin laying new strands of neuro-peptides throughout the marketplace, never again referring to the way things used to be. You need to concentrate solely on establishing your new positioning. It takes time, but the key is not to think in terms of trying to erase old memories, but to instil new perceptions by creating what amounts to a new market category.

THE CONCEPT OF REPOSITIONING YOUR COMPETITORS

Sometimes you can find yourself at a distinct disadvantage because your main competitor has been able to create a perceptual, and possibly unfair, advantage in the public mind. What can you do about it?

In *Positioning*, Ries and Trout give the example of Scope, a then new entry into the personal mouthwash market. The market leader was Listerine, which had an arguably unpleasant taste. In fact, Listerine's advertising strategy at the time was to use the line:

The taste you hate – three times a day.

Scope hit the market with an advertising campaign that effectively knocked Listerine from its number one position by referring to it as 'medicine breath'. Listerine has never fully recovered from this perceptual body blow.

A similar thing happened in the case of aspirin. For many years, aspirin was by far the largest selling pain-relief product in the United

States. No self-respecting household would be without its pack of aspirin in the medicine cupboard. Then Johnson and Johnson came into the market with Tylenol. Before the launch of Tylenol, however, the boffins undertook all kinds of research and discovered isolated instances of stomach bleeding caused by aspirin – not a lot, but enough. Tylenol delivered the *coup de grace* to aspirin with the devastating meme:

Tylenol, for the millions of people who should not be taking aspirin.

As a direct result of that campaign, Tylenol not only displaced aspirin as the number one painkiller nationally, but today Tylenol is reported to be the biggest selling pharmaceutical product in American drugstores. By adopting this stunning strategy, Scope and Tylenol were able to reposition their competitors with spectacular results. If things ever reach the stage where all else has failed, this option is open to you.

SOCIAL PROOF

Another way to position yourself through your advertising is to tap into the concept that Robert Cialdini, author of *Influence: The Psychology of Persuasion*, calls 'social proof'. We tend to like and trust people who are 'just like ourselves'. Social proof is an extremely potent instrument of influence. We've all had the experience at one time or another of seeing a group of people looking up at something. The urge to look up to see what they are looking at is almost irresistible. Sometimes school children do this as a prank.

Many social behavioural experiments have been set up whereby a student will lay on the ground feigning illness. A group of fellow students will then walk by, taking no notice whatever. Other passersby, seeing the students take no notice, also just keep walking. In other circumstances, these very same people would probably not hesitate to help. Perhaps they feel that the students know something they don't, and don't want to make fools of themselves. Unfortunately, many people have died on crowded streets as a result of this odd quirk of human nature, particularly in big cities like New York.

Social proof is the basis of the almost universal success of testimonial-style commercials, in which the consumer identifies with the customer depicted in the commercial. We see 'similar others' telling us how wonderful a product is. Even though we know at an intellectual level that the sponsor has arranged the endorsement, there is a very real pressure to believe the person's story.

For that reason, it makes a lot of sense to choose actors for your radio and TV voice-overs rather than regular station announcers. You can choose a voice that taps right into the comfort zone of your target audience. Actors tend to sound more like ordinary people and are generally more believable, because engaging people's emotions is their special skill.

Another of Robert Cialdini's potent instruments of influence is the principle of authority. If some person in a position of authority says that something is okay, then there is a powerful pressure to take that person's words at face value. Cialdini tells of a social science experiment in the United States in which a casually dressed man deliberately walked right off the footpath into the busy traffic to see if anybody would follow him. Of course, no one did. Then the same man, dressed to look like a top executive and carrying a briefcase, repeated the experiment. This time a number of people followed him into the traffic.

This is why live reads work so well on radio. In exchange for large sums of money, many radio personalities are quite prepared to 'go off at the mouth', endorsing your product or brand. The results are often spectacular. Because these people tend not to sound like regular voice talent, their authority, personality profile and vocal style lend a product or brand a level of credibility it might not otherwise enjoy.

In the visual media, TV and print, you can create the same effect by carefully selecting the individuals who appear in your advertisements. Do they convey the feeling of 'similar others' in your prospect's mind? It's worth taking the time to choose your talent with this in mind in order to maximise that feeling of connection and empathy with your customers and prospects.

INSTANT MARKET SEGMENTATION THROUGH THE USE OF MUSIC

Finally, if you use TV or radio, you can instantly align your product or brand with the right kinds of people within your target market through the astute use of music.

Music acts as a kind of mental barcode, and instantly puts people into a specific frame of mind. Imagine you're watching TV or listening to the radio, and a commercial comes on. Before anybody opens their mouth to speak, the opening few beats of music prepare you mentally for what is to come.

With some forethought, you can very quickly and easily create a distinct feeling of connection in people who relate strongly to that particular type of music. It might be screaming rock, a string quartet, a rippling harp, a contemporary instrumental track, or an emotive piece of sound design. Whatever it is, the moment your prospect hears it, it instantly sets him or her up with the right mental predisposition for what follows.

One aspect of music in advertising that is not generally appreciated, or even understood, is the Pavlovian effect of conditioning. Over time, the opening sounds of certain commercials recreate in us the famous experiment by Dr Pavlov and his salivating dogs. Instead of hearing a bell, we hear a guitar riff or perhaps a drum lick, or maybe a musical sound effect. Most people in the eastern states have to listen for less than a second before they recognise a Strathfield Car Radio commercial. The driving rock music speaks directly to consumers within their target market.

Many older Australians will vividly recall a series of radio commercials for Bonnington's Irish Moss cough syrup. They used to begin with the words 'sip ... sip ... sip', with a violin playing ascending sliding notes which mimicked the words. A simple musical device like that can be worth quite literally millions of dollars in increased revenue to a company with the wit and the foresight to adopt it. For this reason, you're well advised to pay careful attention to the type of music you use for your TV and radio commercials. The music you select should evoke a feeling identical to that generated by even the mention of your company or product name.

Be sure to take your time over this, or you run the risk of sending out mixed messages into the marketplace. Think of your music in terms of memes. What does the music tell your prospect about your product or brand? Is it congruent with your product or brand? If the feeling of the music you use is more up-market, for example, than the feeling of your product, people will tend to have an adverse reaction when they come to do business with you, without quite knowing why. Of course, the reverse is also true. Because of its ability to instantly touch people emotionally, music is a wonderful tool to help you to connect with your prospects very easily.

><

Activator One, then, is the first of five building blocks. It will enable you to create advertisements that will break down the first barrier to the Inner Circle. That barrier or area of resistance is people's need to comprehend what your company or brand name *means,* and exactly how and where to pigeon-hole you.

To bring Activator One online, you need to do the following:

1   Have your product, company or brand name become synonymous with something special. Identify the market niche you intend to dominate, and modify your operations to give that attribute an overt presence. Specify and dramatise it to the point that the people in your target audience perceive you to be a specialist, and take you seriously at that level.

2   Verbalise that market position as the 'long version'. This will invariably be too long and clumsy, but should say all the right things.

3   Refine the long version, distil it, strip it down to its bare essentials, and after all that, super-simplify it until you have a sparkling, clean identity meme. Often when you encounter a great meme, there's a tendency to think: 'That's easy! Anybody could do that.' But when you actually set about creating one from scratch, you'll probably find that it's not as easy as it looks.

Remember the acronym: 'When you need a meme, just call in the TEAM'. Reread the section on memes, and you should find all the material you need to get things moving.

As you work your way through the book, you will realise that ultimately, all five Activators become linked in various ways to produce a synergistic, cohesive whole. You will find that a good strategy is to link Activator One to Activator Three, which deals with influence and leverage. That way, you can kill two birds with the one stone, by creating a compound meme which neutralises both Hot Zones simultaneously.

> •
>
> **>> The expression of Activator One is:**
> **Take ownership of and project a specific market**
> **niche within your industry.**
>
> •

THE MAIN POINTS

•

1 >> WHO *ARE* YOU?

•

There is a world of difference between a prospect knowing your name, and understanding what it *means.*

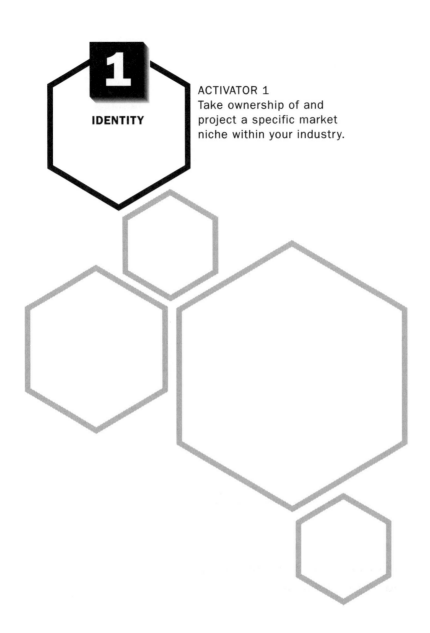

1

IDENTITY

ACTIVATOR 1
Take ownership of and
project a specific market
niche within your industry.

**THE WAM
RAPID RESPONSE SYSTEM**

•

2 >> PEOPLE HAVE A NEED TO PIGEON-HOLE AND CATEGORISE

•

If *management* is not clear about exactly who you are, then it should come as no surprise to learn that the public hasn't a clue who you are either. People have a need to pigeon-hole and categorise you before they can relate to you and make intelligent buying decisions.

•

3 >> POSITIONING

•

According to Ries and Trout's positioning theory:

> The human mind contains slots or positions which a company attempts to fill. This is easy to do if the position is empty, but difficult to do if the position is owned by a competitor.

In order to communicate with the marketplace effectively, you must create and project a clear and powerful identity. As Jack Trout points out:

> If you don't have a simple, differentiating idea to drive your company or brand, you'd better have a great price.

•

4 >> POSITIONING STATEMENT

•

Creating a positioning statement is possibly the single most effective way to identify your product or service accurately in the minds of your prospects. Your positioning statement should ideally appear at every opportunity, along with your company name, preferably integrated into your logo. Woolworths has executed this to perfection. At the time of writing, the size of 'the fresh food people' line has grown visually to about two and a half times the size of the 'Woolworths' line.

•

5 >> POLARITY

•

The concept of polarity in relation to positioning means that ideally you should position yourself in a way that is diametrically opposite to your main competitors. If your competitors appeal to the older market, then you should consider appealing to the younger market. If they are focused on price, then you focus on something quite different, but equally or even more important to your prospects. In this way, you effectively remove yourself from competition, because you're appealing to a completely different market segment.

•

6 >> PRE-EMPTIVE MARKETING

•

Pre-emptive marketing is one of the most powerful but little under-stood concepts available to you. Whoever is first into the public mind with an idea owns it. Once it has been established, competitors are effectively blocked from using the same idea, as not only is confusion likely to be created, and therefore risk, but people tend not to like or respect blatant imitators.

•

7 >> THE FIVE WORD TECHNIQUE

•

The Five Word Technique is a very effective way to begin the position-ing process. It gives you the direction you need to define your ideal market segment, and also lays the groundwork for you to begin the process of developing a meaningful positioning statement.

•

8 >> SOCIAL PROOF

•

We all tend to like and trust 'similar others', people who are just like ourselves. Using people in your advertising who relate directly to your target market can help to align your product or brand with the right kinds of prospects, and have a big influence on your levels of consumer response.

•

9 >> AUTHORITY

•

If a person in a position of authority says that something is okay, then there is a pressure to take his or her words at face value.

•

10 >> MUSIC AND POSITIONING

•

Never underestimate the ability of music to instantly target consumers in a TV or radio commercial. Music acts as a kind of mental barcode that immediately switches people into a frame of mind which anticipates the mood of what is to follow. That is why you should be careful to leave the selection of any kind of advertising music to people who have the skill, and who understand the critical nature of what they are doing.

Having knocked out the first barrier to the Inner Circle, the next step is to take a close look at the emotional connection by engaging Activator Two ...

CHAPTER 4

EMOTION

'Do you have any idea what I really want?'

You cannot sell anything to anybody if you cannot first create,

or stir within them, an emotion. STUART WILDE

Activator Two is about emotion. There is only one reason why people have ever bought from you in the past, and why they will ever buy from you in the future, and that is because they want to change the way they feel. It's that simple.

This means that there is a very strong emotional connection associated with every purchase, and that you had better tap into it in a big way if you are to have any chance of optimising your advertising and marketing dollars.

'Do you have any idea what I *really* want?'

'What kind of question is that?' you ask your customer. It's obvious what you want. If you've come in to buy my product, then my product must be what you want. Right? Wrong!

The simple fact is that nobody on the face of the earth ever bought a product or a service. People don't buy products and they don't buy services, they buy *emotional states of mind.* If you find this difficult to swallow, think it through for a moment. Think about anything you've ever bought in your lifetime. Isn't it true that in the final analysis, the real reason you bought it was to *feel* better in some way?

When you look through and beyond the product, on the other side there is *always* an emotion, a meaning beyond the meaning, a truth beyond the truth.

Take, for example, a person who has just bought a new BMW convertible. What has he or she just bought really? A lump of technology? Whatever it was, it absolutely wasn't just a car, or even transport. If that were all that was wanted, a second-hand Volkswagen would have done.

The emotional trigger may have been something like prestige, status, style, pride, insecurity, jealousy, sex, ego, fun, exhilaration, or a sensational driving experience, but it certainly wasn't just the car. The product itself is never more than the means to an end. And that end is always an emotion. That's why we talk about emotional hot buttons.

Look at anything at all that you have bought in the past week – a tube of toothpaste for example. Ask yourself why you bought it. You will probably come up with an answer like: 'To clean my teeth.' Then ask yourself why you want to clean your teeth. You might then come up with something like: 'To make my breath fresh.' Then ask yourself why you want to have fresh breath. And so on. Inevitably, you will arrive at the real answer: 'Because having a fresh mouth makes me feel good', or 'Because I want to feel better than the way I feel now.' And the need to feel better underlies every buying decision and purchase we make. Feeling good, or bad, is what emotions are all about.

So if you can agree that what the customer really wants is an emotion, then why in the world would you want to offer them your product? In the final analysis, your product turns out not to be the real product at all, but simply the precipitator of an emotional experience.

You should be making the *emotion* the hero of your advertising, and by the way, this is how you get it – through your product. A means to an end.

Take a look at a Johnson's Baby Powder commercial. Are they selling baby powder? No. They're selling you the cutest baby you ever saw, tapping into one of the most powerful emotions there is. The maternal instinct. And does it work? You'd better believe it!

Coca Cola doesn't sell Coke, it sells fun and exhilaration. Levi's doesn't sell jeans, it sells sex. Rolex doesn't sell watches, it sells prestige, and makes an unmistakable statement about a person's social status. Emotion, the precursor of self-interest, is the real driving force in the marketplace. So why not tap into it in a big way?

THE POWER BEHIND THE PURCHASE

What motivates people to buy? Actually there are many reasons, but it's a good question, and one that's worth looking at from an interesting perspective.

A large proportion of the power of advertising is ultimately derived from fear; specifically, fear of the unknown. Fear causes negative emotion and stress, and the vast majority of people spend a great deal of their lives in a state of stress, anxiety and varying degrees of negative emotion. In other words, they feel lousy a lot of the time.

This is due to the fact that people generally tend to be negative in their attitudes to life rather than positive. Of course there are many positive people in the world, but they represent only a very small minority.

If you doubt this, take a look at the news. Look at what sells. The TV shows, soaps, videos, movies, newspapers and magazines that people rely on for their entertainment and information are characterised by violence, trouble, strife and more negative emotion than one person could handle in a lifetime. It's a sad thing, but that's the way it is.

TAPPING INTO THE POWER OF EMOTION

One of the most powerful forces in human nature is the need to move away from discomfort and towards comfort. Nature in its wisdom guides us through life with this simple but extremely effective set of 'traffic signals': pain and pleasure. Pain is nature's warning and pleasure is nature's approval, as long as short-term pleasure does not produce long-term pain, in which case the rule still holds.

In the English language, there are around three thousand words to describe the various shades of human emotion. The fascinating thing about this is that over two thousand of them are negative. Over two-thirds! That fact alone explains a lot. Because the words we use to describe our experience *become* our experience, we can begin to understand the ubiquitous nature of negative emotion among people generally.

Interestingly, studies have shown that if you ask the average person to list all of the emotions he or she has experienced during the past month, practically nobody is able to list more than ten or twelve, and at least two-thirds of those emotions are likely to be negative.

So what has this got to do with marketing and advertising? Everything!

The fact that people feel bad in one way or another so much of the time means that they have a natural and overwhelming need to feel good again, and one of the most effective ways to change an emotional state is to go out and buy something. This is why emotion is such a crucial element in influencing buying decisions, and why advertising is more an art than a science.

Of course this is not to say that fear is the *only* reason people buy things. We often buy things simply because we feel they'll bring us some degree of pleasure, comfort or enjoyment, without necessarily coming from a position of pain.

Like trying to master the game of golf, trying to second-guess human emotions can be a challenging and frustrating pastime, because people are so unpredictable. Whether we realise it or not, we live in a world that lives or dies through the buying, selling and trading of emotions. The truth is that if you advertise, you're in the psychology business, whether you like it or not.

Next time you're wandering around a shopping centre, it's worth looking at the people you see in a new way, realising that every single one of them is there for the express purpose of trying to create or maintain the emotional state of feeling good in some way.

TYING YOUR PRODUCT OR SERVICE TO AN EMOTION

Viewed from this perspective, it makes a lot of sense to look for some answers to the question 'What is it about my product that has the ability to make people feel good in some way?' You can be certain there is an emotional basis there, because it's the only reason people have bought from you at all. The next question to ask is: 'What else is there about my product that has the ability to make people feel good? And what else? And what else?' If you can come up with some new answers to these questions, you've just uncovered a goldmine that's been under your nose all the time. Your focus as a company should be aimed squarely at people's need to feel good, because ultimately that's the only reason they're going to buy from you.

Effective marketing, therefore, provides a lifeline of hope and promise to people in their ongoing struggle to escape stress and feeling bad, and to get back to feeling good again. That's why as a person who advertises, you have every reason to feel good about yourself. Your advertising and marketing creates a win–win situation whereby your customer gets to feel good and you get to move some product. It's a satisfactory outcome all round.

So how do you go about finding out what people really want? At WAM, we have an interesting theory:

1   If you want to know what people want, ask 'em.
2   If you want people to know something, tell 'em.

It's worth the small amount of money, time and effort it takes to initiate some level of basic research to determine what people really want. If you take the time to ask the right questions, people will tell you.

Remember, too, that when you advertise, it's a mistake to think of the marketplace as a giant amorphous crowd of people. Although you're communicating simultaneously with many people, it's *always* one on one.

The emotional factor is the reason our wants are invariably many more than our needs. Buying something is an attempt to buy at least some level of happiness, and happiness is the ultimate drug.

The good news is that very few people who create advertising are aware of the mental processes involved. For that reason, it's quite possible for a smaller company or brand to overtake a larger one simply by skilfully expressing its emotional appeal as a potent meme. Once contact has been made, the meme downloads quickly and easily into the customer's mind in a way that *overtly* holds the promise of emotional comfort.

WHY PEOPLE BUY

Let's restate some of the more common emotions people experience, and express them as buying motivators. We've listed fifty here, but there are certainly many more. See how many of these emotional motivators relate to your product or brand. This will give you a clue as to how to formulate and articulate the emotional hook that is essential if you're to get the kinds of results you're looking for.

[FIFTY BUYING MOTIVATORS
JUST A FEW OF THE *REAL* REASONS WHY PEOPLE BUY

1	To make money	2	To save time
3	To become more comfortable	4	To become more fit and healthy
5	To attract praise	6	To attract the opposite sex
7	To increase enjoyment	8	To protect family
9	To possess things of beauty	10	To emulate others
11	To avoid criticism	12	To protect reputation
13	To make work easier	14	To feel superior
15	To work faster	16	To be trendy
17	To 'keep up with the Joneses'	18	To be excited
19	To feel opulent	20	To communicate better
21	To look younger	22	To preserve the environment
23	To become more efficient	24	To satisfy an impulse
25	To buy friendship	26	To save money
27	To avoid effort	28	To attain better cleanliness
29	To escape or avoid pain	30	To be popular
31	To protect possessions	32	To gratify curiosity
33	To be in style	34	To satisfy appetite
35	To avoid trouble	36	To be individual
37	To access opportunities	38	To escape stress
39	To express love	40	To gain convenience
41	To be entertained	42	To be informed
43	To be organised	44	To give to others
45	To feel safe	46	To feel younger

47 To conserve energy   48 To pursue a hobby or avocation

49 To be accepted   50 To leave a legacy

These kinds of emotional triggers hold the key to answering your prospect's unspoken question: 'Do you have any idea what I *really* want?' Once you have identified the motivator or motivators that most relate to your product, you have that special ingredient you need to create powerful advertisements that will reach out and touch people in a way that will make them want to buy from you.

One of the most effective ways to lift your advertising response level and win market share is to make emotion the predominant feature of your advertising on a consistent basis. This is what memes are all about: simplifying an idea or concept, and then firing it straight at the heart.

When you start making an *emotion* the hero of each advertisement, you will be adding a whole new dimension to your communications with the marketplace. But there's more to this emotional issue than meets the eye.

A MAJOR DISTINCTION

There's a fascinating story about a woman who once asked Charles Revson, the founder and president of the Revlon Corporation, an interesting question. She asked: 'Mr Revson, what exactly is your product?'

His answer showed an amazing depth of insight and understanding of the marketplace. He replied: 'On the factory floors, our product is cosmetics, but in the department stores, our product is *hope.*'

This quote from Charles Revson is quite profound, and makes the distinction between his *product,* and his *commodity.* When women buy cosmetics, they aren't interested in pretty containers full of chemicals. The thing they really want is the *effect* that they *hope* the cosmetics will create. In the most literal sense, his *commodity* is cosmetics, but his *product* is hope.

So what is your *real* product? You know what your commodity is because you work with it every day, but what is your real product; the thing your customers and prospects *really* want when they come to do business with you? What is your equivalent of hope? Whatever it is, you can be certain of one thing: it will be an emotion.

Now might be a good time to think back over your past advertising. Have you been trying to sell the wrong thing? Whoever came up with that famous piece of advice, 'Don't sell the sausage, sell the sizzle', really knew what they were talking about. When you take your focus away from your commodity and start offering people the thing they really want, your real product, you'll see the results reflected in your bottom line. So how do you figure out what your *real* product is? You ask!

PEOPLE WILL TELL YOU ANYTHING YOU WANT TO KNOW

Begin some preliminary in-house research at the earliest possible moment. Take a look through your database and identify twenty or thirty or more of your regular customers who are representative of the kinds of people you would like to attract through your advertising. You want to find out what around 80 per cent of them feel is the underlying reason they buy your product, or buy from you. The difficulty with this, of course, is that for all kinds of reasons, not the least of which is embarrassment, people may be reluctant to come right out and tell you their innermost feelings. You need to ask them in the right way. To do this, you have to distinguish between first-, second- and third-level questions. Once you approach your in-house research from this perspective, you will begin to get the answers you really need.

FIRST-LEVEL QUESTIONS

First-level questions are those obvious questions that produce obvious answers, which are of little real value. If you sell cameras and you ask a customer 'Why did you buy this camera?', the response is likely to be something like: 'To take pictures, of course!' To get the response you're looking for, you need to dig deeper with a second-level question.

SECOND-LEVEL QUESTIONS

Second-level questions are interested, concerned, open-ended questions that avoid the obvious and demand an intelligent answer. To use the camera example, a second-level question might be something like: 'What kinds of pictures will you be taking?' or 'Is there any particular type of photography that really interests you?' Second-level questions get you into the ballpark, and set you up for a third-level question.

THIRD-LEVEL QUESTIONS

Third-level questions are the most difficult of all to verbalise, but they are the ones that will tell you what you want to know. They are designed to encourage your customers to reveal the underlying emotional basis for the purchase, but in a way that makes them feel comfortable. The key to third-level questions is empathy. If your customers feel you are genuinely interested, then they are much more likely to open up and give you the information you need. You must pick both your customer and your moment carefully.

Using the camera example again, a third-level question might be something like: 'How does it make you feel when you go back over your favourite photographs?' or 'What buzz do you get out of photography that nothing else can give you?' or 'What do you feel you *really* get out of photography?'

Making the distinction between first-, second- and third-level questions will enable you to set up your in-house research questions in a way that fits comfortably with your particular business situation. The approach to third-level questions can vary considerably from one situation to another, and one customer to another. You will need to experiment until you find what works for you.

The idea then is to recognise first-level questions for what they are – dead ends – and avoid them like the plague.

Begin by formulating several second-level questions that might apply to different kinds of situations and people. Then put some time into developing some third-level questions that follow on naturally. You will need different kinds of third-level questions for different types of personalities, but your aim is always the same: to probe gently until you reveal the real emotional pay-off for the customer. If you can uncover this information, it's like solid gold to you.

If, for example, 80 per cent of your customers give you responses which indicate that they feel warm and fuzzy when they take pictures of loved ones or places they value and want to remember, then you gain a valuable insight. Interestingly, the answers to these questions often seem obvious in hindsight, but not at all obvious in foresight.

With some insightful answers to your questions, you are now in a position to set up your advertisements in a way that taps into this basic human need to experience and express love. You do this by capturing that idea as an emotion meme that will download quickly and efficiently into your prospect's mind and begin its work of creating and altering perceptions. The memes you use as the headline statements of your advertisements can vividly express this idea, which you now know relates to something like 80 per cent of your customers.

Having established an underlying emotional response, if you now look at integrating this with an attractive promotional offer, you will have something which is quite irresistible to people in your selected market segment.

Can you see how this approach differs dramatically from the way most advertising is presented? Anybody can reduce the price and come up with promotional offers, but when you add a powerful emotive element, which you know to be relevant to your customers, and express it as a compelling meme, it changes the dynamics of your advertising in a way that is calculated to produce a greatly improved response.

Keep in mind that the essential ingredient in gathering research information is empathy. Ideally you should already know these people to some extent, and perhaps have built up some sort of relationship with them. If you approach your questions from a position of rapport, if you genuinely care about your customers, they will sense that. They will become more open with you, and tell you what you want to know.

Take this idea of first-, second- and third-level questions and apply it to your situation. The response you can generate from this approach is out of all proportion to the small amount of time and effort it takes to implement.

Once you have determined exactly which emotional button to push, your final task is to look at the various ways in which you might be able to articulate it as a meme. It may be that you can best express it in a photograph or an illustration. Often a picture really is worth a thousand words. By the same token, the right words can often be every bit as powerful as a picture. A verbal solution meme like 'Now your child can succeed at maths' can trigger a strong emotional connection in a parent whose child is having difficulties at school.

Once again, go back to the section on memes and call in the TEAM. Try Transplanting, Enhancing, Adapting and Modifying existing memes until you come up with one that seems to be best for you.

Always remember that to be effective, a meme must encapsulate the essence of the idea you want to convey, and be so crystal clear that it takes no effort at all to grasp its meaning. Do that correctly, and you've just knocked down the second barrier to the Inner Circle.

•

>> **The expression of Activator Two is:**
Isolate and identify a specific emotional hot button,
and hit it hard.

•

THE MAIN POINTS

•

1 >> WHY PEOPLE BUY

•

People don't buy products and services. They buy emotional states of mind. When you look through and beyond the product, on the other side there is always an emotion.

•

2 >> TAKE A TIP FROM STUART WILDE

•

You cannot sell anything to anybody if you cannot first create, or stir within them, an emotion.

He's dead right. You can't.

•

3 >> MAKE EMOTION THE HERO

•

People don't care about you or your commodity. They care only about their own well-being and what your product will do for them. Appeal to the heart, not the head. Once you have touched them at an emotional level, people will take the trouble to seek you out and find you. It's in their own self-interest.

•

4 >> THE WAGES OF FEAR

•

The percentage of purchases which have originated as a direct result of fear of the unknown is something we can only guess at, but it is enormous. Fear, negativity and emotional pain seem to be a natural part of the make-up of the vast majority of people, and beyond day-to-day survival, they buy products and services in an effort to feel good.

•

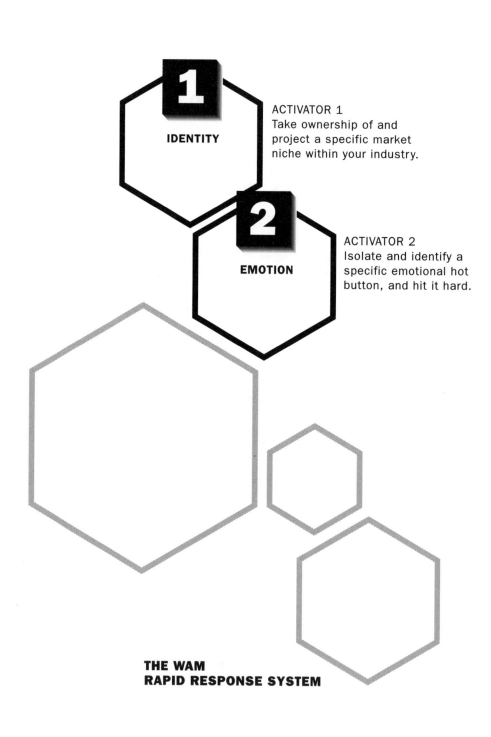

1

IDENTITY

ACTIVATOR 1
Take ownership of and
project a specific market
niche within your industry.

2

EMOTION

ACTIVATOR 2
Isolate and identify a
specific emotional hot
button, and hit it hard.

**THE WAM
RAPID RESPONSE SYSTEM**

5 >> ONE ON ONE

•

Remember that when you advertise, although you seem to be talking to a mass audience, in every case you're really talking one on one to your prospects. Be sure to frame your advertisements with this in mind if you want to optimise your response.

•

6 >> YOUR PRODUCT AND YOUR COMMODITY

•

Take a lead from Charles Revson and do whatever is needed to identify the equivalent emotion to 'hope' for your product, service or brand. Be very certain about which is your commodity and which is your product. Very few business managers get it right.

•

7 >> QUESTIONS ARE THE ANSWER

•

If you want to know what people really want, ask them. If you dig deeply enough and ask the right questions, people will tell you everything you need to know. Make the distinction between first-, second- and third-level questions. Remember, asking the right questions is your best means of finding out what your customers really want when they come to buy from you. If you can relate their answers to one or more of those fifty buying motivators, you're well on your way to achieving the aim of this book: to lift your advertising response and win more customers.

Now it's time to move on and try to answer one of the simplest, but most difficult questions you will ever be called upon to answer, by engaging Activator Three …

CHAPTER 5

INFLUENCE

'Why should I buy from you rather

than one of your competitors?'

Market differentiation has very little to do with fact, and almost

everything to do with perception.

Activator Three is about influence, and specifically about the power of leverage.

If you happen to have one of those rare products, services or brands that is truly unique, then you might want to skip this chapter. However, if, like most companies and brands, there is little if anything to differentiate you from your competitors in the public mind, this chapter will tell you all you need to know to create a full-blown, genuine competitive advantage that will set you apart from your competition.

The motivating, self-serving aspect of an advertisement that excites people and inspires them to action is called leverage. There are two different kinds of leverage to consider: short-term and long-term.

Short-term leverage is the kind of leverage that says 'Buy now at these low prices', 'Buy now while stocks last', 'Hurry hurry hurry!' It is the mainspring that drives direct response advertising.

Short-term leverage is useful for a number of reasons. It motivates people to dig into their pockets and buy now. It helps retailers to move excess stock. It gets the economy moving, and most importantly, it helps to stimulate cash flow. There's no question that short-term leverage should be an integral part of any self-respecting advertising campaign in which consumer response is crucial.

However, if that's all you have going for you, then you've got a big problem, because short-term leverage has at least five serious downsides:

1   You end up shaving your margins to the bone, sometimes to the vanishing point; and the implications of that go without saying. So many advertisers fill their commercials with wall-to-wall product and price, never realising that the majority of their audience hasn't a clue what the real price should be. To these people, a product and price commercial becomes meaningless.

2   In pushing discounting to the level it has, business has taught a whole generation of people not to pay normal prices. Because of that, it's doubtful that things can ever return to the way they were. Full price has become a thing of the past.

3   As the saying goes, there will always be somebody smart enough, or dumb enough, to sell for a dollar less – which means you're playing a game you can't win.

4   Many companies, particularly retailers, tell us that they find themselves under constant pressure to dream up new variations on the discounting theme. Then the moment their ads hit the marketplace, their competitors move in and simply steal their ideas. They find themselves spending far too much time wrestling with advertising rather than doing what they should be doing: running their business.

5   You find yourself locked into a cycle: you advertise and they respond; you advertise and they respond; you advertise and they respond; you *stop* advertising and they *stop* responding. Then before you realise what's happening, you find yourself on a self-perpetuating treadmill.

For all its good points, short-term leverage alone is the way to madness. The answer lies in long-term leverage, an entirely different proposition. Long-term leverage is an overriding, ongoing, obvious reason, beyond price, for a person to choose one product, service or brand over another.

Long-term leverage is easy if you have a clearcut advantage over your competition. Are you the biggest? Does your product last twice as long? Is your product exclusive in some way? Do you hold some kind of patent, formula, technology or system that puts you ahead of your competition? Is there some aspect of your operation that gives you a clear advantage? If there is, then things become greatly simplified.

But what if you don't have a clearcut advantage? Of all the companies and brands we've worked with over the years, no more than 2 per cent at most have anything you could call a clearcut competitive advantage. That means fully 98 per cent of them are operating in an environment called 'market parity'. That's when the customer looks out into the marketplace, sees you and your competitors, and says: 'I don't know. They're all the same; which one's the cheapest?' Business managers who find themselves working in this market parity situation invariably see it as a major problem, and spend a lot of sleepless nights trying to figure out what to do about it.

But the thing about market parity is that like anything else in life, it all depends on how you look at it. If you're prepared to just sit there and accept the status quo, then yes, it can be a debilitating problem. But if you decide you're going to do something about it, then it can actually work in your favour.

You see, a clearcut, genuine competitive advantage is not something that just some fortunate products and brands are born with, like blue eyes or blonde hair. A genuine competitive advantage is something you *create*, and it can be done with any business enterprise at all, including yours, irrespective of the competition.

Imagine a set of scales, with equal weights on either side. They sit there in a state of equilibrium, just like two companies in a state of market parity. However, you need to put only a tiny bit of extra weight on either side of the scales to tip the balance.

Market parity works in exactly the same way. When two or more companies are evenly matched in the public mind, it doesn't take much to upset the balance and tip people over the edge to come down in favour of any one of them. That's what the Rapid Response System is all about; giving your company or brand that extra perceptual impetus that will tip the scales in your favour. It's just a question of knowing how to make it happen.

The good news is that it doesn't matter if you're not unique in any way. To move forward, it's not only possible, but essential to develop a clearcut advantage over your competition. At WAM, we do this for companies and brands all the time, and the key to creating that competitive edge lies in the fact that market differentiation has very little to do with fact, and almost everything to do with perception. If people perceive you to be the experts, then you are. If people perceive you to be just about anything at all, then you are. It's as simple as that.

To develop this perceptual advantage, you need an idea, an angle. We want to suggest that you seriously consider making the decision to become widely known for something over and above what people would normally expect from your kind of company, product or brand.

That word 'normal' represents one of the most insidious and pervasive concepts in the business community worldwide. Everybody strives to appear 'normal'. Pick any business category you care to name, and you'll find it filled with companies and brands the customer perceives as basically identical. Each of these companies and brands goes to enormous lengths to appear 'normal'; to conform to a kind of standard, sanitised, predetermined concept of what that type of organisation should look like. That's why they all look the same.

'Normal' is terrific. 'Normal' is wonderful if you're trying to create mediocrity and conservatism. But if you're trying to differentiate yourself in the marketplace and create a competitive advantage, then 'normal' is less than useless. It's subversive.

The quickest way to get lost in the crowd is to move in the direction everybody else is moving. On the other hand, every innovation, every major breakthrough you can name was brought about by somebody with the courage to break away from the crowd and think in different directions.

To differentiate yourself from your competition in the mind of the consumer, you need to begin by seeing your product, service or brand as an aggregation of complementary niche areas of service which combine to create the whole. This takes into account factors such as design, size, functionality, security, customer service, reliability, performance, availability, brand confidence, value, quality, price, guarantees, back-up service, convenience, shelf appeal, exclusivity, aesthetics, and any number of similar factors.

See yourself through the cynical, indifferent eyes of your prospect. Think about all the things your product or service does for people, all the things it has to offer. Without changing anything else, pick just one of these, and decide to specialise in it. This means choosing the one specific attribute that has the widest appeal to the greatest number of people, expanding it, dramatising it, and holding it out to your customers and prospects in a way that intrigues and excites them.

By narrowing your focus and becoming widely known for some attribute beyond people's normal expectations, you take on the persona of a specialist rather than a generalist, and in the process, you'll find you've suddenly become more attractive and intriguing to the only people who really matter: your customers and prospects.

Buzzing around somewhere in the back of the mind of any person about to make a buying decision is a question: 'Why should I buy from you rather than one of your competitors?'

That fundamental and completely reasonable question is guaranteed to stop most company and brand managers dead in their tracks. They simply do not have a convincing answer. As far as the buying public is concerned, their companies and brands appear to be generic alternatives, as alike as peas in a pod.

Walk through any supermarket and look at the competitive brands. The chances are that beyond price, you will find little if anything to influence you to choose one over another, except perhaps for a great deal of advertising which is big on image and hype, but short on tangible consumer influence.

A glance through any reliable market share statistics report over a five-year period shows a distinct tendency for most competing brands to maintain or lose their market position unless something dramatic occurs to alter the status quo. The market leader tends to remain at the top of the heap, the number two brand tends to drift a little closer to the leader, and numbers three and below tend to drift downward. The tragedy is that so many of these brands ultimately lie down and die because they have not been able to achieve the cut-through of the bigger, more powerful brands.

The same applies to retailers. Take a close look at any number of competitive retailers in any industry you care to name. Chances are, with few exceptions, you are looking at a group of businesses without any real kind of tangible market differentiation. Can you relate to this?

These companies are offering products and services that are basically identical to those of their competitors, leaving price as the only real point of leverage. They see lower prices as being the only practical and reliable way to attract customers in the long term.

As a direct result of this line of thinking, whole industries are teaching the public to hold off, and to buy only during advertised sale times.

The insidious effect of this philosophy is to create a price spiral, gradually destroying any kind of normal profit potential by constantly reducing margins, often to the vanishing point.

The paradox here is that when you look at any reliable study of consumer buying motivators, you will find that price invariably comes somewhere around fourth or fifth on the list. And there is a very good reason for this.

THE PRICE MYTH

People do not buy on price. Price becomes an issue only when everything else is equal. We always buy an integrated package of *value*, of which price is just one feature. We each carry around in our heads a kind of instant 'value package calculator'. Whenever we are considering a purchase of any kind, we intuitively scan the situation, looking for units of value over and above the price component. Does this fit with your own experience?

Value can be expressed in many ways: promotional add-ons, convenience, courtesy, security, trust, scarcity, status, peace of mind, performance guarantees, reliability, being recognised personally, ease of parking, location, expertise, information, experience, advice, after-sales service, brand confidence, and any number of similar attributes. In this context you can see how price, although important, can be made to play a less dominant role in the transaction.

A higher priced item stacked with the right kinds of additional value components can represent a much more attractive option than a similar article with a lower price.

Imagine you're looking through a newspaper and you see an advertisement for a brand-new, wide-screen colour television set, with all the latest bells and whistles, on special for $500. You jump in the car and head for the retailer mentioned in the advertisement to check it out. When you take a close look, it turns out to have been made in Siberia, and has a seven-day warranty. Does the low price still hold the same attraction?

You see, we really don't buy on price, even when we think we do. We buy a value package, and most of the calculating is done at lightning speed at the subconscious level. When you really understand and appreciate this profound insight, it can revolutionise the way you frame your advertisements.

THE ACID TEST

We'd like to suggest you take the time to make an anonymous telephone call. Call your own company, the way a member of the public might. Ask the person who answers the telephone a simple question. It might go something like this: 'I'm just about to buy a (your generic type of product). Could you please tell me why I should buy from (your company) rather than one of your competitors?'

Sound scary?

Then try calling each of your competitors and ask them the same question, and see what they have to say. The chances are that in the case of your own company, and each of your competitors, all you will get will be generalisations about one or more of the following:

1   service
2   quality
3   value
4   price
5   experience
6   convenience
7   product depth
8   product knowledge.

The problem with this is that, although companies and brands may go to extraordinary lengths just to maintain these essential attributes on a day-to-day basis, to keep the balls in the air as it were, as far as the customer is concerned, these things are taken for granted. They represent the bare minimum, their most basic expectations, ground zero.

The inescapable fact is that you cannot take something that is a basic consumer expectation, and hope to use it as an effective instrument of persuasion. It has never worked, and it never will. It's like saying: 'When you buy a car from us, you get *wheels*!'

To compound the problem, all your competitors are saying these very same things, whether or not they're true. To move ahead, you need something else. Something for your customers and prospects to latch onto other than just price. You must find a way to create a dramatic shift in people's perception of value; a highly visible, highly marketable, competitive point of difference; a sense of uniqueness, even though there may appear to be nothing unique about your company, product or brand.

The promise of this book is to show you how to do just that. To take you through a specialised process which will result in a compelling reason for your prospects to buy from you rather than your competitors. This competitive point of difference will then be articulated as a meme, and the effect that this can have on your advertising response is nothing short of extraordinary.

There is, however, a catch. It requires you to become proactive, and to do your part. All the knowledge in the world is not going to have any effect whatever without your active participation. There are certain specific things which you must do in order to produce this tantalising outcome. We urge you to get involved and commit to doing whatever it takes, and you won't believe what it will do for your bottom line.

Before we move forward, you will need an understanding of why things are as they are, and the reasons behind this pressing need to become more competitive. To put things in perspective, you should stop for a moment and consider the sequence of events that has, over time, conspired to produce this difficult and frustrating dilemma of market parity. This will lay the groundwork necessary for you to get your head around what may at present appear to be an abstract concept, but which will soon become clear.

HOW IT USED TO BE

From the dawn of civilisation until just before the technological and information explosion in the latter half of the twentieth century, people of all races and cultures had comparatively simple choices with regard to their buying decisions. Before the development of the petrol engine, people's buying options were largely defined by how far they were prepared to walk or travel in a horse-drawn vehicle.

Before the global trend towards urban development, the market forces in any given town or village dictated the number and variety of different suppliers of goods and services appropriate for that particular community. Long-term relationships between families and suppliers of goods and services formed the basis for the vast majority of buying decisions. Choices of various types of suppliers were limited, and the system was essentially self-regulating, bowing to market forces. Sons tended to follow in fathers' footsteps into the various trades. The truth of this is evident today through common family names like Farmer, Baker and Smith.

THE ADVENT OF MAINSTREAM ADVERTISING

With the development of Gutenberg's printing press came the concept of advertising to the mass market. This was inevitably followed by radio, then television, and with computer technology in the 1990s came home shopping, the Internet, the World Wide Web and the concept of the broadband Information Superhighway.

Back in those heady days, people believed anything they were told via the medium of advertising with a naivety that is hard to believe today. Getting new customers was like shooting fish in a barrel. One only has to look at some of those early posters for things like Coca Cola, cigarettes and alcohol to find the most outlandish claims. These products promised anything from 'toning up the liver' to 'creating a sense of radiant health and well-being' to 'helping to settle the nerves'.

Today we look around us and see that the entire concept of advertising, marketing and retail trade has been turned on its ear through the multiple effects of the technological explosion, the information explosion and the population explosion.

People no longer believe what they're told through advertising. They've been lied to, cheated, conned and bamboozled with outrageous claims for so long that they've become cynical, cautious and more discriminating than ever before, and almost totally lacking in trust. In short, through thoughtlessness and lack of concern for the well-being of the consumer, the advertising industry has created a monster.

WHAT IS A CUSTOMER REALLY?

If we peel away from an individual the layers of culture, education, social status, socio-economic position and geographic location, we are left with a totally fascinating creature.

Our every thought, action, decision and behavioural impulse is motivated by self-preservation. Everything we do from blinking an eyelid through to choosing a marriage partner is based exclusively upon our own self-interest. Even the concept of joining a religious order, or an altruistic act like donating money to a charity, is based on self-interest. Nobody ever made a purchase that wasn't directly motivated in some way by self-interest.

YOUR CUSTOMERS' SELF-INTEREST

Given that self-interest is the greatest single motivator of human behaviour, why in the world don't all suppliers of goods and services focus their every effort on tapping into this wellspring of potential power as their means of attracting customers and gaining the market share they would like to have?

One possible reason for this curious mindset on the part of people in business is the simple fact that they too are people. Because self-interest is the predominant motivator, the very concept of focusing their attention on the wants and needs of others is about as contrary to human nature as you can get. It takes awareness, training, discipline and understanding for a business manager to get ego out of the way and to think exclusively from the customer's point of view.

Managers typically develop skills which relate specifically to their own industry. They tend not to have acquired the awareness, training, discipline, understanding or even the *ability* to focus exclusively on the customer. It is not part of their world. They are company- or product-oriented and inwardly focused to the extent that, quite simply, they do not see another option. There's something about seeing the company name and logo splashed all over the place that is quite irresistible to the corporate ego.

If you doubt this, take a look through the *Yellow Pages*, or any newspaper. The chances are that a large proportion of the advertisements will be either focused on reduced prices, or predictably featuring the company name, logo, address, phone numbers and services available. Many of these advertisements are so introspective that they do not even attempt to involve the customer. Often the company or brand names and the advertisements themselves are basically interchangeable. If you were to keep the advertisements the same and change the company logos around, nobody would be any the wiser.

Unfortunately, far too many of these advertisements are little more than outrageously expensive business cards. They form a monotonous and predictable background pattern in the mind of the consumer, and are routinely and summarily ignored. Transparent among the media clutter, they fall more under the general heading of camouflage than advertising. They become just another tree in the forest, another panel of advertising wallpaper.

To prosper in today's fiercely competitive environment, a company or brand which does not have a clearly articulated marketable point of difference is operating under a very serious handicap, and is under constant threat from more visionary competitors who can enter the market at any time and create havoc.

Without a competitive point of difference, your product or brand essentially drifts, feeding solely on the momentum of the marketplace. Convenience, the law of averages, price advantages and chance become the dominant market forces which ultimately define your level of prosperity. To introduce a strong competitive point of difference is to take control of the situation, and alter the dynamics of the marketplace to operate in your favour.

This is something that any company, product, service or brand, including yours, can achieve. As this book unfolds, you will see possibilities you may never have seen before, and it is entirely within your power to take this concept and make it real. In the special supplement at the back of the book we will take you through a specialised process which, when you implement it, will produce this extraordinary outcome. The system works. All it takes is your active participation and commitment.

THE BASIS OF MARKET DIFFERENTIATION

Market differentiation is a concept that has been around, in various forms, for many years. Before we begin specifically to develop a competitive point of difference for your company or brand, you'll need to gain some specific insights. Let's begin by looking at two relevant points of view. One line of thought which makes a lot of sense comes from Al Ries and Jack Trout in their classic book, *Bottom-Up Marketing*. Ries and Trout approach the subject of marketing in a way that challenges conventional thinking.

STRATEGIES AND TACTICS

Ries and Trout claim that the traditional thinking behind the universally accepted business concept of strategies and tactics is fundamentally flawed. Traditional business practice is to produce a long-term strategy which says in essence: 'This is where we want to be in five or ten years.' Then you have to work out a tactic that is capable of producing that outcome. You tell your people: 'Now go and figure out how to do it.' The strategy is the 'what', and the tactic is the 'how'.

The problem with this line of thinking is that unless you write your competitors' business plans, the future is unknowable. To regard a five- or ten-year plan as something definitive and achievable is unrealistic because it does not take into account things like future changes in technology, unexpected competition, future trends, market variations, or unpredictable strategic moves by your competitors. A long-range plan may be useful as a guide, but can only ever be aspirational in nature, and is more often than not an exercise in wishful thinking.

The essence of 'bottom-up marketing' is that the sequence is flipped over: the tactic is concentrated on first, and then the strategy. The tactic becomes the 'what', and the strategy becomes the 'how'. Ries and Trout define a tactic as a 'competitive mental angle', and a strategy as a 'coherent marketing direction'. The idea of bottom-up marketing is that you first come up with an idea; an angle or concept which you can expand, dramatise, and make the focus of your advertising and marketing. Then you say to your people: 'Now go and figure out a strategy to support this tactic; a strategy that will take us where we want to go.'

Domino's Pizzas in the United States was a prime example of this. Tom Monaghan launched the brand with:

Your pizza delivered hot in thirty minutes or it's free.

Only then did he employ the strategy which supported that tactic, which involved developing a proprietary business operating system from scratch, and then rolling it out first as a national, and then an international franchise operation.

The point which relates specifically to our objective in this chapter is the idea of a tactic being a 'competitive mental angle'. A tactic needs to be competitive rather than simply different if it is to have any leverage. It is a 'mental' thing because its purpose is to get it into the minds of your prospects. And finally, it is an 'angle', an idea. It has to be something big and compelling enough to become the cornerstone of your business activity.

A tactic is an exercise in perception, and, at least as far as advertising and marketing are concerned, perception is more powerful even than reality. Only after you've developed your tactic can you begin to look at formulating a strategy to support it.

Bottom-Up Marketing is well worth reading. It gives many illuminating examples of companies that have prospered through the use of this unconventional but devastatingly effective approach to business.

Ries and Trout have encapsulated these thoughts and many more in a small but highly readable and informative book referred to earlier called *The 22 Immutable Laws of Marketing*. It is required reading for anybody committed to results marketing.

All this talk of tactics and strategies is not just theoretical marketing gobbledegook. It's a down-to-earth, hard-nosed, pragmatic approach that can mean the difference between winning market leadership and sacrificing millions of dollars at the altar of ignorance.

Advertising agencies, particularly big advertising agencies, are often the biggest offenders. They lead their clients down the Institutional Advertising and Brand Image Road, in the belief that brand image and brand personality alone will solve all of the world's marketing problems. In the real world, it turns out that people are not fools, and if products and services don't live up to the expectations generated by advertising that over-promises and under-delivers, then they simply drop out and write it down to experience.

THE DECORE DEBACLE

One of Australia's best known and best loved television commercials of all time appeared as part of the famous De-de-de-Decore campaign first launched in 1988. The full story of this campaign is chronicled by the advertising journalist and author Neil Shoebridge in his fascinating book, *Great Australian Advertising Campaigns*. Perhaps the best way to pass on an accurate account of what happened is to quote directly from that book:

> When the stuttering, sing-along De-de-de-Decore advertising campaign for Decore shampoo and conditioner launched in May 1988, it created a sensation. Children sang the Decore song in playgrounds. Television news and current affairs programmes played the ad and debated its merits. A new version of 'Duke of Earl', the 1962 song that provided the inspiration for the Decore jingle, was released by the man who sang it in the television commercial and sold briskly. In the weeks after it made its debut, the Decore campaign became a member of the exclusive club of advertising campaigns that sneak into the popular culture.
>
> With its snappy jingle and scenes of people washing their hair

in the shower, the Decore campaign provided the power of the advertising. It also proved that advertising alone is not enough to make a product a success. The 1988 television commercial boosted consumer awareness of the Decore brand, which was almost invisible before the De-de-de-Decore ad arrived. It generated huge trial sales of Decore, pushing it into the ranks of the most frequently used brands in the cluttered, $200 million-a-year shampoo and conditioner market. Decore's sales and market share soared in the space of three months. Thanks to the advertising campaign, the Decore brand image was turned around in just eight weeks.

Powerful advertising campaigns can have a downside. Decore became an advertising-reliant product. Every time the De-de-de-Decore ads ran, sales of the product boomed. Every time the ads went off air, sales dropped. More critically, the people who bought Decore once because of the television commercial did not return for a second purchase. Decore made it into the repertoire of five or six shampoo and conditioner brands that consumers buy regularly, but Decore's owner – Reckitt & Coleman Pharmaceuticals – was forced to constantly slash the brand's retail price to generate sales. It was not until 1990, when Reckitt & Coleman changed Decore's formulation and stopped discounting it in supermarkets, that the brand's market share stabilised and the company started to make money from Decore.

Does any of this sound familiar? Earlier in this chapter we noted that there is an unfortunate downside to short-term leverage. You advertise and they respond; you stop advertising and they stop responding. Not having any tangible reason to continue to choose Decore over its competitors, curious consumers tried it once and then went elsewhere.

What Decore failed to do was to access the Inner Circle of the millions of people who tried the brand. These people were attracted by the fun and magnetism of the advertising itself, not by the product. It's not difficult to see why this is a recipe for disaster. When you examine a famous case study like this, you begin to see why the Inner Circle really is the name of the game; it's where all the action is, and ultimately it's where the long-term profits are.

The thing that was missing from the Decore campaign, and so many other campaigns both before and since, is that magic ingredient called long-term leverage; that overriding, ongoing, obvious reason, beyond price, for a person to choose one product, service or brand over another.

The Decore advertising engaged Activator Two (emotion) extremely well, but it then fell over because it failed to engage Activator Three (influence), the subject of this chapter.

The thing that distinguishes long-term leverage from advertising hype is that there is real substance to it. The Decore brand lacked a tactic, a 'competitive mental angle'. If the Decore campaign had been designed around an incisive tactic that actually delivered on some kind of promise, and at the same time turned the marketplace on with that same brilliant execution, things might have turned out very differently.

THE UNIQUE SELLING PROPOSITION (USP)

Rosser Reeves, chairman of Ted Bates & Company in the early 1940s, originated an enduring but widely misunderstood philosophy which he called the Unique Selling Proposition, or USP. Through the inspired use of this brilliant concept, Bates increased its billings from $4 million to $150 million without losing a client, while getting spectacular, sometimes unprecedented sales for its clients. A USP is typically defined as:

> The distinguishing advantage you hold out in all your advertising, marketing and sales efforts.

A USP, by definition, is about *selling*, and is therefore designed to produce a selling response. A common characteristic of the USP is that, being a selling tool, it tends to focus on the commodity rather than the customer. A typical example of a USP for an office printer might be:

> The Okipage 4W has the lowest maintenance cost of any printer.

That USP unquestionably puts the Oki printer ahead of many of its competitors. At least it is holding out something of tangible value to the marketplace. However, it turns out that the most effective advertising doesn't focus on the product at all; it focuses on the customer. Instead of talking about the commodity or the brand, and using words like 'I', 'we', 'us' and 'our', commercials that work best of all talk about the customer, and use words like 'you', 'your' and 'you'll'.

In formulating our philosophy for the WAM Communications

Group, we looked closely at the many different points of view regarding the idea of market differentiation, and came to the conclusion that a contemporary approach to the USP concept was the answer. We then began to refine the process and gave it a few original twists.

At some point, as the philosophy which underpins this book began to develop, we found ourselves questioning the appropriateness of the term 'Unique Selling Proposition', as seen from our perspective. The problem for us revolves around the idea of 'selling'. Although selling is the universally accepted way of approaching business, there is an inbuilt downside. If you feel that somebody is trying to sell you something, what do you do? You become defensive and back off, because you feel your security is being threatened.

In his classic book, *Scientific Advertising*, Claude Hopkins makes the observation that:

> Any attempt to sell, if apparent, creates corresponding resistance.

This line of reasoning led us to a conclusion which flies in the face of conventional wisdom:

•

>> **Advertising is not about selling. It's about buying.**

•

When you adopt this line of thinking, all the rules change. Suddenly you're not trying to create a sale; you're trying to create a *purchase*, which has a completely different set of dynamics. You suddenly find yourselves operating in a world of attraction, not coercion. As we noted in Chapter 2:

•

>> **Attraction happens *when we become attractive*,
not when we come on strong.**

•

We realised that if we really do believe advertising is not about selling, but about buying, then the 'selling' mindset which is implicit in the term Unique *Selling* Proposition, must of necessity be inappropriate within that paradigm. This distinction has had a major impact on the way we go about the process of creating a marketable point of difference for our clients.

When you see yourself as a sales person, your natural focus is on persuasion, but when you see yourself as a 'buying facilitator', your natural focus is on rapport. This line of thinking brought us to the realisation that we needed a more appropriate name, a name which reflected this alternative mindset in a meaningful way. As a result of this, we adopted the term Customer Buying Advantage (CBA).

CUSTOMER BUYING ADVANTAGE

A CBA is defined as:

> The ultimate point of difference your customers and prospects find both curious and irresistible.

It is a compelling idea, or angle, which is encapsulated in a simple, bold statement, and articulated as a meme. This statement must do eight, and *all* eight, of the following things:

1   It must be a big idea, capable of supporting a major advertising campaign for at least five years.
2   It must represent immediate and relevant value to the customer.
3   It must attract attention.
4   It must distinguish you from your competition.
5   It must fill, or appear to fill, an industry gap.
6   It must motivate people to take action.
7   It must lock your brand name permanently and indelibly into the concept.
8   It must work as a headline in print, and must also fit comfortably within a ten-second copy window in a TV or radio commercial.

This magic memetic statement then becomes the focal point of every communication with the marketplace.

The reason a good CBA is seen as both curious and irresistible is that it is articulated as an intriguing statement *about the customer* that provides the single, most compelling reason to choose one product, service or brand over another. This statement is then expressed as an attraction meme, which transforms it into a devastating marketing tool.

•

>> **A Customer Buying Advantage is the perceptual magnet that attracts and draws people out of their apathy and makes them want to buy from you.**

•

A CBA is not complicated, just elusive. The definition will become clear as we get further into the concept. You will see that a CBA is articulated in as few words as it takes to express that ultimate point of difference in a way that is both intriguing and irresistible to the customer.

The difference in attitude at our business development seminars since this particular innovation has been striking. In the early days when we were looking for a USP, two interesting things happened:

1   From the outset, our clients found it difficult to believe it was possible to create a USP for them in particular, because they believed there was nothing unique about their product. They felt intimidated by the idea of uniqueness, which tended to affect their ability to believe in a positive outcome.

2   When we ultimately developed a USP for these clients, although we did not make the connection at the time, it invariably turned out to be expressed from the company or brand's point of view rather than the customer's. This had the effect of weakening the communication.

When we coined the term 'Customer Buying Advantage', the real breakthrough became apparent immediately. We found we had created two very different outcomes:

1   Because our clients were not confronted with and intimidated by the word 'unique', they had no difficulty in accepting the challenge implicit in the word 'advantage'.

2   Because we were looking for a 'buying advantage' rather than a 'selling proposition', our collective focus was now on the customer, not the product. This resulted in a very different type of outcome, because it spoke directly to the prospect. The term 'Customer Buying Advantage' itself acts as a filter which guarantees a customer-focused outcome every time.

A USP, by definition, is about *selling*. A CBA, by definition, is about *buying*. This distinction produces a ripple effect in the thought process, which leads to a completely different attitude and therefore a completely different outcome.

THE VISIBILITY FACTOR INHERENT IN YOUR CBA

If you ask people who have seen the movie *Schindler's List* the scene they best remember, it's invariably the emotive scene in which the only colour on the screen is the red coat on a little girl as she walks down the street. Your CBA creates this effect in the marketplace. In a sea of mediocrity and apathy, a compelling CBA stands out like a single red carnation in a field of white.

As well as creating massive visibility, your CBA is the ultimate business stabiliser. It keeps you honest. As long as you continue to deliver the dream, customers have a reason to choose you over your competitors. When you stop delivering, people will see right through you and abandon you in droves.

A well-crafted CBA can be so powerful and effective that it is possibly the next best thing to having a licence to print money. It is worth any amount of time and effort you are willing to devote to it.

THE NEED TO NARROW YOUR FOCUS

Consider for a moment the idea of trying to hammer a nail deep into a piece of wood. Obviously the sharper the point on the nail, the deeper it will go with a minimum of effort, and once it's in, it's there to stay.

We're not suggesting your advertising works something like that. We're suggesting it works *exactly* like that. To drive your advertising message deep into the public mind, you need to narrow your focus.

You need to narrow your focus until your advertising has a sharp, hard point on it, and that sharp, hard point is your CBA. The remainder of your advertising message, the supporting information, is like the shaft of the nail. Once the point has gone in, the rest just follows naturally, as it has with Woolworths' 'fresh food people' concept. Woolies still advertises specials and promotions (the shaft of the nail), but there is no doubt whatever that the point (the fresh food people) is very sharp indeed, and has been driven deep into the public mind.

If your advertising response has not been all you have hoped for, maybe you've been using a blunt nail.

With all of this in mind, we have reached the stage where we can begin the process of digging, identifying, refining and articulating a CBA specifically for your company or brand.

WHAT DOES A CBA LOOK LIKE?

It is at this point that the ideas and concepts outlined in the previous chapters begin to take on a new relevance. In order to find what you're looking for, you need to adopt the role of a detective on the one hand, and an artist on the other. In particular, you need a kind of CBA profile; you need to know what to look for so that you'll recognise it when you see it.

Your objective is not just to create a CBA, but to create a *pre-emptive* CBA that you can own, and that your competition can't steal.

So what do we know about your CBA in light of what we have learnt to this point? Actually, a surprising amount.

1   It will be a meme: a short, lucid statement which taps directly into some kind of strong emotional need on the part of your prospect. It will slip easily into your prospects' minds, and appeal strongly to their sense of self-interest in a big way.

2   It will give you the aura of being a specialist.

3   It will be designed to *attract* attention, to elicit a buying response rather than be expressed as a 'sales pitch', and expressed in terms of 'you' rather than 'we'.

4   It will not contain any detailed information; it will need to be something above and beyond the normal expectation of your prospects, something compelling that your competitors do not appear to be offering.

5   It will be congruent with the identity embodied in your positioning statement. It is quite possible, often desirable, to create a compound meme which embodies both your positioning statement *and* your CBA. Your prospect should be able to relate immediately to your CBA and find it both engaging and credible.

6   It may well be something that every single one of your competitors is doing, but which nobody is talking about. The Heinz Peak Nutrition Process mentioned earlier is a classic example of this. Once you have established a strong idea in the public mind, any attempt by your competitors to steal it is likely to be viewed by the consumer as just another 'me too' tactic. People think perceptually, not logically; like Woolworths and 'fresh'. Whoever is first into the public mind with a concept owns it. This is the essence of pre-emptive marketing.

7   It will be expressed as a statement *about the customer*, something that elicits a 'double take' response. It should have the ability to turn your prospects' heads, or make them look twice to make sure they saw or heard correctly. It should contain that ingredient known as 'the wow factor'.

8   The articulation of your CBA will be a creatively crafted, edited, simplified and polished version of a broader and possibly more complex idea; a simple but intriguing meme, designed specifically to slip quickly and easily into the mind of anybody in the market for whatever it is you sell.

9   Ideally your CBA will have been developed from something which already exists, but has become so familiar, so integrated into the system, that it has become basically transparent. Although it has been right there under your nose, you've never recognised it for what it is.

EXAMPLES OF CBAs IN ACTION IN THE MARKETPLACE

To this point, we have talked a lot about CBAs. Now the time has come to see exactly what they look like in real life. Once you can see what others have done, you will find the task easier to comprehend.

Perceptually, it's another world. People who have never contemplated the possibility of creating a genuine competitive advantage never fail to be amazed at what can be done, and, as we noted earlier, it can be done with any company or brand at all, including yours.

It is the *articulation* that will make or break your CBA. It must be expressed in a way that engages 'the wow factor' – the more unusual or outrageous the better.

In order to give you a feel for this whole CBA issue, we're going to walk you through the process by outlining the first few examples in some detail. As you read through the background to these examples, you will begin to realise that there was a time when none of these companies had any real market differentiation at all, maybe just like you. It just took a little lateral thinking and a system to dig it out.

KNEBEL KITCHENS

As far as the core business is concerned, Knebel Kitchens is really not very different from its competitors, except perhaps for its excellent use of technology and its high standards of production and design. Unfortunately, to the customer, these things are basic expectations and do not constitute a means of enticement. When we looked at ways in which Knebel's advertising and marketing might be improved, we immediately began thinking in terms of a CBA.

However, the more we looked, the more it became evident that despite their design innovations; their policy of using the traditionally superior screwing-and-gluing method of construction rather than stapling; their premium-quality plantation beech dowels imported from Scandinavia; their custom-made, high-strength hinges imported from Austria; and many other unique features, there was nothing individually strong enough to run up the flagpole and hold out as a competitive point of difference. Knebel, like so many companies, was in a situation of complete market parity in a highly competitive, price-driven market.

We then began looking for something *peripheral* to the core business. This brought up the topic of guarantees. When we asked about Knebel's guarantee, it turned out to be for five years, when the industry standard was between five and ten. The magic happened when we asked the next question:

'What would happen if we owned a Knebel kitchen for fifteen years and one of the doors fell off?'

They replied, 'We'd fix it.'

We asked, 'Even though it was out of guarantee?'

They replied, 'Yes.'

Wow!

Then we asked, 'How about if we owned a Knebel kitchen for twenty years and the laminate started to peel?'

'We'd fix it.'

We asked them, 'Why would you do that?'

They replied, 'Because we're proud of our kitchens and we would not want an unhappy customer.'

Knebel was in effect giving a lifetime guarantee on its product without ever telling anybody about it!

As a result of this line of thinking, we developed a CBA for Knebel which, to our knowledge, is unprecedented in the kitchen industry:

> Your beautiful new Knebel kitchen has been built to stand the test of time. That's why it comes to you with the famous Knebel Lifetime Guarantee.

There are several things worth noting here which will help you in formulating your own CBA:

1. 'The famous Knebel Lifetime Guarantee' is a security meme.
2. You might think that by giving such a guarantee, people would tend to take advantage of Knebel, and that the company would be putting itself at risk as a result. Strangely enough, in practice this has been found not to be the case. Despite public opinion, people tend to be basically honest. Experience has consistently shown that claims on this type of guarantee tend to be less than one per cent of sales. The amount of new business the guarantee generates renders any claims against it negligible in the long term.
3. The Knebel CBA is expressed from the customer's point of view. It speaks in terms of 'you' rather than 'we'. It's about the customer, not just the commodity.

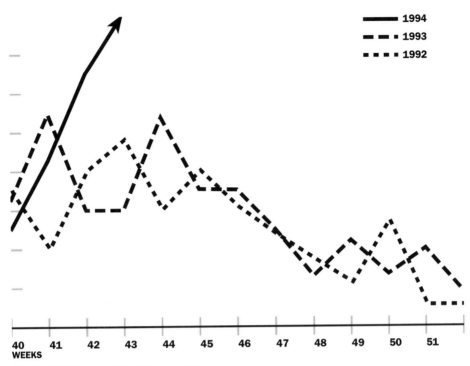

1994
1993
1992

40 41 42 43 44 45 46 47 48 49 50 51
WEEKS

Knebel Kitchens > 92–94 order intake

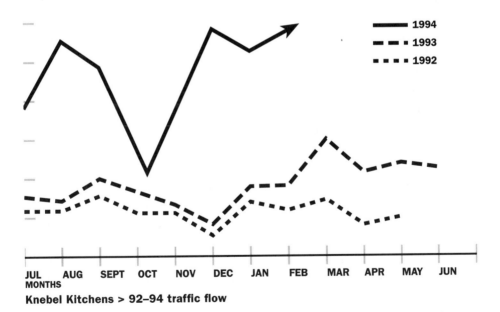

1994
1993
1992

JUL AUG SEPT OCT NOV DEC JAN FEB MAR APR MAY JUN
MONTHS

Knebel Kitchens > 92–94 traffic flow

The Knebel Lifetime Guarantee was launched in October 1994,
creating a massive, immediate and unprecedented jump in sales.

4   The CBA takes the emphasis away from price by creating a greatly enhanced value package. It taps directly into what are arguably the dominant emotions involved in the purchase of a kitchen: peace of mind and security. Provided the design and price are in the ballpark, security is a powerful motivator. With its competitors locked in a price spiral, Knebel effectively sidestepped the issue of discounting and emerged with a message much more relevant to its target market. Its commercials said in effect: 'For around $X per week, you can own a beautiful new Knebel kitchen, with the famous Knebel Lifetime Guarantee.'

5   By engaging the principle of risk reversal and assuming the risk in such a bold and daring way, Knebel effectively lowered the barrier of entry, making owning its product a much more viable proposition. The logic from Knebel's point of view is that if anything is going to go wrong with a kitchen it will invariably happen in the first five years, which was already covered by its original guarantee. Experience has shown that the chances of anything relating to design and workmanship going wrong much after that time are negligible. Should this happen, Knebel has always recognised its responsibility to do whatever it takes to make it right.

6   Another major advantage of offering the Knebel Lifetime Guarantee is that if a Knebel owner should have problems at some time in the distant future, it will be so unusual that Knebel will have the opportunity to jump in and fix it, and in the process, turn a complainant into an advocate. This type of experience can then form the basis of quite spectacular commercials that engage the power of customer testimonials.

7   By adopting the lifetime guarantee tactic, Knebel has pre-empted this concept within the kitchen industry. As in the case of Woolworths and 'fresh', if a competitor should be so foolish as to try to copy or steal this idea, it would immediately create confusion in the minds of its prospects, and therefore incur a degree of risk out of line with any likely benefits.

8   The Knebel CBA is not just something superficial. It is quite real, having been developed from something which already existed but had never been articulated. It's a classic example of taking the invisible, and making it visible.

9   The Knebel CBA fulfils all eight of the CBA qualifiers outlined earlier. It's a big idea capable of supporting a major advertising campaign. It represents immediate and relevant value to the customer. It attracts attention. It differentiates Knebel from its competitors. It fills an industry gap. (Try asking your average kitchen company for a written lifetime guarantee.) It motivates people to action. It ties the Knebel name into

the concept. It works as a headline in print, and it fits comfortably within a ten-second copy window in a TV or radio commercial.

10   Perhaps the most relevant aspect of this CBA from a learning perspective is that we made certain that Knebel did not simply offer 'a lifetime guarantee'. We took the concept and locked it permanently to Knebel's name: 'The famous Knebel Lifetime Guarantee'.

Because the concept has become part of its identity, Knebel now owns that concept in the marketplace. As long as Knebel chooses to stay with that idea, competitors are well advised to consider the concept outlined earlier in this book, and adopt an opposite polarity: an equal but opposite area of focus.

If you simply come up with an idea, however brilliant and innovative it may be, you can be certain that one or more of your competitors will immediately respond by copying you. You may well have had first-hand experience of this.

The secret lies in the idea of tying your name to the concept and driving it into the public mind as quickly as possible. The law of pre-emptive marketing will then ensure that competitors will copy you at their peril.

ROBBO'S SPARES

Robbo's Spares is a chain of retailers specialising in automotive spare parts and accessories, catering mainly to the home mechanic. Like Knebel, Robbo's Spares operates in an environment of total market parity, competing with a host of similar retail chains that offer essentially the same kinds of products and services.

In looking for an angle, we noted that, like many companies, Robbo's had for some time been offering special discounts to its regular customers. Your first thought here may be: 'Big deal – everybody does that.' However, after going through a gradual process of elimination we began to recognise untapped potential in this basic practice, which was already an established part of the system. Ultimately we arrived at the idea of discontinuing the practice of offering discounts to regulars, and replacing it with the 'Robbo's Mates Rates Card'.

Customers now have a very good reason to become repeat customers, and to drive right past each of Robbo's competitors in order to take advantage of 'Mates Rates'; and they do. This CBA has proved to be extremely effective for Robbo's, and is articulated in the following simple ten-word attraction meme:

Now you can buy at Mates Rates from Robbo's Spares.

As a final touch, the Robbo's people have come up with an innovative twist. Robbo's sales dockets are divided into two sections. On the first part the purchases are listed and totalled in the normal way. On the second part the new amount is separately calculated and displayed, taking Mates Rates into account. This gives customers an on-the-spot graphic reminder of the advantage in buying from Robbo's.

This is another instance of a CBA which draws its power from the fact that the company was already providing the benefit, albeit in an ad hoc, fuzzy kind of way. The right attitudes were already in place. All that remained was to:

1   recognise the CBA potential in that single facet of its business, to the exclusion of all others (very easy in hindsight, but another matter altogether in foresight)

2   apply perceptual and creative thinking to design and shape the CBA, and then to articulate it as an attraction meme.

That magic statement 'Now you can buy at Mates Rates from Robbo's Spares' complies with all eight of those CBA conditions mentioned earlier. It's a big idea capable of supporting a major advertising campaign. It represents immediate and relevant value to the customer. It certainly attracts attention. It differentiates Robbo's from its competition. It fills an industry gap. It motivates people to action. It locks the Robbo's name indelibly into the concept. It works as a headline in print, as well as fitting comfortably within a ten-second copy window in a radio commercial.

If you had something like this going for you, what kind of effect do you think it might have on your bottom line? Your CBA might not relate to price at all, but one thing's certain: when you combine the long-term leverage of something like 'Now you can buy at Mates Rates from Robbo's Spares' with the short-term leverage of 'And this week you can save even more with these specials', you have a package with the ability to deliver a whole new level of advertising response.

Geoff Ward, founding member of the Robbo's group, tells us that the Mates Rates CBA has been a resounding success. At the time of writing, Mates Rates customer membership accounts for 14 per cent of total turnover, and is growing steadily. When you take into account the fact that every repeat sale under the Mates Rates program is free of customer acquisition costs, you can begin to appreciate its true value in terms of bottom-line profits.

COLLINS BOOKSELLERS

If you think that when you've seen one bookshop you've seen them all, look again. Collins Booksellers came up with a classic CBA which deserves a mention here. Basically, they identified various quality books on their shelves with stickers offering a 'Good read guarantee'. This means that if you bought one of these books with the sticker and it turned out that you didn't like it for any reason at all, you simply returned it and received a full refund. No questions asked.

When we ask people if they would be prepared to offer something like that, the answer is invariably the same. Nearly everybody feels that the public would simply take advantage of them. And they're right. Some people do. But from Collins' point of view, it makes perfect business sense. The Collins marketing people tell us that customer returns were in fact less than half of one per cent. Amazing but true.

The Collins people carefully select the books carrying the guarantee, and the security offered by that sticker may be just the incentive that entices a person to try out a new author, somebody they would not ordinarily have considered. If that customer is happy with his or her choice, then Collins has just created a potential market for all of that author's books. But as we mentioned previously, the real power of a CBA is not so much in the idea itself as in the articulation of the idea.

When you encounter the Collins CBA executed in big lettering in a shop window as you walk by, it's enough to turn your head and stop you in your tracks:

Yawn, and Collins refunds your money.

That statement is just so outrageous and out of the ordinary, it makes you ask yourself: 'How can they do that?' But it makes perfect business sense. It's an intriguing statement about the customer. It provokes curiosity. That is the secret of a well-articulated CBA.

It's worth noting that Collins Booksellers management made the decision to change their promotional focus from time to time. There are advantages and disadvantages to this strategy. The upside is that there is always something new to attract customers. But the downside is that, because of their transient nature, none of these promotional ideas is around long enough to become imbedded permanently in people's minds. As a result, the retailer has not become generally known for one single, compelling, distinguishing feature. If it were, it would almost certainly have a greater competitive advantage in the market-place in the long term.

This example from Collins proved yet again that a CBA which can produce a significant increase in sales, while incurring customer returns of less than 0.5 per cent, is an extremely worthwhile proposition.

MELITTA COFFEE

Melitta is widely considered to be Europe's favourite coffee, but had been experiencing a decline in market share in Australia because of a number of factors.

One of the problems in marketing coffee is that people cannot iden-tify the various brands in a taste test, or by aroma. They can certainly identify the type of bean used, but not the brand. Because taste and aroma are among the most desirable aspects of coffee, this presents a distinct problem when your aim is to develop a compelling point of difference. Coffee tends to be very much a parity product.

Because Melitta was an excellent product to begin with, we decided to present a leadership stance to the marketplace. We set out to posi-tion Melitta as a premium brand in the public mind by creating the presupposition of premium quality and taste. The idea was to begin with the proposition that Melitta was a highly desirable brand, and to encourage coffee drinkers everywhere to speculate on possible reasons for its good taste.

To achieve this, we created an abstract entity which we called 'The Melitta Secret'. This resulted in a TV campaign featuring a selection of people who fitted Melitta's demographic and psychographic profiles, specu-lating on possible answers to a question, articulated as a curiosity meme:

What's the Melitta Secret?

The strength of this approach is that the question is never an-swered, but leaves the consumer intrigued. This opens the door to all kinds of promotional opportunities – the public can be asked to speculate on what the Melitta Secret might be, with a prize for the winners, for example. People are given a reason to try the brand out of curiosity.

The results of this campaign for Melitta have been spectacular. The 'Melitta Secret' meme has the ability to stick in the minds of people for many years to come, like the 'Which twin has the Toni?' advertisements from the 1950s.

If this concept had been applied to an inferior brand of coffee, it would have paved the way for a repeat of the Decore debacle. The Melitta campaign worked because when customers responded to the advertising and tried the brand, they were delighted, because Melitta really is a premium quality brand.

'What's the Melitta Secret?' is a CBA with the latent power to influence positively customer buying decisions over an extended period of time. The effect of this has been to alter the dynamics of the marketplace in Melitta's favour, resulting in a corresponding increase in market share, as well as a significant increase in supermarket shelf space.

'What's the Melitta Secret?' was Melitta's most successful advertising campaign in ten years.

CIVIC VIDEO

Civic Video has been using a marketing device which seems to be unprecedented in its industry, an environment of almost total parity. Civic created its 'Satisfaction Guarantee', which really makes you look twice to see if you got it right the first time. It is articulated as follows:

> The Civic Video Satisfaction Guarantee:
> Enjoy the movie or swap it free!

If you rent any first release movie and find you don't enjoy it, you simply bring it back, and Civic will invite you to choose another one. Free.

Invariably people's first reaction to this is one of disbelief. How could they possibly do that? People would take advantage of them. And if you thought that, you'd be right – as Collins Booksellers discovered, around 0.5 per cent! If you had a CBA like that, which cost you basically nothing but attracted a disproportionate increase in business, you may begin to appreciate the power of this devastating concept.

><

Following are some examples you might want to consider as a guide to what is possible when you are formulating your CBA.

You'll find that the following examples have all come from the line of thinking we propose in this book. They tend to have 'the wow factor' that engages consumer curiosity.

Note, however, that like many brands, both Federal Express and Domino's Pizzas lacked the foresight to lock their brand names into their concepts. Without a memorable link between the brand name and a concept, it takes much longer, and costs much more in media expenditure, to achieve a high level of brand recognition than would otherwise be necessary.

[CBA EXAMPLES
(Memes are indicated in bold type)

Kentucky Fried Chicken	Cooked the Colonel's way with **11 Secret Herbs and Spices.**
Knebel Kitchens	Your beautiful new Knebel kitchen has been built to stand the test of time. That's why it comes to you with **the famous Knebel Lifetime Guarantee.**
Lite n' Easy	**Lose weight for life with Lite n' Easy.**
Melitta Coffee	**What's the Melitta Secret?**
M & Ms	**M & Ms melt in your mouth, not in your hand.**
Robbo's Spares	**Now you can buy at Mates Rates from Robbo's Spares.**
Federal Express	**Absolutely, positively overnight.**
Domino's Pizzas	**Your pizza delivered hot in thirty minutes or it's free!**
Video EZY	**The Video EZY Guarantee: Get it first time or get it free.**
Collins Booksellers	**Yawn, and Collins refunds your money.**
Civic Video	**The Civic Video Satisfaction Guarantee: Enjoy the movie or swap it free.**
Harvest Homes	**Love it or we'll level it.** (Amazing, but true!)
Prospect Credit Union	Protect your credit rating with **The Prospect Painless Pre-approval in just 30 seconds.**
Tylenol	**For the millions of people who should not be taking aspirin.**

... You get the idea.

Now is a good time to stop for a moment and review our progress to this point. Remember the question that led us to this CBA issue in the first place: 'Why should I buy from you rather than one of your competitors?'

It's a question that has begun to take on a whole new shade of meaning in light of these examples of companies and brands that have made it happen. It's worth reiterating a point we made earlier in this chapter. There was a time when none of these companies had any real marketable point of difference. They all found themselves in much the same position you possibly find yourself in right now.

Was there anything special about any of these companies that may have predisposed them to the ability to formulate and adopt a CBA? While it may appear that way in hindsight, the answer would have to be no. Any company, service, product or brand has the latent ability to formulate and adopt a CBA. It just takes a little time, effort and know-how, which eliminates many companies from the contest.

Maybe you still have doubts and feel that in some way your company is a special case and because of this, there is really no possibility of your developing a CBA. Let's look at an extreme example of an industry that is about as difficult as it gets in terms of market parity: bottled water.

Imagine for a moment you were in the business of trying to create and market a premium-priced brand of non-imported bottled water. How in the world could you even begin to come up with anything even resembling a CBA for something as basic as water? There is one brand which has been able to accomplish it: Pureau.

With supermarket space already crowded with product, Pureau had the foresight to develop a proprietary system which produces water guaranteed to be 100 per cent free from impurities. Pure, clear water. Not only can you actually taste the difference, but when you see it alongside competitive brands in the supermarket, it even *looks* clearer. The Pureau competitive advantage is expressed as a simple security meme which appears on a yellow sticker on each bottle:

Pureau is the *only* water guaranteed salt and bacteria free.

The following statement appears on the back of the sticker, lending a high degree of credibility to the brand:

Commonwealth Government National Food Authority Standard
S5 states in part that packaged water must have no more than

100 micro-organisms per millilitre. Independent laboratory tests carried out on every batch of Pureau consistently show NIL micro-organisms per millilitre.

By adopting this stance, Pureau has tapped into a fundamental area of self-interest to many health-conscious people. Not only does this simple statement assure us that Pureau does not contain bacteria or salt, but it leaves us with the distinct feeling that perhaps other brands may!

The concept was supported by a campaign of simple but effective illustrated advertisements with memetic headlines that read:

Your yoghurt needs bacteria, your water doesn't.

and

Your chips need salt, your water doesn't.

Could any of the other bottled water companies have done the same? Of course they could. But when you're looking at the different options available to you in your local supermarket, that security meme beckons you with a simple message which is difficult to ignore: a good reason to buy from Pureau rather than its many competitors.

It's interesting to note that if you happen to be into bottled water, the Pureau competitive advantage performs three distinct functions.

1   It engages the customer's attention at a basic level of self-interest. Who wants to drink bacteria? Nobody!
2   It effectively positions Pureau in the marketplace. Pureau really has taken ownership of an engaging idea.
3   It effectively answers the question: 'Why should I buy from you?'

Strong as it is, the Pureau competitive advantage has not been expressed as a CBA. It focuses on the commodity, not the customer. We believe it would have more power if it were to be articulated in a way that involved the customer. Perhaps something like:

Enjoy Pureau. The only water guaranteed 100 per cent free from bacteria and salt.

or

You'll love the pure, fresh taste of Pureau. The only water guaranteed 100 per cent free from bacteria and salt.

There are two simple questions a person might pose to one of your customers, the answer to either of which could well hold the key to identifying your CBA:

1 Why did you decide to buy *that* one?
2 Why did you decide to buy from *there*?

If you can turn these questions around and think perceptually, they may give you the vital clue that will lead you directly to your CBA.

Your concern that there is nothing unique about your particular product or brand is ill-founded. In searching for that magic point of difference for our clients, we rarely, if ever, focus on the core operation. We invariably turn our attention to something which is external or *peripheral* to the core operation, and then through the power of concentrated focus, expand it, dramatise it and raise it to the level of the extraordinary.

If you re-look at our CBA examples, you'll notice that none of them focuses on the core business. In every case, the CBA is based on some external issue. A CBA can be an elusive thing. Sometimes it can hit you in a flash, and sometimes you have to dig deep to find it. It may be that from our discussion to this point, you feel you're already halfway there. You could well have all the information you need to create a CBA for your company or brand right now.

However, if it's not at all obvious, and you can see the value in developing a CBA, you might like to consider taking your team through that specialised process we mentioned earlier. (See the special supplement at the end of the book.) Clients who have done this tell us it has been one of the most exciting and rewarding experiences their companies have ever encountered.

Creating a CBA requires your total commitment and involvement, but the rewards are beyond anything you can presently imagine. If you do this well, in a very short space of time you can join that elite group of companies and brands that have broken free from the shackles of market parity. These are the organisations which have been able to create a clear market differentiation in the public mind and, in the process, have become attractive to the consumer. When this happens, you find that instead of creating sales, you're creating purchases. As a result, you discover what it's like to be where the action is: inside the Inner Circle.

•

>> **The expression of Activator Three is:**
Create and articulate your Customer Buying Advantage, linked to a compelling offer.

•

THE MAIN POINTS

•

1 >> SHORT-TERM LEVERAGE

•

Short-term leverage is designed to motivate people to buy now. For all its good points, short-term leverage has five serious disadvantages:

i   You end up shaving your margins to the bone, sometimes to the vanishing point.

ii   In pushing discounting to the level it has, business has taught a whole generation of people not to pay normal prices.

iii   As the saying goes, there will always be somebody smart enough, or dumb enough, to sell for a dollar less; which means you're playing a game you can't win.

iv   You can find yourself under constant pressure, particularly if you're a retailer, to dream up new variations on the discounting theme. Then the moment your ads hit the marketplace, your competitors move in and simply steal your ideas.

v   You find yourself locked into a cycle: you advertise, and they respond; you stop advertising, and they stop responding. Before you realise what's happening, you find yourself on a treadmill.

•

2 >> LONG-TERM LEVERAGE

•

Long-term leverage is an overriding, ongoing, obvious reason, beyond price, for a person to choose one product, service or brand over another.

•

3 >> MARKET PARITY

•

Market parity describes a market environment which the customer perceives to consist of look-alike alternatives. Although in reality they may differ in many respects, perceptually they appear to the consumer to be as alike as peas in a pod.

•

4 >> THE PRICE MYTH

•

People do not buy on price, even when they think they do. They *always* buy a package of value, of which price is a component. A low price is attractive only when certain value mandatories are present in the total package. An item stacked with the right kinds of added-value

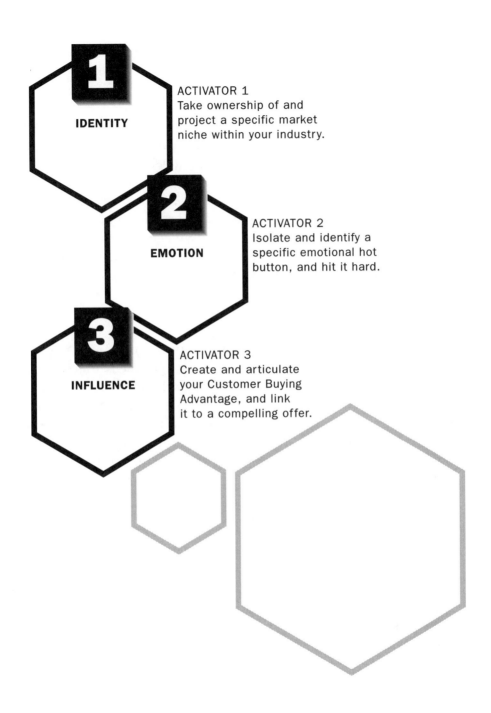

1

IDENTITY

ACTIVATOR 1
Take ownership of and
project a specific market
niche within your industry.

2

EMOTION

ACTIVATOR 2
Isolate and identify a
specific emotional hot
button, and hit it hard.

3

INFLUENCE

ACTIVATOR 3
Create and articulate
your Customer Buying
Advantage, and link
it to a compelling offer.

**THE WAM
RAPID RESPONSE SYSTEM**

components can represent a more attractive proposition than a similar item at a lower price.

•

5 >> THE ACID TEST

•

Try calling your own company and asking the question: 'Why should I buy from you rather than one of your competitors?' Then call each of your competitors and ask the same question. The chances are that all you will get will be generalisations about basic consumer expectations. Fully 98 per cent of companies, products and brands do not have anything that represents a clearcut competitive advantage in the marketplace. This creates a golden opportunity for you to move in and change the dynamics of the marketplace to work in your favour.

•

6 >> YOUR CUSTOMER'S SELF-INTEREST

•

Given that self-interest is the number one motivator of human behaviour, why don't all suppliers of goods and services focus their every effort on tapping into this wellspring of potential power? One possible reason is that because self-interest is the predominant motivator, the very concept of focusing their attention on the wants and needs of others is just contrary to human nature. Understanding this and turning it to your advantage can make an extraordinary difference to your advertising response.

•

7 >> STRATEGIES AND TACTICS

•

In *Bottom-Up Marketing*, Ries and Trout challenge convention by defining a tactic as a 'competitive mental angle', and a strategy as a 'cohesive marketing direction'. They point out that the companies which have made the most spectacular gains in market share are those which have begun with an innovative 'angle', or idea, and then developed a strategy to support it.

•

8 >> THE DECORE DEBACLE

•

In many ways, the 1988 Decore campaign exposes the flawed thinking behind a great deal of the advertising undertaken by some of the biggest advertisers in the world today, and validates the concept of the Inner Circle. People are not fools, and if a product or brand fails to live up to the advertising hype, then its managers should not be surprised when people try it once, and then drop out. The message of this book is that it is not only possible but essential to develop a clearcut competitive advantage if a product or brand is to survive and prosper in today's increasingly competitive market environment.

•

9 >> THE UNIQUE SELLING PROPOSITION

•

A USP, by definition, is about selling, and is designed to create a selling response. Consequently, it tends to be focused on the commodity. A USP can be an extremely effective marketing tool, but it turns out that the most effective advertising focuses on the customer, not the commodity. To enable us to achieve this consistently, we felt that a further development of the USP concept was required.

•

10 >> THE CUSTOMER BUYING ADVANTAGE

•

A CBA, by definition, is about buying, and is designed to create a buying response; to create a purchase rather than a sale. A CBA is a simple, bold statement that does eight, and all eight of the following things:

i   It must be a big idea capable of supporting a major advertising campaign for at least five years.

ii   It must represent immediate and relevant value to the customer.

iii It must attract attention.

iv   It must distinguish you from your competition.

v   It must fill, or appear to fill an industry gap.

vi   It must motivate people to take action.

vii It must lock your brand name permanently and indelibly into the concept.

viii It must work as a headline in print, and must also fit comfortably within a ten-second copy window in a TV or radio commercial.

The reason a CBA is such a powerful marketing tool is that it is not just some kind of mindless advertising hype. A CBA is a compelling instrument of influence, based on a genuine synthesis between what consumers want on the one hand, what your competitors are doing on the other, and what you can deliver consistently, with a high degree of excellence.

•

11 >> NARROW YOUR FOCUS

•

When you try to become all things to all people, you become nothing to anybody. When you narrow your focus, when you decide to become widely known for something beyond people's normal expectations, you take on the persona of a specialist rather than a generalist. When you do this, you make yourself more attractive and intriguing to your customers and prospects, and you'll find you've broken through another barrier to the Inner Circle.

•

12 >> EXAMPLES OF CBAs IN THE MARKETPLACE

•

The CBA examples in this chapter are here for you to model when you're formulating your own CBA. Begin with the final articulation, and then work backward. As you do this, you'll begin to understand how they were developed, and at the same time get a feel for the process involved in developing a CBA for your own company or brand.

><

Before you can access the Inner Circle, there are two more Hot Zones to contend with. You can have people understand who you are, you can touch them emotionally, you can give them a reason to choose you over your competitors. But if they can't bring your name to top of mind at the moment of a buying decision, then you've got a problem.

Let's annihilate it by engaging Activator Four …

CHAPTER 6

ACTIVATOR FOUR

RECALL

'How do you expect me to remember your name

at the moment I'm ready to buy?'

One of the major reasons people don't respond to advertising

is that by the time they're ready to make a buying decision,

they've forgotten who the advertiser was.

Activator 4 is about the distinction between brand awareness and brand recall. It's quite possible that a large number of people know the name of your company or brand very well at the intellectual level. If we were to ask any of these people: 'Do you know of (your company or brand name)?', they'd answer 'Yes'. However, the big questions are, do they think of you when they are actually about to buy whatever it is you sell, and if not, why not?

In order to access the Inner Circles of total strangers, you have to begin by making it easy for people to bring your product or brand name to top of mind at the moment it is most needed: the moment of a buying decision.

There are basically two ways to create massive brand recall in the minds of your prospects. The first is the way the big multinationals do it. First you create an 'institutional' commercial – an image commercial which says in effect: 'We're these wonderful people with this great product. Come and get it!' Then you throw obscene amounts of money at it over an extended period of time. There is no question that this strategy works. It happens all the time, and has created many market leaders in the process. But there is a much more cost-effective way.

A MAGICAL MOMENT IN TIME

At the heart of every strategic marketing effort lies the opportunity to capitalise on, to take advantage of, a magical moment in time.

There is a specific moment, when a person, your prospect, suddenly realises he or she needs to buy something in order to satisfy some emotional need. Metaphorically, the mind lights up like a Christmas tree, as minute channels of electrical energy, tiny impulses, scan the data banks of the mind looking for information which might solve the problem.

The mental process begins with a non-verbal question. The mind formulates it in a way that is very clear, but which sidesteps the need for language and words. This unspoken question could be something like 'Where am I most likely to find this?', 'What options are there?', 'What happened last time we needed this?', 'What problems did we have?', or any number of variations.

This is where memes enter the picture. The information in the mind appears to be made up of files containing edited, condensed or stripped-down versions of our experience. This information is accessed, scanned and processed at lightning speed. The magic happens in that instant when the mind makes a neuro-association. A synapse occurs, and it connects.

And there, as clear as crystal, right there in your prospect's mind, is the answer. It may present itself as a single name, or several viable options.

The key to brand recall is to set up a system in the mind of your prospect which optimises the likelihood of your name being brought to top of mind in that magical moment in time.

Although the human mind represents the pinnacle of human evolution, and although technology is unlikely to succeed in replicating its enormous computing and intuitive capabilities, it has one intriguing characteristic. It is inherently lazy. It will do practically anything to avoid the simple act of thinking.

Certainly in an emergency, or when it is cranked up and in harness, working on a problem or a project, particularly in a work situation, it performs just fine. Sometimes it excels itself and amazes you with its creative ability; but take away the pressure, and it drops back to the level of minimum effort. Maybe it's smarter than we give it credit for! However, this inherent 'laziness' holds the key to brand recall. The reason for this is simple.

If the mind has the choice of either thinking, or looking for a shortcut, it will go for the shortcut every time. In order to take the line of least resistance, the mind takes the option of rapidly scanning memes. This basically eliminates the need to sift through massive data files.

Think about it. If somebody said to you, 'Quick, we need to buy a mobile phone. Now!', would your first instinct be to react rationally and think, 'Well ... I'll look up the *Yellow Pages*. There must be four hundred suppliers in there'? Possibly, but probably not. If you're like most people, you'd instantly bring one, two, three or maybe four suppliers to top of mind, if you're lucky. The chances are that you'd end up buying from one of these suppliers.

•

>> **People tend to operate from a mental shortlist, and if you're not on that shortlist, then you're not in the game.**

•

The process of creating brand recall is not what it seems. To communicate with another person on any level requires two distinct operations:

1   The message has to be sent.
2   The message has to be received.

In the case of most of the advertising we see around us, the message is sent, but not received, for reasons which will soon become evident.

If you have been getting a less than satisfactory response from your past advertising, then the issues we are addressing in this chapter and in the previous chapter will have a profound effect on the way you structure your advertising from this point on. Activators Three and Four, influence and brand recall, should ideally go hand in hand. To achieve influence without brand recall is arguably worse than useless. You can very easily find yourself subsidising your competitor's advertising. To achieve brand recall without influence is a more useful outcome, but having the ability to achieve both in one hit is what it's all about.

THE MYTH OF AUDIENCE REACH

In order to squeeze the most out of your advertising budget, there is a little known, and even less understood concept you need to grasp: the myth of audience reach.

What does this mean?

When most people advertise, they are basing their media buying decisions on a false premise. They buy air time or print space on the basis of audience ratings, and a corresponding dollar value is assigned. The larger the audience, the higher the cost to advertise in that medium. So far so good.

The problem is that although your advertisement may physically reach a predetermined number of people, the majority of them are deaf, blind, or both, to your message. Most of those people will not be in the market for whatever it is you have to offer right then and there. The law of averages prohibits it.

THE WAM REACH MODEL

The marketplace consists of three distinct groups of people: the Nows, the Soons and the Laters.

THE NOWS

The Nows are those people who will actually go out and buy from either you or your competitors some time in the period from the moment your ad hits the marketplace until about forty-eight hours into the future. These people are ready to buy right *now*. They have the money and the motivation, and they have probably shopped around and decided exactly what, where and when they are going to buy. If you were to run an advertisement which influenced some of those people to re-consider and buy from you instead of your competitor, then you would win market share. This is what direct response advertising is all about.

Because there are only so many people within any given market segment, marketing is a game in which you try to hold onto your exist-ing loyal customers and divert people away from your competitors. In the overall scheme of things, the Nows constitute only a very small proportion of the whole, but are the most powerful group to address because they are about to buy.

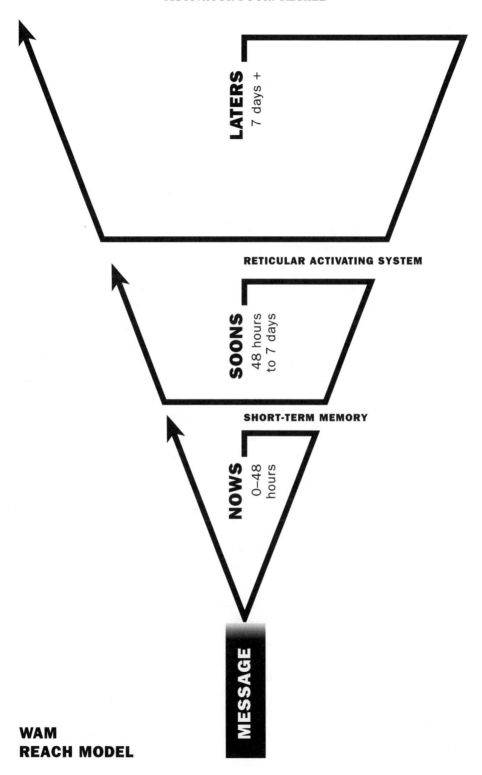

LATERS
7 days +

RETICULAR ACTIVATING SYSTEM

SOONS
48 hours
to 7 days

SHORT-TERM MEMORY

NOWS
0–48
hours

MESSAGE

**WAM
REACH MODEL**

THE SOONS

The Soons are the next most powerful group to consider. These are also real people who will actually go out and buy from either you or your competitors some time from about forty-eight hours after your ad hits the marketplace until about seven days into the future. These people also have the motivation, they may have done some research, and maybe they have already decided where they will buy, but for some reason they're holding back. They're not quite ready; they're waiting for something. Maybe they're waiting for the money, or for something to happen, but by definition they will buy, and soon.

Have you ever seen or heard an advertisement for something that really interested you, but felt that you were not quite ready for it? Then maybe a week or a month later, some polarising event occurred and you suddenly needed whatever it was, and you needed it *right then*? And no matter how hard you tried, you couldn't remember who the ad was for?

So what did you do? You went right out and bought a competitor's product by default. The horrifying thing about this from the point of view of an advertiser is that when this principle works against you in the marketplace, *you find you have been subsidising your competitor's advertising!* It happens all the time. It's the first of two brick walls that you can run up against: people's short-term memory. And it can cripple your advertising if you don't know how to handle it.

The solution lies in your ability to crash right through people's short-term memory and beyond.

THE LATERS

The Laters are that massive group of real people who will buy from a week after the advertising until a year or more into the future. These people, by definition, will also buy from either you or your competitors, but don't know it yet. They are not aware that, as time goes on, they will ultimately become Soons, and then Nows.

THE RETICULAR ACTIVATING SYSTEM – THE ULTIMATE FILTER

The problem with the conventional approach to advertising is that when you stop advertising, people stop responding. You find yourself on that self-perpetuating treadmill with no real chance of backing off for fear that business will drop off – as it probably will.

The purpose of the Nows, Soons and Laters concept is to make the point that if you can reach out and touch *all* of them simultaneously in a way that promotes strong brand recall, even though the Soons and Laters are not yet ready to buy, then you can consider backing off a little. People will then respond even when you are not advertising because they have been conditioned to recall your name at the moment they're ready to buy. Does that concept make sense to you?

However, before you can hope to achieve this, you have another brick wall to crash through. This second brick wall is absolutely devastating, and in effect, routinely wipes out most of your audience in one swoop. And the amazing thing about this particular brick wall is that practically nobody knows about it. In psychology it's known as the Reticular Activating System (RAS), and until you get a handle on it, you are probably going to continue to waste a lot of money on ineffective advertising. Let's explain.

As we live our lives, information is coming at us at an incredible rate. There are conversations all around us, traffic noise, birds, dogs barking, telephones, air conditioners, advertising messages of all types, children, arguments, television, movies, newspapers and magazines, and so many other stimuli, that if the mind did not have some filtering system, some means of focusing only on those things which seem to be relevant at the time, it would be in danger of going into overload. As a result, the evolution of the human mind over time has produced the RAS – the ultimate filter.

Have you ever been in a crowded, noisy room, and suddenly become aware that your name has been mentioned somewhere on the other side of the room? It may have been uttered softly, but you still picked it up. How does this happen?

Have you ever bought something that you have never seen before – a car, or perhaps an item of clothing – only to find it everywhere the moment you bought it? Was it everywhere before you bought it? Of course! You just didn't see it.

Have you ever gone looking for your car keys and, although they were quite literally before your eyes, you didn't see them? After you had looked unsuccessfully in all kinds of places, becoming more and more frustrated, you finally came back to the original spot and *there they were*. Most people seem to identify with this phenomenon, and are often unsettled by it. People often call it 'selective blindness'.

At our business development seminars, people tell us that this kind of thing happens to them all the time, and they've sometimes wondered if they were going a little crazy. In fact, this is something that most of us experience, sometimes at the most inconvenient times. What's happening here? The simple fact is that people are, as peak performance coach Tony Robbins puts it, 'deletion creatures'. We see only those things we focus on, and delete everything else from our consciousness.

THE REASON WHY MOST ADVERTISING IS IGNORED

The reason we did not see the car keys was that we were physically *incapable* of seeing them, because of a phenomenon known in psychology as a 'scotoma'.

A medical term, scotoma is defined as 'a mental blind spot, or a gap in the field of vision'. The Scotoma Effect is the key to understanding why most people are blind to your advertisements. Like the car keys, if people are not in the market for your product or service right then and there, their RAS simply deletes it from their reality by creating a scotoma, which renders them effectively blind to your message.

Imagine that you bought a new set of car tyres about six months ago. You are now not in the market for tyres, and the whole topic of tyres has faded from your consciousness. You could be reading a newspaper featuring a full-page advertisement for 'Half price premium quality tyres for this week only', and the chances are that you wouldn't even see it. Your eye will be attracted by some other headline that engages your interest, and you become yet another person to confirm that most advertising is ignored.

So how do you get around this intriguing situation? The secret lies in sidestepping the short-term memory process altogether and tapping into a different part of the brain; the part that recalls things like multiplication tables, poetry and nursery rhymes from your school days, long after most other memories from that time have faded.

When you're calculating something and you say to yourself: 'Nine nines are eighty-one', you're not *remembering* anything; you're hitting 'play', and triggering a high fidelity digital stereo recording created in childhood. When you say 'Mary had a little lamb, its fleece was white as snow', you're not *remembering* anything. Once again, you're simply hitting 'play'. These things never fade in the way that memories fade, because they are hardwired into the brain, and are there to stay.

The most effective way to create massive brand recall involves developing a 'mnemonic recall trigger' for your product, service or brand. A mnemonic is 'something intended to help the memory'; basically a mental shortcut.

Most of us remember being taught 'I before E, except after C' at school. Do you remember it because you had to write it out five hundred times? No. You were probably told only once, and it has stayed with you for life. People tell us that to this day they can't write words like 'brief', 'believe', 'conceive' or 'receive' without bringing that mental shortcut to mind just to check the spelling, to make sure they've got it right.

The interesting thing is that you never think about 'I before E' until you encounter one of those words like 'receive', 'conceive', or 'brief'. At that magical moment, the instant your mind perceives the problem, it searches for a solution. In an instant it retrieves the mnemonic recall trigger 'I before E, except after C'. It is precisely this process that holds the key to achieving massive brand recall.

'Thirty days hath September, April, June and November' is another sticky mnemonic recall meme that many people use on a regular basis, particularly if they happen to be writing out a cheque at the end of the month.

The reason these kinds of phrases seem to stick so firmly in our minds is that they are memes, and, like all memes, they operate under the evolutionary law of the survival of the fittest.

Mnemonics are used as mental shortcuts in all kinds of learning situations, from mathematics, to learning the sequence of coloured wires in electrical cable, to music. The sequence of sharps when setting a key signature in music is G, D, A, E, B, F, C.

This can be tricky to remember until you learn a particular mnemonic that is set out as a telegraph message: 'Go Down And Enter By Force. Charlie.'

You get the picture. Mnemonics help us to recall certain things in a different way. Most of the time we don't need them, but when we do, they're there in an instant.

What is the reason for this curious aspect of recollection, this human affinity with mental shortcuts? Why does it exist?

THE NATURE OF AUTOMATIC RESPONSE

The overriding objective in human design is the survival of the species. Because survival typically depends upon split-second decisions and actions, analytical thought is not an option in a life-threatening situation. Instant action is required.

For this reason, the mind has developed an extremely effective second line of defence, a system of automatic response. The mind asks, in effect: 'What did we do last time this happened?' By instantly accessing past references and outcomes, the mind is able to sidestep the thought process to the extent that many people in the world today live out most of their lives on 'auto pilot', and almost never engage in the act of contemplative thought.

As a species, we have developed over the last few centuries at an exponential rate. For most of us, the life-threatening situations which were the basis of this system of mental shortcuts no longer exist in today's world of industry and commerce, or at least not to anything like the same extent. Nevertheless, we're left with the system and we use it all the time, even though we may not be aware of it.

APPLYING THE CONCEPT OF MNEMONICS TO ADVERTISING

As far as advertising is concerned, there are three characteristics of the human mind which, collectively, have been shown to produce extraordinary results in the area of brand recall:

1   When the mind is faced with the prospect of actually thinking versus taking a mental shortcut, you can count on the shortcut every time.
2   The mind has a natural affinity with mnemonics, and is able to access them at blinding speed.
3   The mind has a natural affinity with memes, to the point where they play a pivotal role in our survival mechanism.

It is a simple matter to set up a system of recall in the mind of the consumer by consistently following a two-step process:

1   framing and articulating your product or company name as a mnemonic, a sticky meme
2   using the laws of influence to produce selfish motives in the customer to buy.

Under these conditions, when a person encounters the need for a generic product or service, the mind will recall the selfish promise offered via the advertising stimulus to which it has been exposed. It will then immediately scan for a mnemonic, because a mnemonic represents the line of least resistance. That magical moment in time happens in the instant that the mind suddenly matches the two in a flash of insight.

If you happen to be the only one in your market segment with a well-crafted mnemonic recall trigger and a selfish promise to the end user in the form of a CBA, you have a devastating advantage over your competitors.

Contrary to popular belief, you don't need a massive budget to achieve a high level of brand recall, although of course more is better. What you do need is a recall meme, a sticky mnemonic recall trigger and enough media weight to drive it into the public mind with consistency and repetition over time. Repetition is the key.

What the vast majority of advertisers fail to understand is that brand recall without the use of a mnemonic is linear. That is to say brand recall builds slowly, if at all, through a process of *addition* over time through repetition.

When you introduce a powerful mnemonic recall trigger, you bring a whole new set of dynamics into play. The graph curve becomes *exponential* rather than linear, gaining its momentum through the power of multiplication rather than addition. This is because mnemonics are such an integral part of the natural operating system of the human mind.

Advertising that deliberately and consistently utilises the power of mnemonics results in increased brand recall over time. Quite literally, you can make one advertising dollar do the work of three or four.

THE NATURE OF MEMORY AND BRAND RECALL

For our purpose here, memory can be said to fall into three broad categories:

1   **Short-term memory**

Short-term memory is extremely volatile, and its purpose is to allow us to deal with the here and now. It can last anywhere from a few seconds to about forty-eight hours, depending on the context. The horrors of short-term memory become evident when you've just been introduced to a group of complete strangers, and it's important you remember their names. It's a situation most of us know only too well. To use the computer analogy, short-term memory resembles RAM (Random Access Memory, which is volatile in nature). When you turn your computer off, the RAM evaporates and is gone forever. By conscious effort, however, it is possible to extend our range of short-term memory to create something we can regard as mid-term memory.

2 **Mid-term memory**

We use mid-term memory for important but temporary issues, such as remembering people's names in a social situation – particularly if we feel we're likely to meet these people again in the near future.

However, unless we consciously and deliberately tag and file these important pieces of information so that we can retrieve them quickly and easily, we often find they are not available right then and there. Without a clear point of reference, the mind goes into search mode, scanning through a lifetime of accumulated random information. 'It's right on the tip of my tongue' is a familiar expression. When this happens, the best thing to do is to put the matter out of your mind, and then some time later the required information just appears, usually too late to be useful.

3 **Long-term memory**

Long-term memory seems to fall into three broad sub-categories:

i   General knowledge, which includes our professional knowledge and expertise, as well as the vast body of information we use to cope with life on a daily basis.

ii Special names, faces, events, experiences, odours, sounds and feelings, all tied strongly to past and present emotional states.

iii Material learned over time through repetition, memes and mnemonics. This material has become hardwired and resides in a part of the brain which contains things such as poetry, music, multiplication tables, historical dates and places, brand names, and the vast array of mental shortcuts we have devised to help us to deal with the volatile and limiting aspects of both short- and mid-term memory. The distinguishing characteristic of mnemonics is that they are able to be accessed and recalled instantly and effortlessly.

With all this in mind, you need to look closely at the way that your advertising is formulated, so that it zeroes in on that magical moment in time, that moment of truth when somebody makes a decision to buy. When this occurs, you take advantage of the nature of memory and create the outcomes you want so much to achieve.

Because mnemonics are hardwired into the brain, people who are very old and even senile can remember long tracts of verse, poetry and music from their childhood, but have difficulty remembering what they did five minutes ago. People at our seminars tell us that they may not have seen a Marshall ad for two years, and then one day they find they have a flat battery. In the space of an instant, they find that the line 'Holler for a Marshall' has sprung to top of mind; an awesome demonstration of the power of mnemonics.

The key to making all of this work for you is to *frame your product or brand name as a sticky meme, which functions as a mnemonic recall trigger.* As it happens, 'Holler for a Marshall' is a classic mnemonic recall trigger, which explains why it has worked so well.

Two pharmaceutical products which employ mnemonic recall triggers to good effect are Spray Tish and Demazin. In the case of Spray Tish, the 'Tish' part of the brand name itself obviously relates to the act of sneezing, and constitutes an association meme which is quite likely to bring the product to top of mind for anybody in the act of sneezing. The Demazin people ran a TV spot in which the actor replicated the act of sneezing by going: 'D ... D ... Demazin!' Both memetic approaches are quite valid and demonstrate a high level of insight.

A CONVINCING DEMONSTRATION

At our business development seminars we tell our audience that we'll speak a line, and as a group, they're to respond with whatever immediately comes to mind. Then we give them something like:

- 'Good on you Mum, ... '
- 'Take me away, ... '
- 'Have you driven a ... '
- 'Holler ... '
- 'Drive in and jive away ... '
- 'Oh, what a feeling ... '
- 'I feel like a ... '
- 'TDK ... '
- 'We're Woolworths ... '
- 'Which bank? ... '

and so on.

After they have given us the responses to ten or more of these lines in loud unison, we ask them: 'How did you all do that? Did you all go out and practise? Did you all go out and write them down five hundred times? No. You're wired.'

Have you ever made a conscious effort to remember 'Good on you Mum, Tip Top's the one', or 'Take me away, P & O'? If somebody were to hold a gun to your head and say 'Forget "Good on you Mum, Tip Top's the one", or I'll blow your brains out!', you'd discover that you would be *incapable* of forgetting it. That recollection is a physical part of your anatomy. It's part of that valuable 'real estate' Tip Top *owns* in your mind, whether you like it or not. The good news is that if it works so well for all those other insightful companies and brands, it will work for you too. All you have to do is to work the system.

Interesting, isn't it? We're *all* wired to give those responses. This goes a long way to explaining why so many companies that have their names expressed as mnemonic recall triggers also just happen to be at or near the level of market leader.

It's a sobering thought that when you articulate your name as a mnemonic recall trigger and project it out into the marketplace through your advertising and marketing, *you actually take away the element of choice as to whether or not people remember your name.*

Think about that for a moment and you'll begin to comprehend the enormous untapped potential locked away in this simple but profound concept; one you should be using at the earliest opportunity, particularly if your competitors are not aware of it.

Be aware also that there are purely visual mnemonics. The McDonald's golden arches, Ronald McDonald, the Michelin tyre man, the stylised 'W' in the Westpac logo, the Jolly Green Giant and the Coca Cola bottle shape are all good examples of this. You can recognise them from a kilometre away.

Famous cities also have their visual mnemonics, which are some of the best known identity memes in the world. Acting as memetic icons, they create instant recognition and countless tourist dollars: the Eiffel Tower, the Parthenon, the Pyramids, the Golden Gate Bridge, the Colosseum, the Empire State Building, gondolas, London Bridge, the Sydney Opera House and the Sydney Harbour Bridge are just a few of many.

You know you have a good visual mnemonic when people can see it in isolation from a distance, and immediately make the connection and identify you. You can't have too many things going for you when you're trying to promote brand recall.

To be effective in the long term, every advertisement must have a residual effect. Getting your name out into the marketplace through the prudent use of mnemonics comes under the heading of 'marketing by stealth'. If your competitor is not aware of the concept, which is invariably the case, you gain a considerable competitive advantage.

FRAMING YOUR PRODUCT
OR BRAND NAME
AS A MNEMONIC MEME

So how do you go about creating a mnemonic meme for your product or service? The first thing you must do is to make the distinction between a mnemonic and a slogan. A slogan is usually little more than corporate fluff, a glib throwaway line that somebody dreamt up once, and it somehow stuck. The common theme of slogans is that they usually mean nothing at all. Nevertheless they adorn buildings and boardroom walls everywhere, despite their doing nothing except perhaps stroke the corporate ego.

'We're the good guys in real estate', 'The best in the West', 'Our quality and service brings customers back', 'You'll love our service', 'We'll look after you', 'Committed to excellence', 'Leadership through products', 'For your complete building service', 'All the difference in the world', 'Big job or small, we can handle it', 'Try it, you'll like it', 'We won't let you down', 'Above all, we aim to please', 'Committed to total quality', 'We sell for less', 'All we slice is the price' (a golf shop), 'Our policy is to do a good job at a reasonable price': these slogans have been taken from actual advertisements, and while the sentiments they express may signify something deep and meaningful to the people who pay for the ads, they mean nothing at all to the people who matter: their prospects. By and large, slogans such as these tend to be far too patronising and vague to qualify even as attempts at positioning statements, although that was probably their original purpose.

The real tragedy with slogans like these is that they do nothing at all to promote brand recall. The advertisements could have been much more effective had they enhanced recall by engaging the simple concept of mnemonics.

In advertising parlance, a mnemonic recall trigger, or recall meme, is referred to as a 'strapline'.

HOW TO CREATE AN EFFECTIVE STRAPLINE

To qualify as a legitimate strapline, a recall meme must satisfy the following requirements:

1   It must be short and catchy, and roll off the tongue easily. Six words or less is ideal, but as many as ten can be effective. Generally, however, shorter is better. Less is more.

2   It must be expressed in the vernacular, in everyday speech; the way people actually speak.

3   It must contain the product name. 'Have you driven a Ford lately?' is a classic example of this. The product name is cocooned firmly within the line, and when you recall the mnemonic, the name comes right along with it. Another effect of a well-crafted strapline is that it is virtually impossible for a person to confuse your brand name with that of a competitor.

Could you imagine coming up with 'I feel like a *Carlton* or two?' or 'Good on you Mum, *Buttercup's* the one?' The strapline seems to put the mind onto the mental equivalent of railroad tracks which guide the consumer unerringly to the correct brand name.

To demonstrate this point, in our business development seminars we ask people if they can recall those commercials that feature the tag line 'I feel better now', which most people can. Then we ask them to identify the advertiser. Those commercials have been running nationally for many years now on all of the major media, with a multi-million dollar advertising budget. In our experience, somewhere around 80 per cent of people across the board believe those advertisements are for MBF. About half of the remainder think it's HCF.

These people are then quite surprised to learn that the advertiser is actually Medibank Private. They can recall the mnemonic, but it does not contain the product name, and is therefore arguably less than worthless, particularly if the commercials have created consumer response for MBF or HCF by default.

4   It must not be an 'add-on'. A line like 'Acme telephones – people to people communication' is broken in the middle, and is therefore intrinsically weak. When you try to recall it, it could just as well be 'Anybody At All telephones – people to people communication'. In real life, people tend to remember the latter half and forget the crucial part, the name they're meant to remember. To be effective a strapline must be expressed as a single, flowing, cohesive thought.

If you can make your strapline rhyme in some way, so much the better, although it is by no means essential. 'Doors Plus, no fuss' and 'Good on you Mum, Tip Top's the one' are good examples of this. Both of these lines have served to create massive brand recall because of their intrinsically 'catchy' nature. However, a word of caution is in order here. Depending on the nature of your product or service, particularly if your company projects a particularly formal or conservative persona, there is a possibility that rhyming may have the effect of trivialising or demeaning your image. For some products or brands it is ideal. You will know instinctively if it's right for you. For example, 'Which bank?' is a mnemonic meme which has worked extremely well in creating massive brand awareness and recall for the Commonwealth Bank, without rhyme. Although it doesn't contain the name of the bank, 'Commonwealth' has been linked visually to the mnemonic with great frequency, resulting in a potent compound meme which has become firmly imbedded in the mind of virtually every Australian.

Alliteration works wonders. Alliteration involves beginning two or more words in close succession with the same sound, to produce a memorable effect. 'I feel like a Tooheys or two' is a classic example of the effect of alliteration in advertising. The interesting thing about this is that originally it would have worked as well, or maybe even better, as 'I feel like a Fosters or two'. But having heard it one way, it becomes locked in and permanent. The T–T sound and the F–F sound in these two examples illustrate the catchy nature of alliteration.

FOUR OPTIONS IN THE FORMULATION OF A STRAPLINE

In developing the Rapid Response System to this point, we have focused on creating:

1   an identity through the articulation of a positioning statement
2   a strong emotional connection
3   a CBA
4   a strapline, or mnemonic recall trigger.

This leaves us with an interesting set of options in the formulation of the strapline itself. Should your strapline cover your market positioning, the emotional connection, or your CBA, or should it work simply as a recall device?

The answer is that there is no definitive answer. It all depends on your individual situation. An ideal outcome for you may be that all four expressions are identical, as in the case of Woolworths, as we discussed in Chapter 1:

Activator One (Identity):   'We're *Woolworths* the fresh food people.'

Activator Two (Emotion):   'We're Woolworths the *fresh food* people.'

Activator Three (Influence):   '*We're Woolworths the fresh food people.*'

Activator Four (Recall):   '*We're Woolworths the fresh food people.*'

But therein may lie a potential problem.

Consider, for example, what would happen if a competitor such as Big Fresh were to move ahead in a big way and over time begin to dominate the 'fresh' idea in the public mind, possibly by coming at it from another angle. In this event, Woolworths could find that its strapline is no longer viable, and another strategy is required. If this were to happen, Woolworths would be walking away from an intellectual property of incalculable value – an unlikely scenario, but by no means impossible.

The big lesson here is that you must decide whether or not your particular CBA is likely to remain viable in the long term for whatever reasons. If you're convinced that it will, then by all means weave it into your strapline and it will do an excellent job of delivering that message to the marketplace and, in the process, continue to build brand equity.

If, however, you feel your CBA could alter in the foreseeable future, perhaps as a result of technological change, then you should seriously consider keeping your CBA and your strapline separate. That way you can change your CBA at your discretion without in any way jeopardising the brand equity you have been steadily accumulating over the years.

It could be that, for whatever reason, your CBA may not slip easily into the role of a strapline. It is not worth compromising the articulation of a great CBA simply to try to perform two tasks at once.

It may be that you address two distinct market segments, such as a consumer and a trade division. This may create a need to cross-market on two different levels, which could create the necessity for a dual identity, and possibly dual CBAs. Knebel, referred to earlier, is a case in point.

Knebel has a strong consumer division, as well as a strong commercial division that specialises in installing kitchens in multi-storey townhouses and home units. This has created the necessity for Knebel to articulate two distinctly different CBAs, in order to address each of these markets, each having its own individual set of priorities. It is important to note that Knebel is focused on making these two CBAs a reality, not just empty words.

For this reason, Knebel has used three separate lines in combination, depending on the situation.

The CBA (expressed as a security meme) for Knebel's consumer market is:

The famous Knebel Lifetime Guarantee

The CBA (also expressed as a security meme) for Knebel's commercial division is:

Knebel. The on-time kitchen company.

This alternative approach for the commercial division addresses a completely different need and a different market segment. The strapline which Knebel has used for recall throughout, is:

I've got a Knebel kitchen on my mind.

This arrangement works well, and is ideal for a company in Knebel's more complex circumstances.

On the other hand, you can have a situation like that of Camera House. Its CBA happens to work admirably as its strapline:

Take better pictures or your money back at Camera House.

In this case, the same statement performs two distinct functions: recall and influence.

The Camera House positioning statement, however, describes its stated purpose simply and clearly as 'The better pictures people', and all of its efforts are focused on being just that: doing whatever it takes to help its customers to take better pictures. This is achieved through providing unbiased product information, advice, tips and assistance on technique and specially designed training seminars for enthusiasts. Note that the positioning statement for Camera House does not attempt to promote branding. 'The better pictures people' is a positioning device which was incorporated into the Camera House logo to form a compound identity meme.

You can see from the above examples how one line can be made to perform several quite separate roles simultaneously, by functioning as a powerful compound meme.

STRAPLINES AND BRAND EQUITY

There is no question that a brand which owns a little piece of the minds of millions of people is in a position of power in a buy-out or takeover situation. If you were to investigate the logistics of buying a company like Strathfield Car Radio, you would find that the 'Drive in and jive away' intellectual property component of that company's assets has a considerable negotiable value, an enormous goodwill factor over and above normal stock, plant and equipment.

Each time a commercial containing a powerful mnemonic recall trigger hits the airwaves, it has a residual effect in the minds of untold thousands of people. It does this without engaging their conscious awareness in any way, adding yet another strand to the string of molecules which supports that idea in memory. The effect over time is staggering.

The question to ask yourself is: 'Am I simply running advertisements, or am I advertising in a way that creates brand equity for the future?' If you aim to do the latter, then in formulating your strapline, you need to take some calculated risks. There is no way around it. You have to weigh up the possibility of changing either your CBA or your positioning in the foreseeable future, and articulate your strapline on that basis. Understand that as you get your strapline out into the marketplace, you are building up valuable brand equity as you go.

Creating a powerful strapline is one of the most productive things you can do to lift consumer awareness and create massive brand recall. This is because a strapline taps into their consciousness at a subliminal level, so that in effect, they don't know that they know – until one day they find your name at top of mind at that magical moment in time.

Have a think-tank session with your key people and see what you can come up with. If you stick to the guidelines listed in this chapter you can't go far wrong. Take some time over it. Refine it, polish it until it sparkles, and you won't believe what it can do for your company or brand.

Now that you're aware of the concept of a strapline, you'll notice the good ones; spectacular sticky recall memes like: 'I like Aeroplane

Jelly', 'Just remember "O" for O'Brien', 'Raine and Horne looked after me', 'Good on you Mum, Tip Top's the one', 'Take me away, P & O', 'Have you driven a Ford lately', 'Join the Pepsi generation', 'It's Mac time now at McDonald's', 'Holler for a Marshall', 'Ah McCain, you've done it again', ' 'Udson with a haitch', 'I like Bing Lee', 'TAB, the adrenalin bet', 'Drive in and jive away at Strathfield Car Radio today', 'I feel like a Tooheys or two', 'TDK does amazing things to my system', 'We're Woolworths the fresh food people', 'Oh what a feeling … Toyota!', 'Which bank?'

It is worth noting that a strapline is not just an aural thing. It should appear in print, on radio, on TV, and in every communication you have with the marketplace. Notice how the great ones do it, model yourself on them and you won't go wrong.

Experience has shown that the effectiveness of a strapline is multiplied when you put it into a musical context. 'I feel like a Tooheys or two' is a strapline that works very well in print, or through the spoken word, but when you set it to music, magic happens. It instantly becomes many times more memorable, and provides the opportunity for repetition – the mother of learning.

In Chapter 3, we touched on the concept of music in advertising. However, we did not mention the topic of jingles. There is major distinction to make here.

What the world does not need is yet another jingle. David Ogilvy is on record as saying: 'If you don't have a good idea, sing it!' The word 'jingle' in the musical context is an actual word with a dictionary definition, and means in effect, 'little song'. A jingle is a singing commercial, and is unlikely to influence anybody to do anything.

There is, however, an alternative. You could be forgiven for thinking that 'Drive in and jive away' is a jingle, but it is not. It is a 'melodic mnemonic', a concept created for the specific purpose of promoting brand recall. Not all, but most of the great straplines have been put into a musical context. These music tracks are not jingles at all. They are melodic mnemonics, because their purpose is not to sing an advertising message, but specifically to create massive brand recall through the use of a mnemonic recall trigger. For this reason, a melodic mnemonic is much more than just music. It's a devastating marketing tool.

Putting your strapline into a musical context allows repetition that is effective without being abrasive. 'I feel like a Tooheys', 'Take me away, P & O' or 'TDK does amazing things to my system' would not have been nearly as powerful but for the emotional and repetitive qualities of music.

>> **A jingle is a singing commercial, but a melodic mnemonic is a velvet sledgehammer.**

Before you consider investing in a jingle, it might be a good idea to ask yourself the following question – it could save you a lot of money: 'Is this music for the sake of music, or is it a pivotal part of a coherent marketing strategy?'

An interesting aspect of this issue came to light when we began asking a new question at our seminars: 'Is everybody here familiar with the Strathfield Car Radio advertising?' In the eastern states, the answer is invariably 'Yes'. The next question is: 'Given all the years you have been exposed to those commercials, can anybody give us one single, accurate piece of product information from any Strathfield commercial, ever?'

Considering the enormous media weight the Strathfield people have put behind their advertising over the years, you would think that this would not be an unreasonable expectation of an entire audience.

To date, nobody has ever been able to come up with so much as one single piece of accurate product information. Not one! So then we ask, 'Then what *can* you remember?' Of course, the answer is always the same: 'Drive in and jive away … ' We rest our case.

Whatever you do, take the time to develop a great strapline for your product, service or brand. It will become your secret weapon for crashing through those two formidable brick walls that delineate the Nows, the Soons and the Laters, to create advertising which has the capability to transcend the passage of time, and touch people even though they may not have seen or heard one of your advertisements for months, or even years.

As we mentioned at the beginning of this book, successful long-term advertising requires the use of *all five Activators*. Until all five Activators have an overt and consistent presence in your advertising and marketing, people do not have the information and the motivation they need in order to make intelligent buying decisions in your favour. One, two or three of these memetic building blocks will produce a positive outcome, but if you want to really make your advertising take off and fly, you need to make use of all five, simultaneously and consistently.

The technology behind the WAM Rapid Response System acts as an underpinning, a sub-structure for your advertising. It provides a solid framework that gives strength, weight, substance, form and definition to each advertisement you produce.

>> **The expression of Activator Four is:**
Create massive brand recall through the use
of recall triggers appropriate for the medium.

THE MAIN POINTS

1 >> A MAGICAL MOMENT IN TIME

All of your advertising and marketing efforts should ultimately be directed towards that magical moment in time, that instant in which your prospect makes a decision to buy.

2 >> THE LINE OF LEAST RESISTANCE

The human mind is intrinsically lazy. If it is faced with the prospect of thinking or taking a shortcut, it will go for the shortcut every time. This is the basis for the principle of mnemonics, the key to massive brand recall. If you happen to be the only one in your market segment with a powerful mnemonic and a selfish promise to the end-user, you have a devastating advantage over your competitors.

3 >> THE THREE LEVELS OF MEMORY

Memory falls into three broad categories: short-term, mid-term and long-term. Mnemonics belong to that part of long-term memory which transcends the passage of time. In later life we may have difficulty remembering the name of the person sitting next to us in a fourth grade English class, but we can remember 'I before E, except after C' without any effort at all, because it is hardwired into our memory.

4 >> THE MYTH OF AUDIENCE REACH

When most people advertise, they are basing their media decisions on a false premise. The law of averages dictates that most of the people who are exposed to your advertisement will probably not be in the market for your product right then and there.

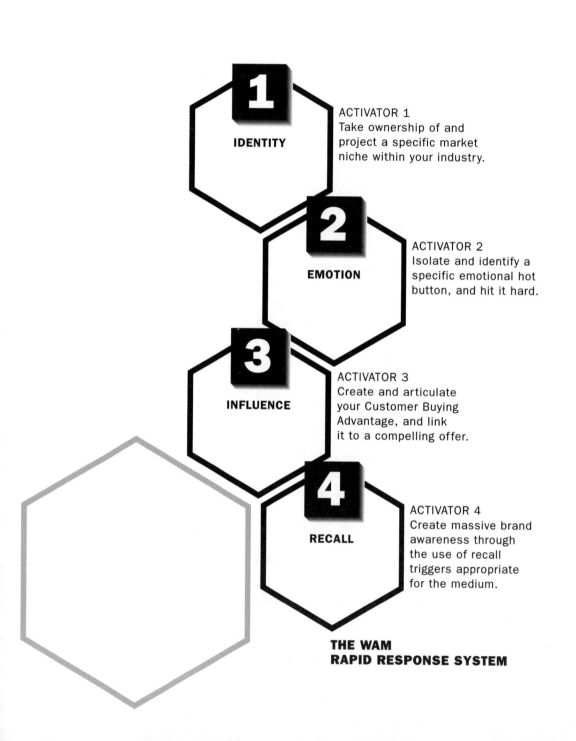

1 IDENTITY

ACTIVATOR 1
Take ownership of and
project a specific market
niche within your industry.

2 EMOTION

ACTIVATOR 2
Isolate and identify a
specific emotional hot
button, and hit it hard.

3 INFLUENCE

ACTIVATOR 3
Create and articulate
your Customer Buying
Advantage, and link
it to a compelling offer.

4 RECALL

ACTIVATOR 4
Create massive brand
awareness through
the use of recall
triggers appropriate
for the medium.

**THE WAM
RAPID RESPONSE SYSTEM**

Your prospect's short-term memory and the Scotoma Effect created by the RAS ensure that most of your potential audience is wiped out in one swoop. Your secret weapon to crash through both these brick walls is a well-crafted and powerful mnemonic recall trigger.

•

5 >> FRAMING YOUR COMPANY OR BRAND NAME AS A STRAPLINE
•

In framing your name as a mnemonic, you must first make the distinction between a slogan and a strapline. To qualify as a legitimate strapline, it should be short and catchy, expressed in everyday speech, contain the product name within it, possibly have a rhyming or alliteration element to it, and it should be in one piece, not an add-on.

•

6 >> JINGLE VERSUS MELODIC MNEMONIC
•

If you use TV or radio, it is important that you make the distinction between a jingle and melodic mnemonic. Before you decide to invest in a jingle, ask yourself: 'Is this music for the sake of music, or is it a pivotal part of a cohesive marketing strategy?' A jingle is a singing commercial. A melodic mnemonic is a velvet sledgehammer.

We've covered a lot of ground to this point, but now we have to put it all together and make it fly, and to do that, we need to bring Activator Five on line …

CHAPTER 7

A C T I V A T O R   F I V E

COMMUNICATION

'How do you expect to break through

the media clutter to connect with me?'

Communication is about bridging the gap between minds.

Fix communication, and most of the world's problems would

vanish overnight.

Activator Five is about communication, and specifically about breaking through the media clutter and connecting with your customers and prospects. No matter how many advertisements you produce over time, Activator Five will keep you on track, enable you to achieve consistency, and help you to ensure that each will perform to its maximum potential.

Effective communication means getting in tune with the way people think, and harmonising with the psychology of the marketplace. Psychology is defined as 'the study of mind', and to get your advertising and marketing on track, you need to do a lot of thinking about thinking.

Ultimately there are four fundamental reasons why people don't respond to advertising:

1   They were not in the market at that particular time.

Solution: A good strapline and a good CBA, expressed as memes, will transcend the passage of time, and cause a person to associate the two and bring them to top of mind at that magical moment in time: the moment of a buying decision. This means that you can impact on customers even at times when you're not advertising.

2   They were in the market, but were not given a good enough reason to respond.

Solution: Separate yourself from your look-alike competition with a powerful CBA, articulated as a meme, and linked to a compelling offer.

3   By the time they were ready to make a buying decision, they had forgotten who the advertiser was.

Solution: Develop a well-crafted strapline articulated as a sticky mnemonic meme.

4   They were never actually exposed to the advertisement for any or all of three reasons:

   i   The advertising was either in the wrong media, or in the right media at the wrong time.

Solution: Plan and buy media space wisely.

   ii   Even though these people may have been physically present when the advertisement was run, it failed to flag them down because of bad communication.

Solution: Familiarise yourself with the communication basics outlined in this chapter.

   iii   They were either Soons or Laters, and the Scotoma Effect ensured that even though the advertisement may have been right there before their eyes, they didn't actually see it at all.

Solution: Because mnemonic memes sidestep the short-term memory process altogether, a sticky strapline, a mnemonic recall trigger, can reach back through time to bring your name to top of mind months, even years, after people last heard or saw it.

To deal with these issues, and to make certain that nothing slips through the net, Activator Five is divided into four sections:

1   the right execution

2   the right money

3   the right media

4   the right people.

1 THE RIGHT EXECUTION

Before you even begin to create a new advertisement, the first thing to consider is that all advertising should be based on a desired outcome. What exactly do you expect to happen when your ad hits the marketplace? Do you expect people to call a particular telephone number? Do you expect people to visit retailers and ask for your product by name? Do you expect to create a massive boost in sales? Maybe you're in the process of establishing or altering your positioning and you want people to perceive your product or brand in a different way. Well that's fine, you can do all of those things. But there's something you need to understand right up front:

>> **Advertising is an object lesson in cause and effect. If you want to produce a spectacular effect, then you have to be prepared to put a cause in place that's capable of producing that kind of effect.**

If you run a commercial that says basically: 'Need one of these? Then buy from us', you're probably not going to get a very good result. On the other hand, if you were to say 'Today only, everything's free!', you'd have a mob of people trying to kick your door down. The answer lies in striking a balance between these two extremes. You must always tie your expectations directly to the law of cause and effect; it puts the responsibility for the outcome of your advertising directly where it belongs – with you.

The secret to good response communication lies in a tried and proven device which is expressed through the acronym AIDA. The value of the AIDA principle is evident when you recognise the fact that it is used religiously by the people who live or die on the effectiveness of their advertising: the direct response marketing people throughout the world.

The beauty of the AIDA concept is that it can be executed at any level at all, from a high-budget television commercial, or a stylish advertisement in a glossy magazine, to a 'down and dirty' direct response ad in your local suburban newspaper.

AIDA indicates a sequence:

ATTENTION ➤ INTEREST ➤ DESIRE ➤ ACTION

Let's look at the first letter of the AIDA acronym: A for *attention*.

Without a doubt, the best way to grab people's attention is through the use of a compelling headline, and this can be the ideal showcase for your CBA. Without the help of a well-crafted CBA to deliver your promise in a sharp, concise way, you would have to use many more words to articulate your thoughts, and there would be no consistent focus from advertisement to advertisement. This holds true for any medium at all, whether it be TV, print or radio, outdoor, or any type of direct mail.

Research has shown conclusively that when you decide on a headline statement, you gamble 80 per cent of the pulling power of your advertisement. It's a very useful discipline to take the time to create at least twenty good headlines for any advertisement, and then select the best.

Remember that to get the most out of your headline, you should always express it as a meme. A headline is no place for 'clever' wordplay or cryptic statements. It must be so super-simple that people can instantly comprehend exactly what it means, and it must tap directly into their sense of self-interest. Here are two useful definitions of a headline statement for you to consider:

A headline should be the most selfish promise to the end user.
JAY ABRAHAM

A headline should be a lifeline of hope.
GEOFF AYLING

Next time you set out to create a headline for an advertisement, try framing it with these definitions in mind. You can see that by setting up the opening statement of your ad like that, you're creating the exact environment your prospect's mind needs, if you are to short-circuit the Scotoma Effect. Your prospect has a need, and your headline statement must speak directly to that need in a way that promises a positive outcome with the minimum of effort, a lifeline of hope.

The effect of a headline can be greatly enhanced by juxtaposing it with an intriguing illustration. Executed intelligently, the two can work together to form a compound meme, effectively replicating itself in the mind of anybody who happens to be interested in whatever is being advertised at that particular time. One glance is all it takes for your meme to connect and perform its covert function of altering consumer perceptions, attitudes and, consequently, behaviour.

Flick through a copy of *Reader's Digest* some time, and you'll see a collection of advertising and editorial headlines that have been created by some of the most skilled people in the business. These headlines reach out and grab people's interest in a way that is quite irresistible.

Keep in mind that a headline is not something that happens just in print. A good headline will greatly enhance the pulling power of any advertisement at all – television, radio, print, outdoor, direct mail, the Internet, or anything else. If you don't connect with your prospect in the first couple of seconds, you probably won't connect at all.

Having grabbed your prospect's **attention**, you have to now move to the next phase and create **interest**. This is where Activator Two, Emotion, often enters the picture. If you've done your homework and understand the *real* reason for the purchase, you can create copy which speaks directly to that emotion and touches a nerve in your customers and prospects.

If you have done all your groundwork correctly, and if your CBA and your emotional connection truly reflect the things your customers and prospects want to hear and feel most of all, there is no way you can fail to **interest** these people in what is to follow.

The next phase is to create a feeling of **desire** in your customers and prospects. When you're setting up the **desire** stage of your advertisement, we suggest you take a long, hard look at all of the product *features* that form part of your normal routine, and flip them around so that they are expressed as *benefits*. This is because features invariably relate to the product or service, and the benefits invariably relate to the customer. In creating **desire**, you will need to think in terms of rapport rather than persuasion, empathy rather than inducement.

The most effective advertising doesn't focus on the product at all; it focuses on the customer. For this reason, at the WAM Communications Group we've created a culture which includes something called the 'We' Police. This entails going through each advertisement with a fine-tooth comb and locating any reference to words like 'I', 'we', 'us' and 'our', and replacing them with 'you', 'your', 'you'll' and 'yours'. There are times when this may be inappropriate, but as a rule of thumb, make certain the 'you' words outnumber the 'we' words by a ratio of at least five to one.

The final phase of the advertisement is to call for some kind of **action**. This can be extremely subtle, or it can be quite forthright, depending on the context.

The **action** phase of your advertisement relates directly to your outcome, and it's a good time to be thinking about tracking consumer response. How do you presently determine whether or not your advertising has been effective?

In the United States, consumers respond to print response coupons in a big way. These response coupons are specially coded, using a different key number for each publication. This enables the advertiser to track the performance of the various print media, and has very obvious benefits when it comes down to figuring things like cost per lead.

Australians have not been conditioned to respond in this way to such an extent, which can make it more difficult, but not impossible, to track consumer response in the print media. For example, some newspapers and magazines will allow you to book a 'split run'. This means that one version of an ad goes out to half of their readers, and another version to the other half. These two ads may contain different prices, offers, response mechanisms or phone numbers, allowing you to test one advertisement against another.

There are things you can do to track response in the electronic media. If you are advertising on radio or TV for example, you can use separate dedicated telephone numbers for each medium, station or channel used. That way you can track the performance of each, which allows you to adjust and optimise your media schedule as you go.

Another good idea is to create a survey chart listing all the radio and TV stations, with boxes underneath each entry, divided into times of the day or night. Radio, for example, might be segmented into Breakfast, Drive, Morning, Afternoon, Drive and Evening and so on, and you can do the same kind of thing for TV.

You are now in a position to survey your customers at the point of sale, to determine which medium was the best performer. You must, however, be cautious with this line of consumer tracking. Thirty years of experience has taught us that people can be notoriously unaware of when or where they saw or heard a particular advertisement.

Often we hear stories from our clients about customers who were quite adamant that they saw a particular offer on TV, when there was no TV used for that campaign. They actually saw it in print or heard it on the radio. The efficiency of the RAS is such that people often extract from a commercial only the bare minimum of information they need to get what they want. All you can really do is to keep this in mind, and do what you can to validate your results.

Depending upon the type of advertisement you're creating, *action* can have a number of different connotations. You may ask people directly to come in and buy, to send in a coupon, to enter a competition, to bring in a sample, or you might ask that they call a phone number.

The AIDA concept provides an excellent framework to use in

formulating your advertising, because it has been tried and proven for many years now, and it works.

The right execution involves creating a synergy by overlaying and integrating each of the five Activators, the concepts at the heart this book. With practice, you'll develop the skill of weaving all of them into each advertisement smoothly and seamlessly.

COMMUNICATION GUIDELINES

The technical aspects of advertising – producing print layouts, scriptwriting, research, and radio and TV production – fall outside the scope of this book, but you will find an excellent range of reference material in the Reading List section at the back. However, there are some general guidelines which should be taken into account whenever you're about to create a new advertisement.

Whatever you do, decide to make the effort and conscientiously set about creating a clear and concise positioning statement. Understand the difference between your product and your commodity as we discussed in Chapter 4, and have the appropriate emotional hot buttons at your fingertips. Create and articulate your CBA and let it do its job of attracting attention, differentiating you from your competition, filling an industry gap and motivating people to action. Learn to model the market leaders and frame your company or brand name as a sticky mnemonic recall trigger.

You should then try to narrow your focus still further by combining two or more of these statements in the form of a compound meme. We saw examples of this with 'The fresh food people' concept for Woolworths, 'Absolutely, positively overnight' for Federal Express, and 'Update' for Ron Hodgson Motors. By stacking memes in this way, you perform three very useful functions:

1   You make it extremely simple for people to understand what you're all about.

2   You create more space for supporting information in your advertisements.

3   You'll find it easy to set up a template format for your ongoing advertising. For example, you might decide to express your CBA in the form of a headline statement in order to capture people's attention. Then at the end of your advertisement, you might decide to follow the Woolworths pattern and integrate your equivalent of 'The fresh food people' just above your logo as a permanent fixture. Or you might follow the Ella Baché and Fisher & Paykel idea of placing your positioning statement below,

but as an integral part of your logo. P & O integrated their strapline into their logo by having the words 'Take me away' in cursive script just above the logo in a way that created a clear memetic package.

The right execution means ensuring that you habitually and strategically weave these memetic statements into every advertisement so that it cuts right through the media clutter and impacts on your customers and prospects whether they're ready or not.

The power of the WAM Rapid Response System lies in the fact that although people can, and do, routinely filter out your advertising via the RAS and the Scotoma Effect, they cannot filter out covert memes, and they cannot filter out mnemonic recall triggers. The reason for this, as we discussed in Chapter 6, is that both mnemonics and memes are a fundamental part of our survival system. We are simply recognising that simple fact and then turning it to our advantage.

The right execution involves finding the ideal balance between lucid communication and aesthetics. It's here that a lot of advertising becomes derailed. For example, many advertisers persist in reversing white out of black in their print ads, even though research has proved conclusively that when you do this, reader comprehension drops through the floor. The same thing happens when you put either your headline or body copy in capitals. Even though it is possible to read it, research has shown that people shy away from material which has been set out in capitals.

Then there is the typeface issue. People have become accustomed to reading 'serif' type, the typeface normally used in newspapers and books. The serif is the name given to those little terminal 'flags' which are integrated into the design of the typeface. There has been a lot of speculation as to why people prefer reading serif type. Some experts feel that the serifs create a kind of 'tram track' effect which helps to guide the eye along each line of print.

Whatever the reason, the research figures speak for themselves. In 1982, Australian journalist-typographer Colin Wheildon undertook a landmark research project which spanned a seven-year period, from 1982 to 1988. The study was received with acclaim as valid and valuable, and has been recognised by universities in the United States, Britain and Australia, and by newspaper and magazine groups in Australia, New Zealand, the United States and mainland Europe.

The study revealed the surprising fact that even when the most efficient methods of typographic communication are used, only 67 per cent of people clearly understand what they have just read. This means that even when you get everything right, nearly a third of your audience is not going to clearly comprehend your message. People tend to read *selectively*. Unless there's a good reason to do otherwise, we find it much easier to scan text for the high points, rather than dwell on every word. A sobering thought.

Potential disaster looms when you change to a sans serif typeface (a typeface without the terminal flags). The research showed conclusively that reader comprehension drops to *12 per cent*! It's not that people *can't* read it, it's just that it seems to require that little extra effort of concentration that people aren't prepared to make without a good reason. This is less of a problem in certain magazines that use a sans serif typeface throughout, as readers become conditioned to the effect. To optimise the impact of your advertising, it pays to know which publications use which type style.

As we noted in Chapter 2, people tend to have an underlying resentment towards advertising and see it as an intrusion, an invasion of their privacy. Perhaps this is why readers are reluctant to take anything other than the line of least resistance, except when it appears to be in their own self-interest.

One possible explanation for the comprehension difficulty with sans serif type could be an undesirable optical effect which was identified in 1926 by the British Medical Council. It was described as an 'irradiation', and seemed to set up a light vibration that interfered with the reader's ability to focus clearly on the lines of type, which seemed to move and even merge.

If you decide to go for a sans serif typeface, you run a grave risk of compromising reader comprehension. Skilfully used, sans serif type is certainly useful for creating effects, but if you want to maximise reader comprehension, our advice is to put your body copy in a serif typeface every time. David Ogilvy has been preaching this particular gospel for many years in his various books, but now there is a definitive body of research evidence to support it.

Another point worth mentioning here in relation to print advertising is a phenomenon known as 'eye gravity'. In western countries, where people read from left to right, there is a strong tendency for the eye to travel down the printed page from top-left to bottom-right. For this reason, you should avoid placing a headline statement anywhere below an important section of body copy. Research has shown that, in the absence of an illustration, people will go straight to the headline. Eye gravity then takes over, so the eye moves downward towards the bottom right-hand side of the page. The eye resists moving upward to read any material above the headline. An illustration placed above the headline doesn't seem to produce this problem. The eye tends to look first at the illustration, then at the headline, and if these have stimulated some level of interest, the eye will move on and scan the body copy in order to seek more information.

Another caution: when you are advertising in print, be discriminating in your use of spot colour. There is no question that spot colour is an excellent way to enhance your print advertising. In fact, a research study conducted in the United States revealed that although the use of spot colour added around 20 per cent to the cost of an advertisement, it was noted by 63 per cent more people, resulting in 64 per cent more sales! However, the spot colour road can be the road to disaster. For example, if you decide to make your advertisement more visually attractive by putting your headings or body copy in colour, it's worth noting that while 80 per cent of people will find it aesthetically more attractive, only 10 per cent will demonstrate a good level of comprehension. This effect is exacerbated as the text colour becomes lighter and the contrast diminishes.

This is not to say that coloured text cannot work. It most certainly can, in the hands of the right graphic designer. It all relates to contrast. To keep reader comprehension levels high, there should be at least a 70 per cent colour differential between the text and the background, especially a tinted background.

Whichever way you look at it, if you want to give readers the best chance of comprehending your advertisements, the golden rule is to keep your text to black on white using a serif typeface, and restrict your use of spot colour to illustrations, borders, logos and highlights.

If you'd like to learn more about the pitfalls and perils of advertising in print, we suggest you try to get hold of a copy of an invaluable booklet entitled *Communicating or Just Making Pretty Shapes* by Colin Wheildon.

Now that you have an understanding of memes, and the impact they have on the communication process, you can begin to look at the advertising you see around you in a new way. Start to analyse print advertisements, and radio and television commercials from this new perspective, and give them rating points out of ten. Do this on a regular basis and you'll find you've internalised a wealth of useful information which you did not have before you started this book. You can learn from other people's expensive mistakes and optimise your own precious resources.

2   THE   RIGHT   MONEY

This is where so much advertising comes undone. When you're planning an ad campaign, there are two quite separate issues to consider. The right production budget is essential, but the right media budget is critical. All too often, we see business managers trying to skimp and shave production costs to the bone, and then squandering their media budget on a grossly compromised advertisement which is incapable of working properly. The lesson is to keep your eye on the serious money: the media spend. Remember that it costs the same to run an advertisement that brings in five responses as it does to run one that brings in five hundred.

Nobody is suggesting you should throw production dollars around like a drunken sailor, but there is a point at which your advertising begins to look and sound cheap and nasty. You should never forget that your advertising must reflect the ambience and tone of your company, product or brand.

When people are impacted upon by your advertising, they take from it an impression, or a feeling of what to expect when they go to do business with you. If there is more than a marginal discrepancy, if you turn out to be radically more down-market or up-market than your advertising suggests, then you create that undesirable state of cognitive dissonance in your prospects. They get the distinct feeling that something is not quite right, and they won't trust you. For that reason, be sure you don't shoot yourself in the foot by creating shoddy advertising for want of spending the appropriate amount of money on production.

As a rule of thumb, you're nearly always better off running a well-crafted, strategically sound advertisement with a little less media exposure, than squandering your media budget on a campaign that has little hope of influencing anybody to do anything.

3   THE   RIGHT   MEDIA

You'd think that selecting the right media would be something so basic that it would hardly be worth mentioning. However, in practice we see extraordinary examples of business managers wasting inordinate amounts of money on the wrong TV channels, the wrong radio stations, the wrong programming, or the wrong newspapers and magazines for their particular target audience. Media buying decisions based entirely on the cheapest rates can very often backfire, and amount to a complete waste of money. Unless you're buying distressed space, cheap media space often doesn't represent good value – particularly when a good response is imperative.

Depending on the nature of your particular company, product or brand, planning and booking your own television advertising can be simple, or very complex. It could be that your target audience is so wide that just about any program on any channel will put you in front of enough of the right people to make it worthwhile. In that case, if you shop around for the best run-of-station package you can find, you'll probably get good value for money.

If your target audience is more tightly defined, things become more complicated. There's nothing quite as wasteful as a TV spot in front of a mass audience that has no interest in your product. As far as reaching a specialised niche audience is concerned, there are very few business managers who are really capable of efficiently and effectively planning their own television advertising, simply because it's so difficult to achieve a commercially acceptable level of accuracy.

TARPS

Television programs are rated in terms of TARPs, or Target Audience Rating Points. TARPs are expressed as numbers, which reflect the size of the viewing audience for that particular program. A rerun of Gilligan's Island might rate a 2 or 3, whereas a State of Origin football match might rate in the 30s. Obviously, the higher the TARPs, the more expensive it is to buy a spot in a given program. So far so good.

REACH AND FREQUENCY

The complications set in when you begin to factor in 'reach' and 'frequency' against cost per thousand. Reach relates to the total number of people in your target audience who are exposed to your TV campaign, collectively, over a given timeframe. Frequency relates to the total number of times that group is exposed to your TV campaign over a given timeframe.

Research has shown that in order for your commercial to register at all, a person has to be exposed to it a minimum of 3.5 times. On the first exposure, it's unlikely to create any kind of real awareness. By the second and third exposures it is beginning to make an impression at the subliminal level. Somewhere around the fourth exposure, it begins to take on the ring of familiarity, and you're beginning to make progress. However, because people don't see every ad you run, it becomes necessary to run your ads with as much frequency as possible in order to get the average hits as far above 3.5 as possible.

A very useful means of quickly increasing frequency on both television and radio is to book an 'echo package'. We see echo packages all the time. That's where an advertiser buys a TV or radio package which features a thirty-second commercial right at the beginning of an ad break, and then a fifteen-second cut-down right at the end of the same break. The disadvantage of an echo package is that a fifteen-second commercial costs marginally more than half of a thirty-second commercial (around 60 per cent).

Imagine for a moment you're trying to impact on a particular individual within your target audience. Since there's no guarantee that this person will be watching or listening just when your commercial happens to go to air, you're left to rely on the law of averages. You might happen to connect one day, but the next day he or she is doing something different and you miss out. You can see how it can take a lot of advertising to average 3.5 hits, let alone eight or nine.

The strength of the echo package is that when you do happen to synchronise with this person, you get to zap him or her twice in quick succession. Do this a few times and it doesn't take long to rack up quite a few hits. However you go about it, it's essential to plan your media in a way that puts you in front of as many of the right people as possible, the greatest possible number of times, based on your media budget.

If you're marketing to a tightly defined target audience, the answer could be to locate a professional media planner and buyer. Not only do professional media planners tend to have stronger buying power and better contacts, but they have at their fingertips the latest statistical information, as well as sophisticated computer software that allows them to devise a media spend that delivers the highest TARPs possible within a given budget allocation, balanced against the highest possible reach and frequency figures. The average business manager would find it next to impossible to produce a media plan with that level of accuracy, without the right kind of technology and inside information.

The danger is that, in trying to wheel and deal media time with the various TV channels, you must make critical decisions which are bound to be based on biased information. The resulting ineffective advertising could cost you more than you might have spent on efficient professional media planning and buying. It's something to think about.

Although radio and the print media don't operate in terms of TARPs as such, some radio stations apply equivalent TARP weights to their programming to assist them in formulating their system of rates. The name of the game is to try to optimise reach, frequency and cost per thousand, through the known media preferences of your target audience.

As a general rule of thumb, if you have the choice of going for a larger reach and a smaller frequency, or a smaller reach with a higher frequency, you're nearly always better off going with the latter – as long as the people you do reach fall within the demographic and psychographic framework that defines your primary target audience.

Take the time to analyse your media alternatives very carefully, and expect the information you receive to be biased. It will be – you can count on it. For that reason, if you're going to do your own planning and buying, try to source your comparative data from one of the professional media buying houses, or perhaps a business associate from one of the major advertisers who could help in this area.

4 THE RIGHT PEOPLE

It's here that we find that we've come full circle. We're now talking about Stanley, your Central Demographic Model. Do you have a clear concept of what your version of Stanley looks like? Is it a tightly defined segment of the market, or does it fit more with the statement Alan Morris of Mojo fame made in relation to Coca Cola: 'Our target market is anybody with a mouth'.

Many years ago, we were asked to work on a Revlon cosmetics brand called Charlie. When we asked the client for a description of the typical consumer, the Central Demographic Model for the brand, he produced a photograph of a young, trendy, zany-looking girl. That photograph proved invaluable throughout the entire creative process. Whenever an idea popped, we would simply ask the question: 'Would *she* go for that?' The answer was always obvious.

You might want to consider adopting that idea for your own advertising. It may be a photograph of an individual, or a group of individuals, or perhaps it may be a real person, perhaps one of your customers. However you go about it, it's worth any amount of the time it takes to accurately identify your Central Demographic Model.

A photograph is particularly useful, because you can use it to brief the people who will ultimately be putting your advertisement together. In this context, a picture really is worth a thousand words, and might just save you from disaster by giving all the people in the chain an identical impression of the type of person you want to attract.

DEMOGRAPHIC AND PSYCHOGRAPHIC PROFILES

At this point, it's worth looking at the distinction between your prospect's demographic and psychographic profile. The word 'demographic' relates to a person's geographic location, gender, age and socio-economic status. From this information, it's quite easy to come up with an accurate demographic description of your primary and perhaps your secondary target audience.

A person's psychographic profile relates to his or her mental disposition, propensities and inclinations as a member of the buying public. For instance, the brand manager of a company marketing a particular trendy brand of beer may discover that there are significant numbers of men above the age of fifty-five who buy the brand because it makes them feel young. Without the notion of psychographics, this particular market segment might go unnoticed.

This means that two customers buying the same product could have radically different demographic profiles, but identical psychographic profiles. When the numbers of this secondary group become significant, a good media planner can figure out the most effective way to optimise the media mix in a way that takes both groups into account to the best advantage.

THE ROLE OF MEMORY IN ADVERTISING

Given that most people who are exposed to an advertisement are unlikely to be in the market right then and there, it becomes essential to ensure that people remember your advertising. For that reason, it makes sense to take a look at memory function, and make sure we've covered everything.

According to Glenn Capelli of the True Learning Centre in Perth, research has shown that memory can be improved by up to 40 per cent, simply by following seven simple strategies which he calls the 'seven key factors to memory awareness':

1   **Primacy**

The brain tends to remember the first thing to which it is exposed in a given situation, which explains why first impressions are so important. People are therefore more likely to remember your opening statement than something which occurs later in an advertisement. The concept of expressing your key proposition as a headline statement relates to primacy, and is the basis of the *attention* part of the AIDA principle.

2   **Recency**

The brain also tends to remember the last thing to which it was exposed in a given situation. The last, or *action* part of the AIDA principle relates to recency. By closing your advertisement with a call to action, you're leaving the consumer with the part that really counts. No action, no sale.

3   **Repetition**

Repetition is the mother of learning. When we suggest you favour frequency over reach when you advertise, we're promoting the idea of repetition. As far as frequency is concerned, more is better. There is no substitute for repetition in advertising.

4   **Stand out**

The brain tends to remember things which 'stand out from the crowd'. When you construct an advertisement correctly in the form of layered memes, it will absolutely stand out from the surrounding material. The same applies to your key proposition. It should always be executed in a way that takes advantage of this 'stand out' facet of memory.

5   **Chunking**

The brain seems to work best when it has to remember no more than seven things at a time. This is why many book titles contain the number seven, as in Stephen Covey's *The Seven Habits of Highly Effective People*. One of the secrets of memory enhancement is to chunk things down so that they can be made to fit into seven categories or less. Memes are the ultimate technique for chunking information. When you get it right, your advertising will convey a depth of information without appearing complicated.

6   **Association**

Association has long been recognised as an effective aid to memory enhancement. If a person's name is Peter Hill, mentally draw a hill and write Peter on top. It works. One of the most effective ways to frame an advertisement is to express it in a way that causes people to relate to it. When you do this, you're invoking the principle of association.

7   **Visual**

The brain finds it easier to relate to pictures than words. Words are important, but there's nothing quite like an engaging picture to generate interest in an advertisement. The visual connection is what makes television the most powerful medium on earth. If you're going to use a photograph or an illustration in your advertising, make certain it's a meme; that its purpose is to convey a specific idea in the clearest possible way.

One of the most underestimated and misunderstood facets of the memory process is the principle of mnemonics. Most advertising copy writers certainly don't understand it, but a select few have used it to great effect. Glenn Capelli teaches this eighth aid to recall as an adjunct to the principle of association. When he's speaking to an audience, he groups the first three aids to memory enhancement together as a mnemonic chant: '*Pri*-macy, *rec*-ency, *re-pe-tition*'. Heard in this way, they stick in the mind very easily. By contrast, the second three, 'Stand out, chunking, association', don't work together as a mnemonic and are more difficult to remember.

When you frame your product or brand name as a mnemonic recall trigger, you invoke the same memory enhancement mechanism responsible for the instant popularity of many pop songs. Hear the Beach Boys singing: 'Ba-ba-ba, Bar-Bar-bra-Ann' just once, and you've got it. It will probably stick in your mind forever. Long after the last notes of 'Mustang Sally' have died away, you're likely to still have 'Ride Sally, ride' buzzing around in your head. 'Good on you Mum, Tip Top's the one' works in exactly the same way. There's no doubt about it, a mnemonic recall trigger and repetition together make a devastating team. It makes a lot of sense to take advantage of this knowledge to make your advertising instantly memorable in the same way.

KNOW YOUR CUSTOMERS

Take the time to survey your customers, particularly the kinds of people of whom you'd like to have many more, and find out what television and radio stations and programs they listen to. Find out what newspapers, sections of newspapers and magazines they read, and then plan your media schedule accordingly. You'll find that if you take the time and effort to bring the five Activators to life in your day-to-day advertising, you'll have all the enticement and all the leverage you need to bring in as many new customers as you can handle.

Activator Five, then, is your comprehensive insurance policy against missing out on consumer response by virtue of poor communication. It's quite possible to have a compelling story to tell, but to miss out simply because people didn't comprehend your message, or because you failed to flag them down in the first place.

•

>> **To engage Activator Five, think in terms of communicating through:**

1 **The right execution**
   You may only get one hit, so don't try to be too clever.

2 **The right money**
   The right production budget is important. The right media budget is critical.

3 **The right media**
   To catch fish, you have to go where the fish are.

4 **The right people**
   There's nothing quite as futile as putting an advertisement in front of vast numbers of people who have no interest in your product. Keep your sights fixed on your Central Demographic Model.

•

Keep your execution on track by committing to memory the four fundamental reasons why people don't respond to advertising, and make certain you get them working for you rather than against you. Be sure to make constant use of the AIDA principle; it's an excellent way to ensure that you always set your advertisement up for maximum response.

The WAM Rapid Response System involves systematically and consistently weaving Activators One, Two, Three and Four into each and every advertisement, and then using Activator Five to deliver your message cleanly and concisely to the largest number of people within your target audience as many times as possible, within the constraints of your advertising budget.

THE MAIN POINTS

•

1 >> ACTIVATOR FIVE IS DIVIDED INTO FOUR SECTIONS

•

These sections are:

i   the right execution
ii   the right money
iii the right media
iv   the right people.

•

2 >> THERE ARE FOUR REASONS WHY
• PEOPLE DON'T RESPOND TO ADVERTISING

The reasons why people don't respond to advertising are:

i   They were not in the market at that particular time.
ii   They were in the market, but were not given a good enough reason to respond.
iii By the time they were ready to make a buying decision, they had forgotten who the advertiser was.
iv   They were never actually exposed to the advertisement for any or all of three reasons:

    a   The advertising was either in the wrong media, or in the right media at the wrong time.

    b   Even though they may have been physically present when the advertisement was run, it failed to flag them down because of poor communication.

    c   They were either Soons or Laters, and the Scotoma Effect ensured that even though the advertisement may have been right there in front of their eyes, they didn't actually see it at all.

•

3 >> THE RIGHT EXECUTION

•

Advertising is an exercise in cause and effect, and should always be undertaken with a clear outcome, or expectation in mind. For this reason, you should consider adopting the AIDA principle whenever you're creating a response advertisement. A stands for *attention*, I stands for *interest*, D stands for *desire*, and A stands for *action*. The AIDA principle is used by direct response advertisers because it has a proven track record.

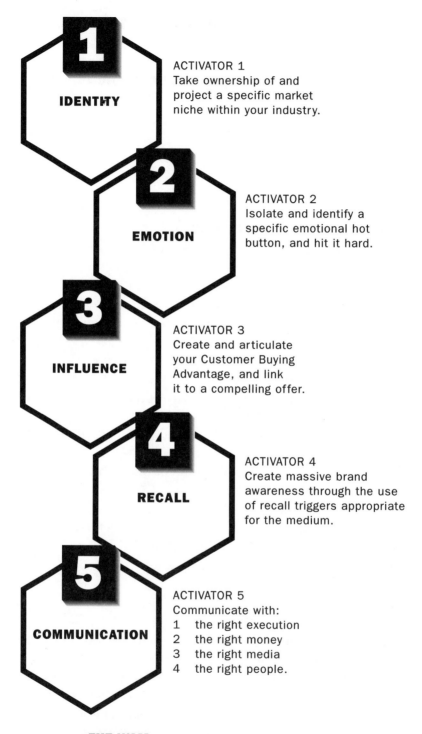

1

IDENTITY

ACTIVATOR 1
Take ownership of and
project a specific market
niche within your industry.

2

EMOTION

ACTIVATOR 2
Isolate and identify a
specific emotional hot
button, and hit it hard.

3

INFLUENCE

ACTIVATOR 3
Create and articulate
your Customer Buying
Advantage, and link
it to a compelling offer.

4

RECALL

ACTIVATOR 4
Create massive brand
awareness through the use
of recall triggers appropriate
for the medium.

5

COMMUNICATION

ACTIVATOR 5
Communicate with:
1   the right execution
2   the right money
3   the right media
4   the right people.

**THE WAM
RAPID RESPONSE SYSTEM**

Remember that when you choose a headline statement, you gamble 80 per cent of your media dollars on its pulling power. It's a good discipline to write at least twenty good headlines before you make your final selection. Remember that a headline should be the most selfish promise to the end-user, a lifeline of hope.

Consider getting hold of Colin Wheildon's booklet, *Communicating or Just Making Pretty Shapes* (see Reading List). It will keep you from confusing communication with aesthetics, and help you to get consistently better results from your print advertising.

•

4 >> THE RIGHT MONEY

•

Often business managers try to cut production costs to an absolute minimum in the name of economy, not realising the negative effect that can be caused by sending the wrong message to the marketplace. Make sure that you keep your eye on the serious money – the media spend. Don't jeopardise it by running advertisements which have been badly compromised by inadequate production budgets.

•

5 >> THE RIGHT MEDIA

•

To catch fish, you have to go where the fish are. There is nothing quite as wasteful as an advertisement in front of a mass audience that has no interest in your product. Media planning and buying is a game in which you must optimise the balance between audience reach, frequency and cost. This may or may not be easy, depending entirely on your particular product, service or brand. If you have a wide mass audience, then buying run of station may well be the way to go. If you have a more finely targeted audience, however, you may be well advised to consult a professional media planner and buyer.

•

6 >> THE RIGHT PEOPLE

•

It's here that we find we've come the full circle. We're now talking about Stanley, your Central Demographic Model. Do you have a clear concept of what your version of Stanley looks like? Consider getting hold of a photograph of your ideal prospect, and use it whenever you're formulating an advertisement. It will keep you on track. A photograph like this is also invaluable when you're briefing creative people, because they are all getting exactly the same impression of the person with whom they're trying to connect. Don't forget to consider not only your prospects' demographic profile, but their psychographic profile as well. This information may be instrumental in opening up new markets that might not have previously been apparent.

><

We've come a long way, but this book would not be complete without taking a close look behind the scenes, as it were, and getting a clear understanding of the way your customers and prospects think …

CHAPTER 8

THE PSYCHOLOGY OF THE MARKETPLACE

When you advertise, assume you're operating in a hostile environment.

The art and craft of creating advertising response can be a complete mystery until you begin to look at it from the perspective of the concepts we've been discussing in this book. We noted earlier that the average person in a large urban environment is exposed to something in the order of two thousand advertising impressions per day, and virtually all of those advertising impressions are filtered out of our consciousness before we're even aware of them, through the devastatingly efficient mechanism of the RAS.

Those advertisements, together with the vast sums of money it took to produce them and place them in the various media, were diverted and demoted to the status of background chatter, as people's minds efficiently screened their consciousness from any irrelevant sensory stimuli. Not an encouraging prospect for those whose livelihood depends on influencing the marketplace.

Or is it?

Our view is that while the system nature has set up *seems* to work against the best interests of those who need advertising to work for them, it actually works very much in their favour. The problem lies first of all in understanding how the system works, and then figuring out how to use it to the best possible advantage. As we noted in Chapter 4, if you're an advertiser, you're in the psychology business whether you like it or not.

The reason people are unable to recall so few of those two thousand advertising impressions from yesterday is disarmingly simple: they weren't in the market for them. Because they weren't even remotely interested in them right then and there, they didn't need to focus on them – so they quite literally tuned them out. This highlights one of the most important functional aspects of the human mind a marketing person can hope to comprehend:

> •

> **>> Left to its own devices, the mind**
> **sees only what it wants to see.**

> •

Invariably, people are able to recall an advertisement for one of two reasons:

1   They were in the market.
2   They found it interesting or entertaining in some way.

Anything else is deleted before it has the chance to become part of their reality.

Remember the Nows, the Soons and the Laters? In Chapter 6 we looked at the WAM Reach Model, which describes the reality that companies and brands experience when they advertise, as they try to extend their reach into the marketplace over time.

Viewed from the perspective of the Reach Model, it should come as no surprise to learn that very few people can remember more than one or two of yesterday's advertising impressions. The RAS is the ultimate filter, and the Scotoma Effect is the advertising equivalent of a black hole.

But the psychology of the marketplace goes much deeper than that. To give you a deeper understanding of what's really going on out there, we'd like to turn your attention to a particular word that holds the answer to virtually all of the mysteries of advertising and marketing: 'paradigm', or 'subjective world view'. This expanded meaning has come into popular usage, but has not yet made it into the dictionaries.

THE POWER OF THE PARADIGM

Edward de Bono notes in *Textbook of Wisdom*:

> A person born with thick corneal opacities cannot see. When in later life, an operation gives sight to that person, the person still cannot see. Everything is a blur of light, colours and disorganised shapes. The person has to learn to 'organise' this information in the brain. That is what perception is all about.

The insight to be gained from this information is that although there are many broad similarities in the way we as people organise our sensory input, there is also a great deal of latitude in the way we interpret and organise this information. There is no 'right' and 'wrong' way in which to organise it. This latitude creates the vast differences in perception between individuals, races, religions and cultures.

We see this all the time, for example, when one individual 'gets' the punchline of a joke, while another person does not. These two people are simply organising information differently in their minds. In the same way, two people can experience an event which one sees as utterly devastating, and the other as a challenge. These two diametrically opposite perceptions will have a dramatic effect upon these people's lives from that time onward.

>> **The ability to mentally organise information in unusual ways is the basis of both humour and creativity. This ability, taken to extremes, is what produces a Gary Larson or an Albert Einstein.**

Your paradigm is the perceptual 'lens' through which you see the world. It is shaped by the arbitrary, subjective way in which you organise the information that comes into your brain via the five senses. Your paradigm is your world view, your personal reality, the way you perceive things to be.

Because the collective paradigm of the marketplace holds the key to your continued growth and prosperity as a company or brand, it's worth taking a close look at the nature of the paradigm to gain some insights into its almost unbelievable power to affect our lives.

In his book *The Seven Habits of Highly Effective People*, Stephen Covey tells a story that encapsulates the concepts of both a paradigm, and a paradigm shift.

To paraphrase his story, Stephen Covey was returning home from the office on a commuter train late one evening, sharing the carriage with just a few office workers, who were relaxing reading their newspapers. At some point, a man with several noisy children boarded the train. The children created havoc, skating up and down the aisles and making themselves generally unpopular with the other passengers.

Stephen resolved to keep his cool, but at some point it all got too much. He approached the father of the children, and explained that the other passengers were weary, and could he please keep his children under control. The father looked at Stephen with tired eyes, and said: 'I'm sorry, they've just left the hospital where their mother died. I guess they don't know how to handle it.'

How would you feel if you found yourself in Stephen's position? Would you just want to shrivel up and die right then and there? One moment you see the situation a certain way, and then in a flash of insight, you find you couldn't see it that way again, even if you wanted to. In that moment, your world turns on its ear. That cataclysmic flash of insight is the paradigm shift that causes people to make dramatic changes in their behaviour.

As we move through life we experience paradigm shifts all the time. Something happens and we experience a major shift in perception from which it is utterly impossible to return. Becoming a teenager is a major paradigm shift, as is your first love, your first job in the workforce, getting married, becoming a parent or a grandparent, or losing a loved one. Each paradigm shift irrevocably alters our attitudes, values, beliefs and patterns of behaviour as we continue to develop and grow as people.

Dr Robert Cialdini uses an interesting device in his discussion groups to demonstrate the nature of perception. He shows the group one of those three-dimensional pictures that require you to look at it in a certain way before you can see the effect. Most people viewing one of these pictures for the first time are unable to see anything except a meaningless repeated pattern.

Eventually, by experimentation and deliberately trying to focus on a point somewhere behind the picture rather than on its surface, the picture suddenly and dramatically 'flips around' somehow to reveal something else entirely: a meaning behind the meaning; the truth behind the truth. It is right there before their eyes all the time waiting to be perceived, but the restrictions of their existing paradigm, the accepted way of looking at pictures, prohibits them from doing what is necessary to see it.

It is not until they deliberately choose to break out of that paradigm, to voluntarily create a paradigm shift and look at the picture in a new way, a way that does not make any 'logical' sense (as seen through the old paradigm), that they are able to access something beyond their ability to see with their own two eyes.

One of these pictures consists of several rows of pineapples lined up in the way we might see them displayed in a fruit store. Try as they might, most people can see nothing but pineapples. But when they persist and look at it a certain way, a perfectly formed crocodile magically appears, seeming to hover about a centimetre above the page.

When you see this for the first time, it is very easy to become struck by the real power of perception. The effect has even more impact when you are doing this with a group of people, and you are the only one who can see the crocodile. It strikes you that you are a group of people receiving exactly the same visual input, but everyone else is seeing something completely different.

If you are fortunate, the implications of this graphic analogy will hit you in a blinding flash of insight, as you really come to understand, perhaps for the first time, the true nature of perception and how it can revolutionise your approach to your advertising and marketing. We sincerely hope it happens for you.

If you choose to see it that way, those three-dimensional pictures are a perfect analogy for the way we use perception to process the world in order to create our individual versions of reality. A number of people viewing the same motor accident will often give quite contradictory accounts of what happened, as many frustrated police officers have found when interviewing witnesses. There is nothing that happens in the material world which is not open to interpretation.

Our purpose in writing this book is to create an environment in which you begin to look at your advertising and marketing in a new way, and for the first time, see a 'crocodile'. If you can do that, then it has all been worthwhile.

COLLECTIVE PARADIGMS

If you happen to be a Muslim, you see the world in a certain way, and you find yourself rigidly constrained by a set of beliefs, values and attitudes which determine your behaviour in virtually every area of life. Muslim women occupy a place in society and keep to tightly disciplined and restricted codes of dress that most women in western society would find intolerable. But for women living within that paradigm, it all feels quite normal and proper. In fact, devout Muslim women would find the liberated mindset of western women impossible to emulate, even if they wanted to.

Moreover, this set of beliefs, values and attitudes is shared by other Muslims in a way that induces them to pray both together and in private, and to perform certain rituals at certain times. They experience the feeling of divine love when they live by these values and beliefs, and guilt, fear and humility when they fail to live by them.

Those beliefs, values and attitudes are not studied, evaluated and taken on board selectively by individuals as valid or even desirable concepts. They come as part of the Muslim 'package'. That is the way it happens in any collective paradigm. When you buy into a collective paradigm of any kind, you also buy into the rules, regulations, values, attitudes and beliefs that give that paradigm its substance and form.

If you happen to be an atheist, you see the world in an entirely different way. You have a very different set of standards which are completely at odds with, for example, the Christian world view. They define your outlook on life, and your behaviour, in a totally different way.

If you live in a paradigm whereby the mere act of some person pointing a bone at you can cause you to die, as is the case with Australian Aborigines, then you simply wither up and die. The act becomes a self-perpetuating belief, a self-fulfilling prophecy with the power to create the biochemical consequences that induce death in that person. If you don't live in that paradigm, then a person can point all the bones in the world at you, and it won't have any effect.

It is truly incredible to realise that the belief system defined by your paradigm locks you into a reality which quite literally has the power of life and death over you. That power can be engaged simply by holding what amounts to quite arbitrary beliefs and perceptions about the way you think the world is.

THE COLLECTIVE PARADIGM
OF THE MARKETPLACE

Although the marketplace consists of a bewildering mix of cultures and social extremes, when it comes to satisfying their material wants and needs, there is a significant collective paradigm overlap in the way that people perceive suppliers of goods and services, and in the way they relate to them.

Make no mistake about it, the collective paradigm of the marketplace has the ultimate power to kill your product stone dead, or to elevate it to the status of market leader. It all depends on how you frame your communications with that vast body of people, your future prospects.

The distinguishing feature of the collective paradigm of the marketplace is that people tend to respond to emotion first, and then use logic to rationalise their decision. To approach your advertising in terms of logical argument is a big mistake. Logic invariably relates to your commodity, whereas perception invariably relates to your real *product* – which, as we have seen, is always the fulfilment of an emotional need.

Next time you find yourself in a heated debate with somebody, you might want to remember the following verse. It also applies to consumers who don't believe your advertising:

It's a total waste of effort
A complete waste of time
To argue with somebody
In another paradigm

If people perceive your product, service or brand to be inferior, then all the supporting evidence you can throw at them is unlikely to alter that perception. You are going to have to think in terms of creating a paradigm shift in the marketplace in order to move forward, and one of the best ways to produce that paradigm shift is to attack at the emotional level with a compelling CBA.

This is where the concept of adopting an equal but opposite polarity comes into its own. If a particular segment of the marketplace sees product X as being better than your product, then maybe you need to consider repositioning your product, talking to a different market segment, and focusing on an equal but opposite attribute which research has shown to be attractive to that group.

As an advertiser, it is important you appreciate that your present system of evaluating what constitutes a good and a bad advertisement is totally bound up with your present paradigm, the way you see the world. The world view you presently hold has a profound effect on the results you are getting in terms of consumer response.

Basically, there are two fundamental ways in which people see the world:

1   through the paradigm of objective reality
2   through the paradigm of subjective reality.

THE PARADIGM OF OBJECTIVE REALITY

If you live in the paradigm of objective reality, then you tend to see the world in terms of dichotomies. Things are either right or wrong, good or bad, logical or stupid, open or shut. You like things to be either black or white. Shades of grey only muddy the water and create difficulties when you're trying to order your thinking.

In this paradigm, if you believe your product or service to be the best, you are also likely to believe that your mission is to convey enough substantiating information to the marketplace through your advertising and marketing to transfer that belief. You hope that as a result, prospects will 'see the light', and come round to your way of thinking.

When you see the world in this way, you believe that there is an objective truth 'out there', which everybody should be able to see, and to act accordingly. In this paradigm, it is patently obvious to you that your view of reality is 'right', and everybody should be able to see that. Anybody with a diametrically opposed view is therefore 'wrong'. If somebody challenges you on some fundamental issue, you will respond by directing them to other people who share your world view and will support your stance.

A most illuminating piece of dialogue to this effect appeared in the TV mini-series *Brides of Christ*. Several novices were out walking, and discussing religious issues with a senior nun who happened to be the disciplinarian of the convent. One of the novices asked the nun how she could be so certain God really existed, and if it were possible that what they were being taught was not really true. The senior nun turned to the novice with an expression of suppressed rage, and said: 'What kind of fool would that make me?'

THE PARADIGM OF SUBJECTIVE REALITY

If you choose to live in this paradigm, then all the rules are different. You understand that reality is completely different for each individual on the planet.

You realise that although we all share the common physical experience of the material world, no two people can ever share the same reality. The confusion arises because the material world is so real to us. It fills our senses with its overt presence. Ten thousand people can stand in front of the Ecole Militaire in Paris, look up in the air and perceive the same Eiffel Tower. Except for perspective, it will look identical to each of them. This is our shared physical reality.

However, our *personal* reality, which is also the reality of the marketplace, is always defined in terms of the sum total of thoughts, feelings, attitudes, emotions and beliefs that we hold about the material world and what happens in it.

The human brain is extremely efficient at determining what things *are* (the Eiffel Tower), but quite arbitrary at determining what things *mean*. (Is it beautiful, or an eyesore?)

This dichotomy lies at the heart of the general apathy consumers display towards products and brands. People may have an identical picture of a product in their minds, but their perceptions and attitudes towards that product may range from wild enthusiasm to indifference, or even aversion, depending entirely upon the arbitrary, perceptual meaning the mind attaches to it.

We get a vivid demonstration of this concept at our business development seminars when we ask the audience 'Which is better, Coca Cola, or Pepsi Cola?', or 'Which is better, BMW or Mercedes?' Questions like that tend to immediately polarise an audience, and there are quite often very vocal advocates for both sides who cite all kinds of 'evidence' to support their particular point of view.

The perceptions and beliefs the marketplace holds about any product or service are just that: perceptions and beliefs. And as we have already discussed in an earlier chapter, belief and reality are two entirely different propositions.

Edward de Bono made some very relevant points about beliefs in his book *Parallel Thinking*:

A belief is a perception which forces us to see the world in a way that validates the perception. If we perceive somebody to be nasty, then we will tend to notice only those aspects of that person's behaviour which validate that perception.

The same applies to companies and brands.

A belief, once established, requires no further evidence from the outside world to sustain it.

This is particularly true of customer attitudes to brands. If a person has come to believe one brand is the best, then the belief becomes reality for that person. Invariably, any evidence to the contrary will either be ignored or discounted as false or biased.

From all this, it should be obvious by now that if you are to influence a reluctant marketplace in a positive way, instead of banging your head against a brick wall, you need to calmly walk around and enter the public mind via the back door. Each of the five Activators will do exactly that. Collectively, they allow your advertising message to glide effortlessly along a smooth track from media to mind, instead of trying to negotiate its way through an obstacle course.

It has been said that it's easy to see further when you're standing on the shoulders of giants. The concepts which underpin this book did not come down in the last shower of rain. In their original form, they sprang from the fertile and insightful minds of brilliant people like David Ogilvy, John Caples, and Claude C. Hopkins, the father of modern advertising, and have proven themselves over time.

We have taken those fundamental concepts, expanded them, combined them with our own experience and thinking, and fitted them together in a way that is well outside the traditional advertising paradigm.

One of the distinguishing characteristics of a revolutionary development of any kind is that not only does it fly in the face of convention, it *works*! The WAM Rapid Response System causes you routinely to do things most advertisers don't do, and consequently, to get results most advertisers don't get. All it takes is your active participation.

One of the most amazing implications of this whole discussion is that all your competitors are locked into their own individual paradigms, and therefore believe their way to be the right way. This means that when you adopt an alternative paradigm, your competitors will not understand what you're doing, and will see you as being 'wrong'. If you go in there with all guns blazing, when they realise what is happening, it will be too late. You will already have gained the advantage.

We sincerely hope that exposure to this material will cause you to make a major paradigm shift, a radical change in the way you perceive things to be. A paradigm shift does not require a bolt of lightning from the sky, just a flash of insight at the moment you're ready to see things in a new way. It's the moment when you look at your advertising and marketing, and for the first time, you see a 'crocodile'.

Effective advertising and marketing is based on the ability to alter perceptions. As we noted earlier, a shift in perception creates a shift in attitude, which creates a shift in behaviour, which of course is the ultimate goal of all advertising.

Having spent so much time in boardrooms throughout the years, at WAM we have become very aware of a phenomenon we call 'boardroom logic'. Boardroom logic goes like this: 'We have this product which is actually superior to the market leader, and what's more, it's less expensive. Therefore, our mission is to convey that fact to the marketplace through our advertising and marketing. When people see the error of their ways, they will switch and buy our product instead, thereby winning us market share.'

It seems so logical in the boardroom, and every day of the week vast amounts of money are allocated to advertising and marketing campaigns based entirely on this line of thinking.

However, the problem with boardroom logic is that the customer doesn't know about it. Living within a completely different paradigm, your customers and prospects use a completely different form of logic called 'perceptual logic'. Using perceptual logic, the customer sees advertising based on boardroom logic and thinks: 'How can your product be better, or even as good as the market leader? And cheaper? If you really were better and cheaper, then everybody would be buying it and *you'd* be the market leader. Something's not right here. I don't believe you.'

In order to get in tune with the way the consumer thinks, you need to make that paradigm shift; to break away from the logic of the boardroom and adopt the logic of the marketplace. You need to become a perceptual thinker.

PERCEPTUAL THINKING

The following story is true, but the name has been changed to protect the identity of the individual under discussion.

Alan Bates had a dream: to own the most innovative and successful communications equipment store in his city. His only problem was raising enough capital to make the store a reality. Through sheer hard work and by leveraging everything he owned, he finally managed to make his dream come true.

The store was truly magnificent. Not only did he stock all the top brands, but the store layout itself was quite striking, like nothing else around. Customers were led through the store along aisles laid out in a series of concentric circles which revealed all kinds of innovative displays and interactive technology. This included a group of computers which allowed customers free access to the Internet, at a time when the Internet was relatively unknown to the general public. All the demonstration mobile telephones were connected and operational, to give customers a hands-on experience of the products. All in all, he seemed to have everything going for him.

To launch the store, he created a series of aggressive product-and-price radio commercials and newspaper advertisements offering crazy, over-the-top deals on mobile phones and other communications equipment. And people stayed away in droves. Nothing he did seemed to work. The more he dropped his prices, the less effective his advertising seemed to be.

In less than six months, he was out of business. What went wrong?

We hear stories like this all the time, and invariably the key to understanding the core problem lies in getting a firm grasp on the way the public perceives companies and brands through their advertising.

In the case of Alan Bates' store, it was probably the combined effect of several factors. Sadly, instead of coming across as an innovator, his advertising pigeon-holed him as just another mobile phone discounter in an already crowded market. His real story remained untold.

It's also quite likely that many of the people exposed to his advertising simply felt it did not ring true, and for a very good reason. In the words of Al Ries in his book *Focus*:

Low prices should always be the natural consequence of some other attribute.

When something sounds just too good to be true, our response tends to be either 'What's wrong with it?', or 'What's the catch?'.

As a newcomer to the industry, Alan Bates had a credibility problem. If someone is offering crazy prices, people need to understand *why* before they feel comfortable responding. Has the retailer overstocked? Is the offer being subsidised by a supplier? Is stock being cleared to make way for a new model? Some kind of reason that makes sense to the consumer needs to be given.

For Alan Bates, another factor was that some of his competitors decided to take him head on and match his prices, knowing that he could not sustain them indefinitely. Not a good place to be.

In an industry characterised by discounting, there's no doubt that he would have been much better off had he focused on the unique, fun nature of the store itself. The odds are that he could have attracted hordes of customers, and need not have focused on price at all. Operating in a market environment in which so few retailers show any signs of innovation, particularly where exciting the customer is concerned, huge opportunities exist for companies of all kinds to show some initiative and take up the shortfall.

THE LANGUAGE DICHOTOMY

Within the context of marketing and advertising, the world consists of two distinct groups:

1   business, which manufactures and sells products and services
2   the marketplace, which uses those products and services.

To survive in business, you have to live in the world of logic and rationality. Your very survival depends on your ability to juggle cash flow projections, wages, profit and loss, legals, logistics, investments, acquisitions, and a host of other things which require logical thinking.

You're firmly established in the Land of Logical Logic, and you speak the Language of Logic, the language of rationality, organisation and systems. That is why so much advertising is focused exclusively on product and price. Logical thinking on the part of business has created a deeply entrenched conviction that discounting will attract customers better than anything else. However, it turns out that price tends to appear somewhere around fourth or fifth on the list in survey after survey, behind things like a better value package, better customer service, convenience, better back-up service, and risk reversal.

The problem you face is that your customers and prospects live in a completely different world. They live in the Land of Perceptual Logic, and speak the Language of Perception, which is the language of feelings, emotions and beliefs.

The intellectual gap between these two groups of people is so vast, it's as though they're from different planets, speaking different languages. Although they use the same words, for all the communication that happens between them they may as well be speaking in Greek and Swahili. They simply do not understand each other.

Whenever advertising fails to produce satisfactory results, you can be certain that if you dig deep enough, the culprit will turn out to be a case of misguided logical thinking. For example, an advertiser will think: 'It's costing me a fortune to run this thirty-second TV spot, so I'll maximise my investment by featuring six products instead of three or four.' This is classic boardroom logical thinking in action, and we hear the resulting cacophony of sound night after night as retailers blast the airwaves with commercials that are virtually unintelligible. The reality is that more is less, and less is more. People's attention span for those kinds of frenetic retail commercials tends to be somewhere around zero.

Using logical thinking, an advertiser may think: 'I'll run a product and price commercial so that people will be dazzled by my low prices.' But the customer on the other side of the box, not having some point of reference, hasn't a clue what the real price should be, and another fat wad of advertising dollars goes down the drain.

Using logical thinking, an advertiser working on a newspaper or magazine ad will think: 'Let's put our name big and bold right there at the top of the ad so that it will grab the reader's attention.' In reality, the only person interested in the advertiser's name is the advertiser. There's something about seeing their name in print that makes advertisers go all warm and fuzzy.

If you take the time to study advertisements that work consistently, year in and year out, you'll find that David Ogilvy was right. Eighty per cent of the pulling power is in the headline. People make sense of newspapers and magazines by scanning headlines as a means of navigating their way through a maze of text. Without headlines, a newspaper would be virtually unreadable. With this in mind, it's easy to see how the advertiser and the reader are very often at odds with one another, and what has to happen for real communication to take place.

Despite the fact that most people who advertise will pay lip service to the idea that advertising should be expressed in terms of benefits rather than features, an evening's television viewing will reveal commercial after commercial focusing exclusively on product features. There are probably many reasons for this odd fact of life, ranging from ego to a lack of understanding of the way people think and the real reasons they do the things they do.

You don't have to think that way. The more you begin to align your communications with the marketplace with the way people think, the more effective those communications will be. Using logical thinking to create effective advertising is usually an exercise in futility. It almost never works because you're speaking a completely different language. The answer is simple.

To communicate with the marketplace in the most effective way, you must first cross over and enter another world and learn to speak another language, the Language of Perception.

Perceptual thinking is a concept that is easy to grasp intellectually, but to make it an integrated part of your approach to business is a practised skill.

Perceptual thinking is not something that comes easily to most people. It is not the natural approach to problem-solving. To be a good business manager is to be a good logical thinker. Logical thinking is essential for all areas of business activity, with the exception of the tactical and creative areas of advertising and marketing. At this level, logical thinking can produce disastrous results, because it can be completely at odds with the way your prospect thinks.

To engage in perceptual thinking is to metaphorically exit your own mind with all its facts, figures, preconceptions, predispositions, prejudices, and intimate knowledge of not only your own business, but of your industry in general. You then enter and occupy, and think with and through the mind of your prospect. From this perspective, logical thinking makes little or no sense.

It's a big mistake to assume your prospect understands anything at all about your product or service. Your prospect almost never sees your product the same way you do. His or her awareness of your product is almost always limited to a vague series of impressions and unsupported conjecture. This awareness can only be perceptual, not logical in nature. From your prospect's viewpoint, however, that conjecture and series of vague impressions equals objective reality; the unequivocal truth.

We know this is true because of the research we at WAM conduct for companies on a daily basis. These people are often stunned by the degree of consumer ignorance of their products and corporate philoso-phies, despite millions of dollars being spent annually on marketing and advertising. Your task is to reframe those past advertising messages that have become dim, fuzzy and diffused, and to translate them into the Language of Perception.

To influence your prospect's belief patterns through perceptual thinking, you have to use the limited information that exists in your prospect's mind as a base, and then build on it. How do you find out what's in your prospect's mind? You ask!

If you can get ego out of the way long enough to ask the right ques-tions, and are not shocked by the answers, people will tell you every-thing you need to know in order to get your advertising and marketing communications in tune with the way they think. Their reality may not be your reality, but it's the only one you have to work with.

You have to create a situation whereby your prospect's 'logical' thinking is the same as your perceptual thinking. Only then can you communicate, and begin to work on influencing people's buying decisions.

After a lifetime of logical thinking, to suddenly engage in percep-tual thinking is way outside many people's comfort zone. It is an un-natural way to think, and is the mental equivalent of walking into quicksand, parachute jumping or firewalking.

When large amounts of advertising dollars and crucial sales are hanging on the quality of your strategic and creative decisions, it's not easy to trust blindly what is, to borrow a term from the computer industry, fuzzy logic. Your comfort zone decreases as the lines of logic become blurred. Logic has become our safety net.

But the fact remains that until you learn to think the way your customer thinks, you're probably not going to get it right. You want to sell to the customer for logical reasons, and the customer wants to buy for perceptual reasons. The two simply do not mix.

Develop the conscious habit of looking at your advertising through your prospect's eyes rather than your own, and determining whether it falls into the category of 'buy from me', or 'this is what I can do for you' advertising. Perceptual thinking is the key to getting all this right.

Here's a simple way to determine your mode of thinking. Ask your-self these two questions:

1   'Am I trying to calculate something here?' If so, then use logical thinking.
2   'Am I trying to influence somebody here?' If so, then use perceptual thinking.

THE NATURE OF BELIEFS

Tom Peters said it all with his famous quote:

Perception is all there is.

Notice he didn't say 'Perception is neat', or 'Perception is half the battle'. Perception really is *everything*, because what happens next absolutely depends on it. Every buying decision is predicated on a belief, and belief begins with a perception.

Depending upon its degree of intensity, a belief falls somewhere within the following sequence of five stages:

1 a perception (awareness)
2 a notion (a gut feeling or idea)
3 an opinion (a firmly held notion)
4 a belief (a firmly held opinion)
5 a conviction (a firmly held belief).
    None of these stages of belief has anything whatever to do with reality.
As Anthony Robbins points out in his bestselling book, *Awaken The Giant Within*:

Most people treat a belief as if it's a thing, when really all it is is a feeling of certainty about something.

A belief is just a feeling of certainty, not a statement of fact. The best product or the best offer in the world will be impotent until it is balanced by a corresponding perception, and creating that perception, that feeling of certainty, is what this book is all about.

Your task as an advertising and marketing professional is to frame your communications with the marketplace so that your prospects are led through this progressive belief sequence over time, to as high a level as possible. A customer who holds a firm conviction that your product is the best there is, is yours for life; as long as you continue to foster that attitude.

IN ORDER TO BELIEVE, YOU MUST FIRST PERCEIVE

It's worth reiterating here that belief is based on certainty, not reality. The two may coincide, but not necessarily. The business world abounds with examples of public perception being at odds with the facts.

Take for example the videotape format battle that went on in the early 1980s between Beta and VHS. Which was the better system really? Does it matter? Anybody who knows anything about it will tell you that without a doubt, the Beta system developed by Sony looked better, worked better, and was unquestionably superior to the VHS format.

Unfortunately for Sony, the battle was lost at the perceptual level in the public mind through superior marketing by the advocates of the VHS system, and the rest is history.

The same thing is happening between Windows for the PC, and Apple. When Microsoft released 'Windows '95', it was touted as the most wonderful innovation ever to hit the computer industry, with features like 'Plug and Play'. Apple users viewed this gigantic marketing splurge with confused amazement, because Apple has had all of these features operating for years, many of them since the very first Apple Macintosh. Anybody who is equally familiar with the Windows and Apple systems will tell you that Apple is without a doubt the best, the most functional, versatile, and user-friendly computer system on the market today.

Apple is the undisputed world leader in the recording and manipulating of digital audio and video, and in desktop publishing and graphic design. You can be sure that the professionals worldwide who use Apple computers exclusively have checked out their options and know what they're talking about.

But the fact is that in the latter half of 1995, Apple found itself in trouble. The sheer media weight of Microsoft's unprecedented, brilliant marketing campaign for 'Windows '95' influenced public perception to the point where Apple's survival in the long term is now in doubt. Perception really is everything.

GETTING YOUR FOCUS ON TRACK

Here's an interesting exercise. Imagine for a moment you have done your homework, and discovered your ideal prospect, your Central Demographic Model. It turns out to be a male who corresponds exactly to your ideal demographic and psychographic profiles, and whose name happens to be John Jones.

Now imagine that your task is to create an advertisement that will absolutely grab his undivided attention. It must rivet him to the point where he would stop the car to listen, or shoosh the people around him so that he wouldn't miss anything. Can you see how you could do that?

When we take people through this exercise at our business development seminars, they tend to come up with all kinds of crazy ideas, none of which is usually very practical. There is, however, one approach guaranteed to get results. You simply start the advertisement with the opening words: 'The following commercial is all about John Jones.'

How do you think John Jones might react if he heard or saw his name in an advertisement? How would *you* react if you heard your name in an actual advertisement? Don't you think it would grab your undivided attention?

The message implicit in that little exercise is so important, so intrinsic, that the following nine words should be framed and hung on the wall in your office:

•

>> **Advertising should be about the *customer*, not the commodity.**

•

Let's take that idea further. Imagine for a moment that technology has advanced to the point where mainstream advertising can now target individuals in the marketplace rather than just reaching them *en masse*.

Under these conditions, how might you now verbalise your advertising message to John Jones? First of all, you'd be able to express it in a way never before possible, as in a personalised letter. You'd be able to say something like: 'John, have you ever thought how good it would be if you could … '

You'd be able to capture his immediate attention, his sense of self-interest, by using his name right there in the advertisement. What do you think that might do to your level of customer response? Do you think John might feel more involved in what you have to say to him? Absolutely.

The good news is that you don't need any further advances in technology to produce that outcome. You can do it right now, in your very next advertisement.

Pick a name, any name, and write your next advertisement specifically to that person, following the philosophy advocated in this book. Your advertisement is then personalised, with that person's name sprinkled throughout it. Then go through and massage the copy, changing all the personal name references to 'you' and 'yours'. Reading that advertisement, this person will still feel and react as though it were addressed to him or her personally.

HOW DOES YOUR PAST ADVERTISING STACK UP?

It's very easy to pay lip service to the idea that advertising should be about the customer, but the acid test is to dig out your past year's advertisements, and also your competitors', and see how many of them were about the customer, and how many were about your commodity. Take a good hard look.

Do they speak the Language of Perception, or the Language of Logic? If you were to pin one of your past newspaper or magazine advertisements up on a wall and look at it from across the room, what would you notice first? Your name? Your company logo? Or would you notice a big fat meme in the form of a headline statement that hits a nerve, tapping directly into your prospect's area of self-interest? Is your advertising about the customer, or the commodity?

If your competitors are operating from a position of logic, then you have the opportunity to move forward and create a competitive edge by adopting the concept of perceptual thinking. Your advertisements will have a far greater appeal because they will be customer-focused rather than product-focused. Remember that people don't care about you or your product. They care only about their own self-interest.

SEPARATING YOURSELF FROM THE CROWD

Only a very small proportion of people who advertise have any real awareness of the concept of perceptual thinking. If you doubt this, take a random sampling of the advertising you see around you and you'll see that it's true. Yet creating effective advertising long term absolutely depends on your ability to work with this fundamental concept.

Interestingly, the people who do understand perceptual thinking tend to be the direct response marketers, the people who live or die on the effectiveness of their advertising. For these people, their survival depends upon advertising which is accountable, tested, tabulated, tracked and measured to the decimal point. You see them as regular as clockwork in magazines and newspapers, on TV and radio day in and day out, year in and year out, running essentially the same advertisements over and over again. Why? Because they work.

Now that you're aware of the concept of perceptual thinking, you'll begin to recognise it when you see it in the media, because you now have a name for it. Without a name, you see these commercials as just being special in some way, without quite being able to define the reason why.

The secret of successful advertising and marketing lies in the ability to get in tune with the psychology of the marketplace. As we've seen, this is often easier said than done. The message in this chapter is that every person on the planet is locked into a totally subjective version of reality by virtue of the way they perceive the world to be; their individual paradigm. Their ability to perceive this subjective reality is clouded by the various kinds of paradigm overlaps which occur within any culture.

As we noted in Chapter 5, one of the most difficult concepts for many business managers to grasp is that market leadership of any kind has very little to do with fact, and almost everything to do with perception. If people perceive you to be the experts, then you are. If people perceive you to be just about anything at all, then you are. That's all there is to it.

If people perceive a competitive product, service or brand to be better than yours, then the most futile thing you can do is to tell them in essence that they're wrong. That only serves to make things worse. You have to think in terms of a paradigm shift. This means invoking the law of polarity and focusing on another equal, but opposite, attribute.

Remember that set of finely balanced scales with equal weights on each side? They sit there in a state of equilibrium, just like two companies in a state of market parity. However, you have only to add a tiny bit of extra weight to either side of the scales to tip the balance. Remember that market parity works in exactly the same way. When two or more companies are evenly matched in the public mind, the power of perception is such that it doesn't take much to upset the balance and tip people over the edge and to come down in favour of one of them.

When you get your thinking in harmony with the psychology of the marketplace, you'll find you have a natural affinity with the concepts espoused in this book, and take to them like a duck to water – and blitz your competition in the process.

THE MAIN POINTS

-

1 >> UNDERSTANDING THE SYSTEM

-

The secret to successful advertising is to understand how your customers and prospects think, and why they do the things they do. Without an understanding of concepts like memes, emotional hot buttons, the RAS, mnemonic recall triggers and scotomas, you're quite literally flying blind. You're walking through the advertising equivalent of a minefield without a map. Do whatever it takes to get an understanding of how the system works, and then make it work for you rather than against you.

-

2 >> THE POWER OF THE PARADIGM

-

Your paradigm is the perceptual 'lens' through which you see the world. It's your world view; the way you perceive things to be. As we go through life, we experience profound, even cataclysmic, perceptual upheavals called paradigm shifts. After a paradigm shift, you can't ever see things in quite the same way, even if you want to. Creating a positive paradigm shift in the mind of the consumer is what opens the door to market leadership.

-

3 >> LOOK AT THE MARKETPLACE AND SEE A 'CROCODILE'

-

If you have never seen one of those three-dimensional pictures, it's worth getting hold of one to see what it's all about. The chances are that the first time you look at it, you won't be able to see anything but a meaningless repeated pattern. If you have the patience to persist, to look at the picture in a certain way, you'll have the unique experience of seeing the picture transform into something completely different; something that was there all the time, but beyond your ability to see because of your existing paradigm, and the accepted way of looking at pictures.

This experience is a perfect analogy of the way you could be seeing the marketplace. Often your old paradigm, the accepted way of approaching advertising, can be holding you back. If you can make the break and see things in terms of memes, Hot Zones and Activators, and the other concepts which underpin this book, before too long, you'll look at the marketplace and see a 'crocodile'; a completely different reality that will put you in harmony with your customers and prospects rather than being in conflict with them.

•

4 >> COLLECTIVE PARADIGMS

•

When you buy into a group or organisation of any kind, you also buy into the rules, regulations, values, attitudes and beliefs that give that paradigm its substance and form. This applies to religions, politics, social organisations and cults, and their effects can be far-reaching and quite profound. The distinguishing characteristic of a collective paradigm is that the individuals within it have a common view of the world and the way they believe things to be, a view that might be completely at odds with the way people outside that collective paradigm see it.

•

5 >> THE COLLECTIVE PARADIGM OF THE MARKETPLACE

•

Although the marketplace consists of a bewildering mix of cultures and social extremes, when it comes to satisfying their material wants and needs there is a significant collective paradigm overlap in the way people perceive suppliers of goods and services, and in the way they relate to them.

The collective paradigm of the marketplace has the ultimate power to kill your product stone dead, or to elevate it to the status of market leader. It all depends on how you frame your communications with that vast body of people, your future prospects.

The distinguishing feature of the collective paradigm of the marketplace is that people tend to respond first to emotion, and then use logic to rationalise their decision. To approach your advertising in terms of logical argument is a big mistake. Logic invariably relates to your commodity, whereas perception invariably relates to your real *product,* which, as we have seen, is always an emotion.

•

6 >> BOARDROOM LOGIC

•

Boardroom logic is the pragmatic, hard-nosed logic characteristic of accountants and business managers everywhere. It speaks the language of mathematics, organisation and systems. Typically, boardroom logic says: 'We have this product which is actually superior to the market leader and, what's more, it's less expensive. Therefore, our mission is to convey that fact to the marketplace through our advertising and marketing. When people see the error of their ways, they will switch and buy our product instead, thereby winning us market share.' It makes so much sense in the boardroom, and every day of the week vast amounts of money are wasted on ineffective advertising and marketing campaigns based entirely on this line of thinking.

The problem with boardroom logic is that the customer doesn't know about it. Living within a completely different paradigm, consumers use a completely different form of logic called perceptual logic; the logic of feelings, emotions and beliefs. The two simply do not mix. The answer is to get in tune with your customers and prospects and become a perceptual thinker.

•

7 >> PERCEPTUAL THINKING

•

To engage in perceptual thinking is to metaphorically exit your own mind with all its facts, figures, preconceptions, prejudices, and intimate knowledge of not only your own business, but of your industry in general. You then enter and occupy, and think with and through, the mind of your prospect. From this perspective, logical thinking makes little or no sense.

•

8 >> THE NATURE OF BELIEFS

•

A belief is nothing more than a feeling of certainty about what something means. Depending upon its degree of intensity, a belief falls somewhere within the following sequence of five stages:

1 a perception (awareness)
2 a notion (a gut feeling or idea)
3 an opinion (a firmly held notion)
4 a belief (a firmly held opinion)
5 a conviction (a firmly held belief).

None of these stages of belief has anything whatever to do with reality.

CHAPTER 9

CONCLUSION

Synergy: (sinergy) n. To produce an effect greater than the sum of the individual parts.

The WAM Rapid Response System grew out of a deep understanding of the psychology of the marketplace, built up over thirty years of working with every conceivable type of product, service and brand, and by observing what worked and what did not. This level of experience has led to the firm conviction that business and consumers are as different as chalk and cheese in the way they think.

Much of the advertising and marketing material available today is based on a technology that is half a century out of date. Ideas and techniques that served so well in the past don't seem to work any more because the customer has become smarter, more sophisticated and more cynical than at any previous time in history.

Brand loyalty is at an all-time low. We have entered an era where people are no longer prepared to pay a premium without good reason. They've discovered that more expensive does not necessarily mean better, nor does less expensive necessarily mean shoddy. There are a lot of house brands out there which are every bit as good as the market leaders; in fact many of them contain the identical product, and are simply rebadged. More than anything, people are looking for real value for their money.

The big difference with retail advertising in particular as we enter a new millennium is that consumers are no longer fooled by bogus claims, patronising offers, contrived discount sales and transparent marketing hype. They see right through it, they're repelled by it, and see it as an insult to their intelligence.

Now more than ever, you need to align yourself with the idea that advertising is about matching products and services to needs. The business manager who can do this in a way that adds real value to the consumer is going to take market share away from the traditional hype merchants and win the day.

Resistance to advertising can be thought of as a type of friction. Humans have been looking for ways to combat friction of all kinds since the dawn of time. Friction causes machinery to wear out before its time and relationships to fall apart, including the relationship between business and the customer.

Conversely, the removal of friction allows freight trains to pull almost unbelievable loads effortlessly along steel rails, and creates the environment for relationships of all kinds to blossom and stand the test of time.

It is the removal of cognitive friction that holds the key to effective advertising and marketing. There are many links in the chain that connects your product, service or brand with consumer preferences in the marketplace. The WAM Rapid Response System has been designed to ensure that every link of this chain is smooth and unbroken, so that your message is delivered cleanly and concisely.

Keep in mind that any time people are not responding to advertising, it is because of any or all of the four basic reasons noted in Chapter 7. It may be simply that they weren't in the market. It may be that they were never exposed to it in the first place either because of poor media planning, or because the advertisement failed to flag them down and connect as a direct result of poor communication skills. Perhaps they were not given a good enough reason to respond, or by the time they were ready to make a buying decision, they forgot who the advertiser was. The WAM Rapid Response System has been designed specifically to flip all of these issues around and get them working *for* you, rather than against you.

You will remember we began this whole discussion with the concept of memes. To be effective in the long term, advertising needs to be built around a big idea, something capable of kick-starting a product or brand and driving it for at least five years. This is why the ability to express ideas and concepts as self-explanatory symbols, contagious memes, is indispensable to the advertising process. Sadly, however, you could probably line up the next hundred advertisements you encounter, and not find an exciting idea between the lot of them. This can only be good news for anybody with the kinds of skills we're advocating and teaching in this book.

If you take the time to study advertisements that have proven to be effective in pulling a massive consumer response, you will find that the thing that triggered the response was a meme. For that reason, it's worth developing the habit of looking at advertising from a memetic perspective, and noting advertisements that use memes to good effect.

Memes have basically four unique attributes which make them quite invaluable, even indispensable, to the advertising and marketing process:

1   They allow the consumer to grasp quite complex concepts in an instant. A person who had never heard of the Sussan fashion chain would have no indication of what the company was all about from the name alone. But the meme 'This goes with that at Sussan' says it all. It takes the idea of an integrated 'mix and match' company philosophy, and condenses it into a self-explanatory symbol in the form of a simple, six-word statement. That is the power of the meme.

2   Because a meme effectively chunks a lot of information into a small space, it gives you the opportunity to build more supporting material into your advertisements.

3   Because of their extreme simplicity, memes enter the mind with impunity at the pre-cognitive level, and immediately begin altering perceptions and changing attitudes. From an advertising and marketing perspective, this attribute alone renders the meme priceless.

4   A meme can be made to be 'sticky', and become hardwired into the mind. As we noted earlier, when you say: 'Nine nines are eighty-one', you are not *remembering* anything. You are basically hitting 'Play', and

activating a high-fidelity digital stereo recording created in childhood. When you recall a strapline at the moment of a buying decision, you are repeating that exact process. Through repetition, a strapline articulated as a sticky recall meme will rapidly cause a product or brand name to become hardwired into the minds of millions of people.

We identified the place where all the action is, and where the long-term profits are: the Inner Circle. As any business manager knows, the cost of acquiring a new customer through advertising can be staggering when you relate it to your total spend. However, if you can induce that customer to come back again and again, a new dynamic called 'marginal net worth' enters the picture, and you can begin to think in terms of factoring in the lifetime value of a customer. For that reason the Inner Circle is the name of the game. Everything about the WAM Rapid Response System is designed to get you inside this intriguing haven of security.

The difficulty with trying to get inside the Inner Circle relates to the friction referred to earlier in this chapter. Standing between you and the Inner Circle are those five very specific and very sensitive areas of resistance in your prospect we call 'Hot Zones'. Because of their primal need for security, people will throw up barriers to your advertising until you do all of the following:

1   Link your product or brand name to an engaging idea. This gives people a crystal clear understanding of who you are, where you fit into their world, and exactly how you might relate to their needs and wants.

2   Cause them to believe that buying from you will result in a significant improvement in the way they feel.

3   Create an environment where they trust you, and perceive you to be a more attractive buying option than any of your competitors.

4   Through repetition over time, hardwire your product or brand name into people's minds as a mnemonic recall trigger; a high-fidelity digital recording which the mind, purely out of its own self-interest, triggers at the precise moment a buying decision is required.

5   Remove the obstacles to communication and allow the friction-free flow of information from media to mind.

These five fundamental issues are encompassed in the five Activators. Your own intuition will tell you that if you can break down all of those five barriers to communication you can't help but put yourself ahead of the game. Most people who advertise don't have the distinctions to even recognise, much less neutralise, those five Hot Zones.

Your main competitors are almost certain to be operating well inside the confines of the old paradigm. If they happen to be with an advertising agency, the odds are that the agency will be operating within a mindset which encourages tricky word play, 'creative' solutions, non-accountable institutional advertising, and aesthetics over communication. If you doubt this, just look around you.

If you make the decision to become proactive and get into the system boots and all, there is no doubt that you will succeed beyond your wildest dreams, if only because there is so little real competition out there. Remember the set of scales. It doesn't take much to tip the balance and bring people firmly down in your favour.

We spent some time discussing the nature of beliefs. Right here and now, believe that no matter how identical your company, product or brand may appear to be in the marketplace, there is *always* an angle. Take the time to identify just one finely focused attribute of your company or brand. This attribute must comply with the following:

1   Unlike a short-term promotional idea, it must have the potential to become your primary focus, your driving force, for many years to come.

2   It must be something the customer finds highly attractive.

3   You must be able to deliver on your promise to a high degree of excellence, on an ongoing basis.

4   It must be something none of your competitors is talking about.

If you can isolate and identify that tightly focused niche, you're only a short step away from developing that lethal marketing weapon called a 'Customer Buying Advantage'. With a CBA in the equation, you suddenly find you have a fascinating story to tell, and your customers and prospects will be more than willing to listen, because it's in their own self-interest to do so.

Ultimately, the extreme effectiveness of the WAM Rapid Response System is derived from the power of synergy. If you look around, you'll notice many advertisers who use one or two of these concepts very well. If you use any one of them on its own, you'll produce an effect. Two is better, and three is better still. But if you religiously utilise *all* of these interlocking concepts consistently and concurrently, their relative relationships change as they interact to produce a multiplier effect. Creating that synergistic effect is what this book is all about.

THE WAM CUSTOMER ACQUISITION SEQUENCE

The ultimate outcome of any advertising and marketing program should be to:

1   acquire brand new customers
2   lock them into a buying cycle – each repeat purchase is then free from the crippling initial cost of acquiring a customer.

There is an initial period when the consumer is basically unaware of your product, service or brand. From that point, as consumers are exposed to more and more of your advertising, the object of the exercise is to lead them through a sequence. Most advertising, however, fails to achieve this.

1   **Brand recognition**
Brand recognition is a low-grade consciousness of your product, service or brand in the public mind. Your advertising has made some impression, but not enough to be effective. This is as far as many advertisers ever get, because of poor communication, or inadequate media penetration, or both.

2   **Brand awareness**
Brand awareness happens when your brand name becomes familiar

to large numbers of people within your target market. In a research situation, a person may say something like: 'Yes, I'm aware of Brand A. I've never bought it, but I'm aware of it.' Brand awareness is crucial to the success of any advertising strategy, but on its own, it is still not enough. You need to progress to the next stage.

3   **Brand recall**

Brand recall occurs when, at the moment of a buying decision, a consumer is able to produce a menu of buying options from top of mind. The moral here is that if you're not on that shortlist, you're not in the game. Mnemonic recall triggers, sticky memes, hold the key. Brand recall is as far as most advertisers go. But to achieve that ongoing buying cycle mentioned above, you need to move on to the fourth and final stage.

4   **Brand preference**

Brand preference happens when a consumer says: 'I can recall Brand X, Brand Y and Brand Z, but I choose Brand X because ...' Making this happen is the object of this book. The secret is to use your existing advertising budget to move people further along the Customer Acquisition Sequence than would normally be possible, simply by working smarter.

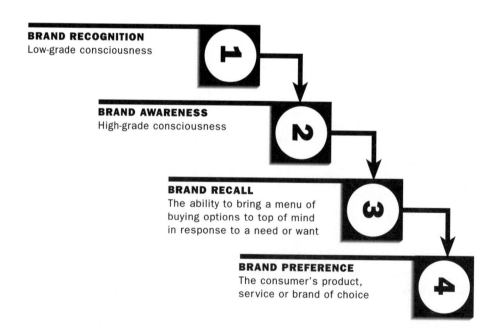

BRAND RECOGNITION
Low-grade consciousness
1

BRAND AWARENESS
High-grade consciousness
2

BRAND RECALL
The ability to bring a menu of buying options to top of mind in response to a need or want
3

BRAND PREFERENCE
The consumer's product, service or brand of choice
4

THE FIVE HOT ZONES

The five Hot Zones stem from the fact that despite the many differences that exist between individuals, there are certain key characteristics of the human psyche which cross all boundaries. They are cross-cultural and common to all age groups, socio-economic groups, religious groups and nationalities. They also have a profound effect on the marketing process, and constitute formidable barriers to the Inner Circle.

Although there are many of these universal human traits, we have identified the five which most impact upon your ability to connect with people through your marketing and advertising. These barriers, or Hot Zones, are so fundamental that they can be regarded as universal laws of nature.

1   **Identity**
    To make sense of a complex world, people have a fundamental need to pigeon-hole and classify everything in order to understand what things mean, and how to relate to them. Your product or brand name must convey a definitive meaning beyond that of simply an industry participant.

2   **Emotion**
    The most important thing in people's lives at any given moment is the way they feel. You must connect with them at the emotional level.

3   **Self-interest**

The number one motivator of human behaviour is self-interest. You must clearly indicate how and why your prospect's sense of self-interest will be best served by buying from you rather than a competitor.

4   **Recall**

People's short-term memory is extremely volatile, and evaporates very quickly. You must provide a way to help people to remember your brand or product name at the time they're ready to make a buying decision.

5   **Resentment**

People tend to have an underlying resentment towards advertising and see it as an intrusion, an invasion of their privacy. Consequently they tend to ignore it. You must find a way to break through this growing tide of resentment and connect with people in a way that they find both appealing and engaging.

To have any hope of success, advertising must find a way to align itself with these human traits or propensities, in a way that causes the ripple of attraction to flow from the consumer to the product, rather than the other way around. It is the failure to do this that causes people to shy away from advertising, particularly if they feel they are being patronised or deceived in some way.

•

>> **Any time an advertisement works, it works only because it has managed to break through at least one of these five barriers. However, very few people who create advertising have even the slightest notion of the existence of these barriers, much less a strategy for routinely dealing with them in order to create a favourable consumer response.**

•

THE WAM RAPID
RESPONSE SYSTEM

People don't run McDonald's. A system runs McDonald's, and people run the system. That is why you can buy a Mac and fries in Melbourne, Manchester or Moscow, and the product will be the same every time. The same principle should apply to your advertising. In order to get it right every time, your advertising should be systemised, and your people should run the system. Each of the five Activators is the antithesis of its corresponding Hot Zone. When you systematically turn these barriers around, you get them working for you, not against you. Minimise your errors, and you maximise your potential.

•

>> **The Rapid Response System has been encapsulated in the following model. This model has been designed to be used as a filter to allow you to evaluate the response potential of any advertising creative or strategic effort. Simply lay the advertisement (or script) and the model side by side, and systematically work your way through the advertisement.**

**Is there a big idea to drive it? Is there a
clear sense of identity? Is there a strong
emotional connection? Have you given
your prospect a feeling that buying from
you will serve his or her best interest?
Have you given your prospect a way to
recall your name six months down the track?
Would your advertisement create a feeling
of intrusion or interest in your prospect?
Evaluate all your advertising in this way, and
you cannot help but get ahead of the game.**

•

ACTIVATOR ONE

Activator One works on the basis that people are going to pigeon-hole
your product or brand whether you like it or not. It's your responsibility to tell them what you want them to pigeon-hole you *as*. If you
don't, they'll either ignore you completely, or give you a default definition of their own, and you probably won't like what you hear. The
purpose of Activator One is to have your product or brand become
synonymous with something special to the customer.

ACTIVATOR TWO

Activator Two recognises the fact that whenever you advertise, you're
in the psychology business. Contrary to popular belief, people don't
buy products and services. They buy emotional states of mind. The
purpose of Activator Two is to identify the emotional basis of the
purchase, and make that the hero of your advertising.

ACTIVATOR THREE

Because self-interest is the number one motivator of human behaviour, it makes sense to tap into this universal human trait in a big way.
The purpose of Activator Three is to give the consumer a compelling,
self-serving reason to choose you over your competition.

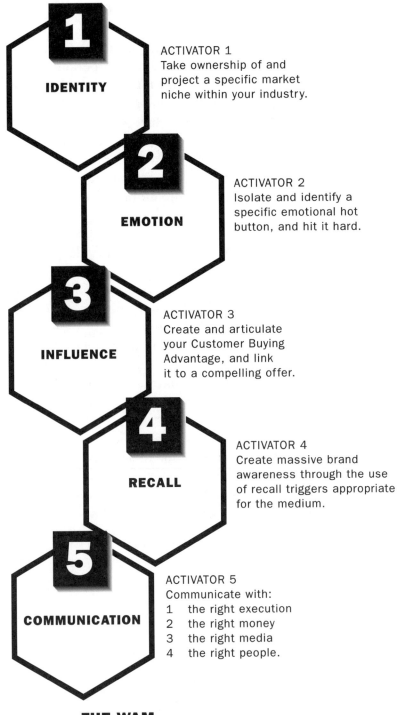

ACTIVATOR 1
Take ownership of and
project a specific market
niche within your industry.

1 IDENTITY

ACTIVATOR 2
Isolate and identify a
specific emotional hot
button, and hit it hard.

2 EMOTION

ACTIVATOR 3
Create and articulate
your Customer Buying
Advantage, and link
it to a compelling offer.

3 INFLUENCE

ACTIVATOR 4
Create massive brand
awareness through the use
of recall triggers appropriate
for the medium.

4 RECALL

ACTIVATOR 5
Communicate with:
1   the right execution
2   the right money
3   the right media
4   the right people.

5 COMMUNICATION

**THE WAM
RAPID RESPONSE SYSTEM**

ACTIVATOR FOUR

Activator Four creates massive brand recall in the larger community through the simple expedient of side-stepping people's fragile short-term memory process altogether, and tapping into a completely different part of the brain. This strategy takes advantage of people's natural affinity with mnemonics, which are in fact high-fidelity, stereophonic, digital recordings that are hardwired into the mind. These recordings are triggered in response to a need or want. The purpose of Activator Four is to bring your product or brand name to top of mind at the precise moment it's most needed: the moment of a buying decision.

ACTIVATOR FIVE

One of the main reasons why people fail to respond to advertising is because they were never actually exposed to it for any or all of three reasons:

i   The advertisement was either on the right medium at the wrong time, or the wrong medium at the right time.

ii   Even though these people may have been physically present when the advertisement was run, it failed to flag them down because of bad communication.

iii They were either Soons or Laters, and the Scotoma Effect ensured that even though your advertisement may have been right there before their eyes, they didn't actually see it at all.

The purpose of Activator Five is to communicate with the marketplace in a way that the consumer sees not as an intrusion, but as a welcome solution to a need or want.

THE WAM REACH MODEL

The marketplace consists of three distinct groups of people which we call the Nows, the Soons and the Laters.

1 THE NOWS

The Nows are those people who will actually go out and buy from either you or your competitors some time in the period from the moment your ad hits the marketplace until about forty-eight hours into the future. These people are ready to buy right *now*. The Nows constitute only a very small proportion of the whole, but are the most powerful group to address because they are about to buy.

2 THE SOONS

The Soons are the next most powerful group to consider. These are also real people who will actually go out and buy from either you or your competitors some time from about forty-eight hours after your ad hits the marketplace until about seven days into the future. Between the Nows and the Soons is a brick wall called short-term memory.

3   THE LATERS

The Laters are that massive group of real people from a week or so after the ad until a year or more into the future. These people will also buy from either you or your competitors, but don't know it yet. They are not aware that, as time goes on, they will ultimately become Soons, and then Nows. Between the Soons and the Laters is a massive brick wall created by the Reticular Activating System. Most advertising is wiped out in one fell swoop, in the psychological equivalent of a black hole called a Scotoma.

><

The WAM Reach Model highlights the fact that even though the media may assure you that you're reaching X thousands of consumers, the fact is that most of those consumers will not be impacted upon by your advertisement because they have filtered it out of existence. It has not become part of their reality. The only way to crash through the barriers created by short-term memory and the Scotoma Effect is through the astute use of mnemonics.

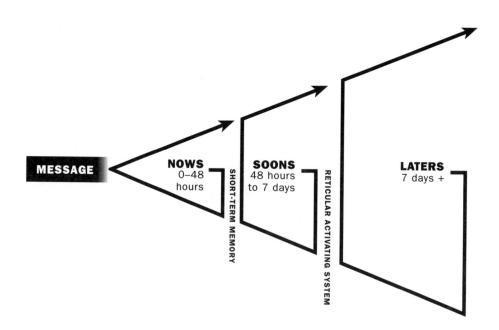

How to create a genuine competitive advantage (even if you're not unique)

Have you ever tried to create a solid, long-term competitive advantage for your company, product or brand? It can be the most mind-bending, baffling and frustrating experience, because it seems impossible. How can you create a sense of uniqueness, when you're really not unique in any way, and basically identical to your competition? It is this paradox that defeats most people who attempt it.

The purpose of this supplement is to guide you through a sequence which will, by a gradual process of elimination, produce this extraordinary marketing tool we call a Customer Buying Advantage (CBA).

Creating a CBA involves bringing all five Activators to life, and integrating them in a special way. You'll then use the power of memes to focus your message, and to communicate it to the marketplace in a way that causes people to want to buy from you.

You are now about to embark on a journey of discovery. In order to make this tantalising outcome real for you, we're going to ask you to do some things you have almost certainly never done before. Fortunately, none of your competitors is likely to have done these things either.

We encourage you to get involved and immerse yourself in the material that follows. Pull together an elite group of around eight to ten of your key people, and take them through this specialised process. The very best way to accomplish this is in the cooperative environment of a CBA workshop.

WHAT EXACTLY ARE WE LOOKING FOR?

We are looking for a way to split you off from the pack. This means developing a simple, powerful, and very specific idea. Your desired outcome is to become widely known for something special, something your customers and prospects value highly.

A common denominator among competitive companies within any industry is that the nature of the core operation tends to be essentially the same. However, people's concern that there is nothing unique about their particular company, product or brand usually turns out to be ill-founded.

>> **In searching for that magic point of difference, we rarely, if ever, focus on the core operation. We invariably turn our attention to something external, or *peripheral* to the core operation. Then, through the power of concentrated focus, we dramatise it, make it larger than life, permanently link your name to it, and then hold it out to the marketplace.**

To accomplish this, you will need to have a firm grasp of the ideas and concepts we have discussed to this point. Then you need to follow a logical sequence of events:

1   Working from a base of solid information, you need to identify and define the area of focus, or niche, which holds the most promise, and progressively work your way to your CBA through a process of elimination.
2   When you have identified the broad outline of your CBA, debate it, refine it, polish it and articulate it as a meme.
3   Make your CBA the cornerstone of your business activity.
4   Ensure that whatever happens, you always deliver on your promise.
5   Make your CBA the central theme of your advertising and marketing efforts.

6   Make certain that everybody in your organisation understands your CBA and its purpose, and is trained to be able to weave it into any customer sales enquiry.

THE FOUR PHASES OF MARKET DIFFERENTIATION

In developing a compelling, marketable point of difference, you will need to think in terms of four progressive phases:

1   **A broad market positioning**

Where exactly are you positioned in the marketplace and why? Are you actually positioned where you think you are? Would your customers and prospects agree with you? Is your Cognitive Identity the same as your Perceived Identity? (See Chapter 3.) Is your chosen market segment still a viable proposition? Do the original reasons why you chose that particular market segment still apply today? Has your broad market segment become overcrowded with competitors? Has your brand name or company name become obsolete? Is it time to consider a change? If not, then at least you have questioned the status quo.

2   **A niche**

A niche is a specific area of focus within a broad market segment. Take Woolworths, for example: there are many possible niches which it could have selected as its single, targeted area of focus. It could have chosen product depth, product range, convenience, pricepoint, wider aisles, service, home delivery, or any number of areas of consumer self-interest. However, it decided to focus on the 'fresh' niche, and captured the imagination of people right across Australia.

In focusing exclusively on this one niche, Woolworths simplified the selection process in the minds of its customers and prospects, and in the process, engaged one of the most powerful concepts in marketing: to own a word in the mind of the consumer. Woolworths still advertises specials, toys, even *petrol*, but the overall focus is always on 'fresh'.

In pre-empting and owning the 'fresh' niche, Woolworths has in effect created a marketable point of difference from nothing. Whether Woolworths is any fresher than its competitors may be a debatable point, but as far as the marketplace is concerned, at least perceptually, there's no contest.

3   **A device**

A device is a mechanism, a workable idea within a niche. You need to search with your eyes wide open. Locating a suitable device to form the mainspring of your CBA may take some creative imagination and some detective work, or it may be apparent from the outset.

A distinguishing characteristic of a device is that it is often something quite unspectacular, even boring. It has become buried within the system, and consequently its potential remains unrecognised. In the case of Robbo's Spares, the device was simply the fact that it was already offering special discounted prices to its regular customers. All we had to do was to figure out a way to transfer that idea into a more spectacular setting.

With Civic Video, the device was centred on the fact that videos sitting on shelves are a negotiable form of 'soft dollars'. If a customer has paid for a rental, it doesn't really matter which video is taken, even if it is exchanged for another. But to the customer, to be given that power represents a significant addition to the overall value package on offer.

The device which launched Domino's Pizzas in the United States was the idea that pizzas could be home delivered, hot, within a thirty-minute radius of the store, and backing that idea with a guarantee. To accomplish this, Tom Monaghan had to simplify his menu options, create new systems, and ultimately establish a franchise operation. The rest is history.

In the case of Nationwide Realty, a little digging and probing revealed the interesting fact that every ten minutes of every working day on average, Nationwide sells another home. We were able to use this device to create the Nationwide Ten Minute Turnaround, which was featured in a national television campaign. This was extended and developed into a visually powerful, stylised Nationwide Ten Minute Turnaround clock, which appeared on the 'O' of Nationwide's 'sold' signs. This simple device appealed both to vendors and buyers alike, because a fast turnaround is the name of the game in real estate.

Whether you realise it or not, lurking within your company's operating system, or within your brand, or your users' perceptions of your brand, or in their attitudes towards your brand, is something with the potential to be taken out, expanded, developed, dramatised and lifted to the level of the extraordinary. There *always* is. It's a matter of knowing what to look for.

A device is like a diamond in its rough state. The skill lies in recognising it when you see it; in seeing potential where you had not seen it before. Your device may have to be lifted out and developed. It may need to be flipped around, or modified to accommodate one or more of your customers' special wants or needs.

4   Articulation

This is the tricky part. It means thinking in terms of the spectacular, and articulating the developed concept as a compelling meme. It should be expressed as an intriguing statement *about* the customer. When you hear a good CBA, it makes you say, 'What ... ?' It comes across as being larger than life, and consequently slips easily and securely into the mind. Take another look through our CBA examples with this in mind. Reverse the process. Try looking first at the final articulation, the meme, and then take a step back and recognise the device, the underlying idea, and then observe how it was articulated. Things are always easier in hindsight. Modelling these real-life examples will help give you the basic skills and the references you will need when you come to articulate your own CBA.

In developing a CBA, there's no room for guesswork. It's far too important. Before you do anything, you need some very specific information. To get that information, you must of necessity go to the only people qualified to give it to you. You'll find these people will give it to you quite freely if you ask. They are, of course, your customers and prospects.

MARKET RESEARCH

You've reached the point where you need to carry out some basic research. If you're concerned about the cost, perhaps you need to ask yourself if you can afford *not* to. You are looking for some very specific information here, not wasting time and money acquiring facts and figures you may already have.

Shop around and source a research company to set up a simple telemarketing program designed to provide the basic information you require. Depending upon your situation and your database, you should try to take your sampling from three different groups of people:

1   Regulars

These are your regular customers.

2   Rejectors

These are people who for some reason chose not to buy from you, but whose names and telephone numbers you captured and still have on file. These were occasions when you lost the sale. Depending upon the nature of their business, many companies and brands may not have this information. It's not essential, but if you have it, it's a bonus.

3   Randoms

These are people who have not yet bought from you, but who qualify as potential customers or clients. They have a need for whatever it is you provide. They are people from within your specified target market, selected according to demographic and psychographic profiles.

The number of people surveyed in each group can vary, but is basically dictated by statistical minimums on the one hand and your budget on the other. The more people you can survey, the more reliable the result. It is not uncommon for a research company to survey as few as six hundred qualified respondents for something as important as an election, and still achieve a high degree of accuracy.

Interestingly, we have found that a simple, professional benchmark research study, in which as few as fifty respondents from each group are surveyed, will reliably identify attitudes, trends and various other indicators, accurate to within two or three percentage points of a major research study. A study like this can also be used to validate previous research.

The purpose of this research is to provide answers to several questions, all of which relate directly to the four phases of market differentiation discussed above.

1   Exactly where do your customers and prospects perceive you as being broadly positioned? How do they have you pigeon-holed, if at all? This includes identifying which word or words these people would use to describe your company or brand.

2   Exactly where do your prospects perceive each of your main competitors to be broadly positioned in the marketplace? How do they have them pigeon-holed? This includes identifying which word or words these people would use to describe each of them.

3   What available niches are there? In Chapter 5, we suggested you see your operation as an aggregation of complementary niche areas of service which combine to create the whole. Each of these segments is a possible niche.

4   Do you or any of your competitors already visibly occupy a viable niche?

5   Of your competitors who occupy a defined niche, how many have a legitimate CBA or a USP?

6   Why do people buy, or not, from you? Why did they choose to buy from your competitors? What extra special service, facility or angle is missing among suppliers generally in your industry, that the consumer

would very much like to see implemented? Where is the gap? This can be the key to identifying your device.

7   Any other information you feel might be important.

It is up to you to brief the research company so that they understand the task at hand. They will then formulate a series of questions, which may or may not need further development. By working together and drawing on their expertise, you must ensure that these questions have the best possible chance of providing definitive answers to these issues.

IN-HOUSE SURVEY

While your external research is being conducted, you have a second but equally important task to undertake: to survey a selected cross-section of your existing customers. These should be the kinds of customers of whom you'd like to have many more. If you find that Pareto's 80:20 rule applies to your organisation, this process can help you to weed out the dead wood, and target the people who can most help you to get where you want to go.

This information is vital. Experience has shown that it can be quite difficult to get staff members to give it the attention and devotion to detail it demands. Make a big issue of it, and assign specific individuals the responsibility and accountability for its correct execution.

Your in-house survey has two important functions:

1   It gives you valuable input from the perspective of the people who are at the coalface: your front-line personnel.

2   It gives you a way of cross-checking and validating the results from your external research.

INFORMATION REQUIRED FROM YOUR FRONT-LINE PERSONNEL

Create a survey form to be distributed to key personnel who are in day-to-day contact with your customers. These people should be carefully selected on the basis of their professional ability, personality, temperament and their natural affinity with people. If your company does not have its own sales team, you'll need to draw people from a retailer or dealer with whom you have a good working relationship.

Whenever it seems appropriate, have these people mention to a selection of your best customers that you are about to commence work on some advertising, and that they would appreciate some feedback. If they have a moment, would they mind helping out by answering a few quick questions? Experience has shown that when customers are approached in this way, when their advice is being sought, more often than not they are quite willing, even eager to oblige. Their comments are like gold and should be recorded with the utmost care.

Create an in-house customer questionnaire based on the questions provided by the research company. You may need to simplify or adapt it so that your personnel are comfortable with it. Be certain everybody understands the importance of having all questions answered. Incomplete questionnaires are of little use, and may actually be misleading.

WHAT DO YOUR CUSTOMERS REALLY WANT?

For the next phase of customer research, you will need to sit down with your key people and formulate a set of second- and third-level questions designed to encourage your regular customers to help you to determine the emotional basis for the purchase.

In Chapter 4 you learnt that second-level questions are interested, concerned, open-ended questions which encourage an intelligent response, such as 'What kinds of pictures do you like to take?', or 'Which area of photography particularly interests you?' Second-level questions are designed to get you into the ballpark.

Third-level questions are designed to discover the real emotional pay-off in buying your product. These are questions like 'What buzz do you get out of photography that nothing else can give you?', or 'What do you feel you *really* get out of photography?' The answers to third-level questions should reveal some kind of underlying emotion. This should then be simplified, and expressed in a single word, like 'fun', 'pride' or 'security'.

When you have these questions formulated, perhaps with different kinds of questions for different kinds of customers, create a questionnaire and have your people survey as many of your regular customers as possible. These should all be customers with whom you have an especially close relationship.

You are looking for an emotional connection common to around 80 per cent of your customers. When you are collating this information, you can chunk it down by grouping similar emotions like 'fun', 'excitement', and 'happiness', and regarding them as one category, which gives you a clearer picture.

Another idea worth considering is to set up a customer advisory group to help you to clarify these issues. This should be a special event, where you bring together a group of your most valued customers at some convenient time, provide some drinks and snacks, and get their views and suggestions on the ideas we've been discussing. The input from a group like this can be priceless, and people are generally only too happy to be involved, because they feel a sense of importance. All you need to do is ask.

When this part of the research has been carried out to your satisfaction, collate customer responses to all *third-level* questions and file them with your other in-house research.

Next, have your front-line people carry out the following, properly, promptly and efficiently:

1   List the ten most frequently asked customer questions. If there are not as many as ten, they are to list as many as they can identify. The questions people ask can provide valuable clues to your direction in formulating your CBA.

2   These questions must be listed in order of frequency. Incomplete lists, generalisations or questions out of sequence are of little use. You are looking for hard information here, so it must be carried out conscientiously.

We find that business managers are often amazed by the seemingly basic things their customers do not understand. Not only will these questions give you valuable insights into what people really want, but you will find you can base entire commercials on this information alone. You can, in effect, hold a mirror up to your prospects, taking their doubts and uncertainties, and reflect back to them a solution, and a positive outcome to their problem.

If any handwritten survey information returned to you is either ambiguous or illegible, be certain to have the person responsible clarify it well in advance so that your research is not compromised.

OTHER INFORMATION YOU WILL NEED

So much for the information to be provided by other people. Now you have some important material to collate yourself. Your CBA is directly influenced by your customers and prospects on the one hand, and your competitors on the other. You need to look very carefully at your competitors, and see exactly what is going on there, and how your CBA should relate to them:

1   Decide whether any of your competitors have anything resembling a Customer Buying Advantage or a USP implicit in their advertising. Because of the thinking and attitudes of business in general, it is unlikely that any will. If any of them do, then all you need to do is to develop a CBA with an *opposite polarity*. This means focusing on some other equal, but opposite attribute, some alternative perceptual high ground.

     If your competitor has a USP or a CBA which is price driven, then you might look at focusing your CBA on customer service, convenience or perhaps product range. Whatever it is, it must be something you can deliver with a high degree of flair, and which is important to the consumer. If none of your competitors has a USP or a CBA, this leaves the door wide open for you to move in and take the initiative. Keep in mind that a CBA rarely focuses on the core operation. It almost always focuses on something external, something peripheral.

2   Take the time to tape, clip or otherwise obtain as many samples as possible of your main competitors' advertising, and collate them. Create and maintain files on your main competitors. Look carefully at each competitor's advertising perceptually; that is, through the eyes of your customers and prospects. There are companies which specialise in supplying this type of information, some for print material, and others for TV commercials. The volume and scope of material available from these services makes them very useful indeed.

     If you were to be brutally candid, honest and unbiased, could you identify one single word or thought that accurately defines each competitor's market niche *from your prospect's point of view*? What part of the market, if any, do they already own in the public mind? The reason for this is that you want to identify a market niche for yourself which has a viable, equal but opposite polarity from that of each of your main competitors; a market niche you can pre-empt and own.

3   Take careful note of any instance of a competitor doing or promoting something compelling and self-serving to the customer that you are not.

4   Carry out a separate analysis of each of your competitors, listing every area you can identify that is peripheral to the core business. This would include things like packaged information, patented processes or designs, exclusivity, special privileges, customer training facilities, special back-up service, extended guarantees, or special finance packages.

Create a chart listing these things in an ordered way, so that you can come back to it and gradually eliminate those areas which do not interest you.

ANALYSING YOUR OWN COMPANY OR BRAND FROM A CBA PERSPECTIVE

Put your own company or brand under the microscope and examine it through the selfish eyes of your customer. 'Become' a customer for a moment and really try to see things the way they do. How does it feel? Would you want to do business with your company under different circumstances? Do your people operate from a position of empathy or sales pressure? Are they sales people, or buying facilitators? Which feels better to you?

To complete your CBA business analysis, you will need to carry out the following:

1   Isolate, identify and list every area of your business activity which impacts, or is capable of impacting, upon your customers in a way that speaks directly to their sense of self-interest. Is there some interesting or curious aspect of your operating procedure that is basically invisible to your customers?

Understand that there *is* something buried within your system that you take for granted, which would excite people if they knew about it. Take the time to think about this from your customers' perceptual point of view, and flush it out. Get it out into the open where you can see it.

2   Go through your operating system with a fine-tooth comb, and isolate and identify any conceivable soft dollar options you already have, or could develop in order to entice your customers. This relates to anything which really costs you little or nothing, but which has a high perceived value.

This could include products or services provided by a third party as a means of extending their reach into the marketplace by tapping into your customer base. Through a joint venture arrangement, and possibly on some kind of reciprocal basis, you could package or bundle these items with your own product or service. This in effect provides your customers with an end-product which has a higher than normal perceived value. This is rapidly becoming common practice, particularly among computer software companies.

SUMMARY

Here is a summary of the research you will need, so that you can keep a check on it, and make sure nothing has been omitted:

•

>> EXTERNAL RESEARCH

•

1   Regulars – your regular customers.
2   Rejectors – people who chose not to buy from you (if possible).
3   Randoms – people who have not yet bought from you.

•

>> IN-HOUSE RESEARCH
•   **(TO BE CARRIED OUT BY YOUR PEOPLE)**

1   Your customers at point of sale.
2   Answers to third-level questions, which give insights into the real emotional basis for the purchase.
3   A prioritised compilation of the ten most asked customer questions.

•

>> MANAGEMENT IN-HOUSE RESEARCH ON COMPETITORS
•

1   List details of any competitors who appear to have a CBA or USP.
2   Obtain samples of your main competitors' advertising for analysis.
3   For each of your major competitors, identify one key word you believe best defines their market niche.
4   List any instances of your competitors offering major services or benefits which you do not.
5   For each of your competitors, list anything significant you can identify as being peripheral to the core business.

•

>> MANAGEMENT IN-HOUSE RESEARCH RELATING
•   **TO YOUR OWN COMPANY**

1   Isolate, identify and list every aspect of your business activity which impacts, or is capable of impacting upon, your customers in a way that appeals to their sense of self-interest. This is your aggregation of complementary niche areas of service.
2   List any soft dollar options you can identify.
3   List any possible niche areas you can identify as being peripheral to your core operation.

IDENTIFYING YOUR IDEAL NICHE

You are now about to enter the final phase of the process. Following are thirty ways to begin the process of creating a CBA. These examples are offered as thought starters, and do not take into account other possibilities which may come to light through your research.

Take the time to go through your research findings like a detective. This includes information derived from your customers and prospects, the research you carried out on your own business, as well as your research on your competitors.

Your aim here is to identify as many additional niche areas as you can that apply to your particular industry, and add them to the thirty alternatives below. When you have created your own expanded list, spend some time on each option, even though it may not seem to be appropriate for your situation at first glance. It may spark another, altogether different train of thought. What would happen if you flipped it around somehow, or adapted it in some kind of unorthodox way?

•

>> **The secret to creativity lies in the ability to put familiar things together in an unfamiliar way. Relating things which are not normally related gets things moving, and makes the sparks fly!**

•

OWNING A POSITION IN THE MINDS OF YOUR CUSTOMERS AND PROSPECTS

For a brand to take off and fly, it must deliberately and single-mindedly set about acquiring and owning a little piece of the minds of millions of people. When we talk about 'owning a little piece of the minds of millions of people', we're not just adopting a figure of speech. It's quite real. We're talking here about owning, lock, stock and barrel, some of the most valuable real estate in the world. It has a geographic location, a physical presence, and it's located somewhere between the ears of your customers and prospects.

At this point, you need to think in terms of what seems to be missing in the marketplace from your customers' and prospects' perspective.

You're looking for an industry gap. Your research should flush some of these things out into the open.

The object is to arrive at that one specific, but elusive aspect of your operation which is of vital interest to your customers, but which none of your competitors owns in the public mind. At the same time it must be something you are comfortable with, and are prepared to elevate to the level of the spectacular. It must be a promise you are certain you can deliver on a consistent basis. You need to narrow your focus, and create the aura of a specialist. This then becomes the basis of your corporate identity.

The key to uniqueness is specialisation. You need to take one niche area of focus, one singular compelling aspect of customer interest and involvement, and make the decision to specialise in it, and become widely known for it. This should not be at the expense of anything else you do. Just develop this niche area until it becomes highly visible to your customers and prospects. Go way, way beyond the norm. Let your imagination run free, just this once, and create in your mind a vision of perfection. What would it look like? Think in terms of executing it to the point where that niche area becomes synonymous with your name in the marketplace, like Nordstroms and service. Exaggerate it and do it to the nth degree. Somewhere within this specialised niche, you will find your device.

The following thirty ways to create a CBA will help you to eliminate the irrelevant. Any additional niche areas you may have added will serve to complete the big picture. Try to home in on an issue which is in line with the findings of your research, an area which your customers see as sorely lacking in their experience.

The very best kind of CBA to adopt is one which already exists to some extent, but has become basically transparent. It's out of sight, beneath the surface, somewhere within your operating system. This means that essentially the mechanism is already in place, and that radical changes and traumatic upheavals in procedure can be kept to a bare minimum. It's 'business as usual', but this time with your CBA on board.

THIRTY WAYS TO CREATE A CBA

1 CUSTOMER SERVICE

Is outstanding customer service something you could conceivably elevate to your main perceptual area of specialisation, your market niche? Do your people already have the attitudes and skills to carry it off in the long term? Is service something your customers and prospects see as desirable, but sorely lacking in your industry? In your research, has the service ethic emerged as a dominant issue? Do any of your competitors already own the 'customer service' niche?

2 QUALITY

Is there a clearcut quality advantage inherent in your product or service? Do you use demonstrably superior materials or methods when you do what you do? Does some kind of unique technology, system or process give you a quality advantage you could translate into an effective CBA? Is outstanding quality something the bulk of your customer base is looking for? What do your research findings have to say about quality or the lack of it? Do any of your competitors already own the 'quality' niche?

3 TECHNOLOGY

Although it may be that you utilise high technology in your operation, is it something your customers and prospects are concerned about, or is it essentially invisible or irrelevant? Is a hi-tech image something you could build on in order to match the customer expectations that came through in your research? If so, does your operation look and feel hi-tech when people come to do business with you? Could the technology route lead you to your CBA? Do any of your competitors already own the 'technology' niche?

4 SPECIFICITY

Is there something about what you do that involves an interesting or unusual specific number of products, steps or processes? Did you know that when Heinz originated its famous '57 varieties' campaign, there were actually 60 varieties? They opted for 57 because it sounded more credible. People tend to accept accurate-sounding numbers as being more believable than generalities.

Building inspector Keith Jeffrey operates a company called Brisbane Home Check. In a profession which is characterised by market parity, his advertisements are quite compelling. They simply hold out the offer:

> Let Keith Jeffrey check 798 areas of your new home – *before* you buy it.

A company called DMF Manufacturing took something which was originally a transparent, routine procedure, and used specificity to gain market share through the development and implementation of 'The DMF 8 Step Project Analysis'. Is this something you could extrapolate and adapt to your situation? Could you make the concept of specificity work for you? Do any of your competitors already own the 'specificity' niche?

5   THE   PRODUCT

Is your product or service itself something so unusual or unique, that it might provide a way of differentiating you in the marketplace? Is your product so unique as to be capable of becoming a generic name like Xerox, Biro or Kleenex? Like Pureau, do you hold any patents or processes with the capability of lifting you perceptually to the level of the unusual or extraordinary? Could your product itself or one of its benefits form the basis of your CBA? Do any of your competitors already own the 'product' niche?

6   CONVENIENCE

Is convenience something you could hang your hat on? Could this be an area that might hold CBA potential for you? Do you have an extraordinary location, or enough locations, outlets or representatives to convince people that you really are extraordinarily accessible? Like Aussie Home Loans, do you have a rapid mobile 'We come to you' service? Is this unusual in your industry? Does your research indicate that convenience is an issue for your customers? Do any of your competitors already own the 'convenience' niche?

7 QUICK RESPONSE

In a world that is becoming more frenetic, frustrated and impatient with every passing day, do you or could you have systems in place which would delight your customers through your unusually quick response? Is this something your research suggests might be of vital importance to your customers and prospects? Does it indicate that they have been let down by your competitors in this regard? Is there anything you could do to ensure that you always keep one jump ahead of your competitors in this area? If you really do have a quick response aspect to your operation, could you pre-empt the idea and adopt it as your CBA? Do any of your competitors already own the 'quick response' niche?

8 AESTHETICS

Do you have particularly stunning colours, materials or artistic features inherent in your product or perhaps your premises? Like Ken Done, does your product involve striking or unique designs? Do you already have a reputation in this area? Are you arguably the best in your industry where aesthetics are concerned?

The ground floor of retailer David Jones' Elizabeth Street (Sydney) store is so uniquely opulent that it rivals Harrods of London or Galerie Lafayette in Paris. Is this an area you could hold out in order to attract more customers? Do any of your competitors already own the 'aesthetics' niche?

9 INFORMATION

Although information may not seem to be a part of your core business, is it possible that over the years you have built up a wealth of information that might be of vital interest to people if only they knew about it? Could you consider organising this information into some sort of regular newsletter which would immediately position you as the experts in your industry? Is this an area that might be worth developing and owning in the marketplace?

Might it be worth considering setting up some kind of information hotline which may be extremely useful to your customers and prospects, and give them a reason to come to you rather than your competitors? Could you then link this service to your name and hold it out as your CBA? Do any of your competitors already own the 'information' niche?

1 0   P E R S O N A L   I N V O L V E M E N T

Nobody likes dealing with underlings, especially when something is important. Is it possible that some or all of your main competitors may have grown big and impersonal to the point where they are not looking after their customers very well? Among the lower echelons of employees generally, apathy and indifference rule supreme.

This is a sore point with customers right across the board. Are you small enough and dedicated enough to make personal involvement the perceptual focal point of your business? If so, you could well have the basis of a good CBA. Do any of your competitors already own the 'personal involvement' niche?

1 1   P R E C I S I O N

Precision is a broad term with many implications. In any area of business activity, from servicing your car to mixing the exact shade of paint to match your living room carpet, accuracy and attention to detail are attributes which are sorely lacking in many businesses today. Is there any way that accuracy or precision could become your chosen point of focus? Would the words 'accurate' or 'precision' grab your prospects' attention in your particular market situation? Could this be something which would hold up as your CBA? Did this come through as being relevant in your research? Do any of your competitors already own the 'precision' niche?

1 2   D E S I G N

Are you well known as a designer? Do you or could you employ any well-known designers in your organisation? Is there something sufficiently unique or different in the design of your product that has been shown to give you a competitive advantage? Although your competitors may have something in the ballpark, is this design idea something you could pre-empt and own?

Victor Kiam, of Remington fame, was so impressed with the design of the product that he bought the company. Is there some way you could twist or bounce off this idea? Could you tie up either local or international agreements which guarantee exclusivity on something with a design aspect which might have a strong appeal to your customers? Do any of your competitors already own the 'design' niche?

1 3 P O P U L A R I T Y

One way to gain popularity is through that powerful instrument of influence called 'social proof', which we mentioned briefly in Chapter 3. If 'similar others' seem to believe something to be okay, then it must be! Is there any way you could use this principle to show the public that because 'similar others', that is, people just like themselves, find your product popular, then it is okay for them to find it popular also?

Popularity is something which may be implied. Social proof can be used as an instrument of influence in persuading people to think and behave in a certain way, creating a feeling of popularity, or at least wide acceptance. A good example of the use of this principle to validate consumer behaviour appeared on the side of a packet of CSR refined white sugar. It read:

> Recent studies by the CSIRO Division of Human Nutrition show that sugar makes up an estimated 10% of the daily energy requirements of Australians. This represents a moderate level of sugar intake, which means that most Australians can feel more comfortable about the amount of sugar in their diet.

Ten per cent sugar in our diet is moderate? Maybe, and maybe not. Has any unintended bias crept into that report? Does the CSIRO indicate just how much, if any, of that ten per cent should consist of refined white sugar and how much should be natural? In any event, a lot of Australians who happen to read that message will more than likely feel that 'If it's okay for everybody else, then it's okay for me.'

This is a classic example of the broad concept which often precedes the articulation of a CBA. In this instance, people are offered evidence in the form of social proof as a reason to abandon artificial sweeteners and come back to sugar.

Although it may have nothing whatever to do with your core operation, popularity tends to breed popularity, which means more customers. Is there any way in which you could formulate your advertising and marketing so that it demonstrates to the public your overt popularity? Do any of your competitors already own the 'popularity' niche?

14 TRUST

There are times when we all have to let go and trust that somebody will do the right thing by us. Trust is something we all need, because it relates directly to security, which is one of the most basic human needs. However, how many businesses are there that hold out trust as their competitive point of difference? Not many. Trust was the basis of the security meme which catapulted Federal Express into a position of market leadership:

> Absolutely, positively overnight.

Another that comes to mind is the pharmacy chain Amcal. Trust is the underlying theme evident in all of Amcal's corporate advertising at a time when their competitors seem to be preoccupied with price. Is trust something you could focus on and develop into your CBA? What does your research say about this? Even though each of your competitors may be every bit as deserving of trust as you are, are any of them saying so? If not, and trust is an issue in your line of business, then the door could be wide open to you. But first you must be certain. Do any of your competitors already own the 'trust' niche?

15 QUALIFICATIONS – TRAINING

Everybody wants to deal with an expert. Do you or your people happen to be more qualified than your competitors? Even if you are not, it is quite possible that your competitors are not using their qualifications as the main focus of their marketing efforts.

Next time you go to buy some sports footwear, check out The Athlete's Foot. They don't have 'sales people', they have 'fit technicians', and 'master fit technicians', and they have a special badge to prove it. This is not just some gimmick, however. The front-line people at The Athlete's Foot undergo regular and intensive training in foot anatomy and footwear technology, so that they are always up to date and can give you the benefit of their knowledge and experience. Can you think of any other footwear retailer who does it like that? Is this an idea you could adopt and perhaps modify to suit your organisation? Interestingly, The Athlete's Foot does not appear to be telling the marketplace about its level of expertise in the way that it might if it had a CBA mindset.

If people see you as being the experts, then you are. Perception is everything. You just need to do whatever it takes to sustain and perpetuate that corporate persona. Is this something you could hold out to good effect in your advertising and marketing? Do any of your competitors already own the 'qualifications' niche?

16 PRICE

By now you may have noticed our lack of enthusiasm for price as a marketing advantage. However, this applies only if you have gravitated towards price as a default tactic. If, like Jewel Food Stores, and the liquor retailer Quaffers, you have deliberately set about building your company policy around competitive pricing, then that is another matter altogether. Do you have systems in place to ensure that your pricing structure is consistently competitive? Does your advertising make the subtle distinction between 'economical' and 'cheap', between 'price' and 'value'?

Like Franklins and Tandy Electronics, is it possible that you could create a *feeling* of thriftiness in the marketplace without necessarily having the lowest prices? Could you capitalise on the difference in meaning between 'lower' and 'lowest?' Do any of your competitors already own the 'price' niche?

17 ADDED VALUE

Does your product or service happen to come with more extras or add-ons than your competitors? Would it be possible for you to do a joint venture with another company that supplies something which has a natural affinity with your product, and which you could package in some unique way? If so, could you consider setting up an exclusivity arrangement with the other supplier which could effectively block your competitors and prevent them copying you? Remember that the perception of an enhanced value package shifts the emphasis away from price.

We recently came across an instance of a supplier selling a product which required a particular type of software to make it operate. This supplier was directing customers to the software supplier in order to create sales. We suggested that he arrange to bundle the software with the product at a specially reduced rate, thereby creating a far more satisfactory end-product. Both parties came out ahead as a result. Could you take some variation of this idea and make it work? Could added value qualify as a viable candidate for your CBA? Do any of your competitors already own the 'value added' niche?

18   RISK   REVERSAL

Sales trainer Tom Hopkins once said:

> Money is a symbol of security. Ten dollars represents everything
> in your world that you can buy for ten dollars. If I ask you for the
> ten and you give it, at that moment there is a twinge of insecu-
> rity. We're here to learn how to make people feel so comfortable
> that not only will they give it to you, they'll *want* to.

Do you, or would you be prepared to, assume the risk when you
sell whatever it is you sell? By assuming the risk, you often remove
the main barrier to the purchase. If you have an industry standard
guarantee, could you learn from a company like Knebel and go out
on a limb, beyond where your competitors are prepared to go?

Don't lose sight of the fact that when you guarantee something,
you don't have to necessarily give away the shop! It just has to be
ethical. It could be that if something doesn't turn out the way it should
have, you could give your customers something: you could refund their
deposit, give them a replacement item, or anything else you care to
designate; just as long as it's done with integrity, and serves to instil a
feeling of confidence and security in your customers.

Do you have confidence in your product? Are you prepared to
stand by your customers should anything go wrong? Like Civic Video,
if you were to adopt some form of extreme risk reversal, is it possible that it would bring you so much extra business that any claims
on your guarantee become negligible? But most importantly as far
as your CBA is concerned, do any of your competitors already own
the 'risk reversal' niche?

19   THE   PEOPLE

Is there something about the people in your organisation that puts you
in a class of your own? Are they better trained? Are they fun people to do
business with? Do they have an unusual affinity with things like expertise, customer service, and going above and beyond the call of duty?

Are there more of them? Do their combined years of experience
add up to something spectacular? If yours is a people-oriented type of
business, it may be that by focusing on your people instead of your product,
you could achieve a very acceptable type of market differentiation and

develop your CBA on that basis. Do any of your competitors already own the 'people' niche?

20 THE SYSTEM

As Michael Gerber points out in his book *The E-Myth Revisited*, companies like McDonald's, Sizzler and so many other franchise operations owe their success more to a system than anything else. People don't operate McDonald's. A system operates McDonald's, and people operate the system. Do you have a system, perhaps that you have developed and patented, which in some way gives you a competitive advantage? Would this system be of interest to your customers if they knew about it? Is it something you could perfect and franchise? If so, is there a way for you to do as we have suggested many times throughout this book, and make the invisible visible? And by the way, read *The E-Myth Revisited*. It could be invaluable to you if you find yourself in this situation.

It may be that your competitors are using the same kind of system but nobody has come out and said so. If it is something that would help you to attract customers in a big way, it could be the very thing you need in order to articulate the concept in your advertising and marketing as a compelling CBA. Do any of your competitors already own the 'system' niche?

21 RANGE

Do you already have a bigger or better product range than your competitors? If your range is not the biggest, but is still very strong, is there any way you could still pre-empt the concept of range in your advertising and marketing? Are there any words you could use that might convey that feeling without coming right out and claiming it? Was range an important issue in your research? Do any of your competitors already own the 'range' niche?

22 ON TIME

Is yours the type of industry where time really is money from your customer's point of view? Do you already have systems to ensure that things happen when you say they will? Would you be prepared to guarantee it? Although Knebel has its 'Knebel Lifetime Guarantee' CBA to address the consumer market, it has adopted the 'On time' market stance for its commercial division. The TV commercial shows the presenter creating a powerful visual meme by tapping his watch every time he says the words 'on time'.

Interestingly, this is a CBA which is not just words, but is quite real. Knebel has a production policy which requires that each kitchen be completed, plastic wrapped and loaded into a trailer *two days* before the production deadline. This is an object lesson in how to create a CBA which derives its power from something that was there all the time, but hidden from view.

23 EXCLUSIVITY

Can people obtain your exclusive product or service anywhere else at all? If so, is there any way you could corner the market by setting up a true exclusivity arrangement? If not, could you pre-empt the idea of exclusivity in the marketplace? If you are a smaller player in the market, would your competitors be in a financial position to out-spend you if you tried to do this?

Even though your product may be exclusive, is there enough consumer demand for it to warrant making it the focus of your advertising and marketing? Does your research indicate that exclusivity rather than some other attribute should become the basis of your CBA? Do any of your competitors already own the 'exclusivity' niche?

24 COORDINATION

Does your organisation live or die through your ability to pull things together on a consistently reliable basis? Do people rely on your ability to meet deadlines? Is it possible that there is some offshoot of the idea of coordination, perhaps time management or networking, that could produce the basis for your CBA? The idea of coordination suggests a desirable outcome such as a trouble-free project or peace of mind, and provides the incentive to come back again. Do any of your competitors already own the 'coordination' niche?

25 SCARCITY

The law of scarcity is a powerful instrument of influence. It is human nature to want that which is in short supply. It could be a commodity, a service of some kind, or maybe exclusive information. People will go to unbelievable lengths to get something which appears to be scarce. If you have something that really *is* scarce, then you have access to a very strong motivator of human behaviour indeed.

Do you have exclusive access to this scarce resource? Does it have significant consumer relevance? Is it likely that new players could enter the market and undermine your advantage? Does your research indicate that your scarce resource is really as desirable as you feel it is? Do any of your competitors already own the 'scarcity' niche?

26 SIZE

Size is a term which has many connotations. Maybe think of it as an idea starter. Is there a way to tie size into your CBA? Apart from meaning more outlets or locations, or greater product depth or product range, could size apply to your product itself? By making it bigger or smaller, could you make it more appealing or more unique from your customer's perspective?

Could size relate to the number of customers who pass through your doors each year? Could it relate to a discount or length of guarantee? Are there any clues within your research which might relate in some way to size in one of its connotations? Do any of your competitors already own the 'size' niche?

27 SAFETY

Safety is the flip side of fear. Because safety relates directly to security and peace of mind, it is a major influence in determining people's buying decisions. It could mean that a person will be safer as a result of using your product or service, or maybe that the product itself is safe to use. Could you enlist the help of some authority, either a respected individual or maybe an agency of some kind, to endorse the safety aspects of your product or service and develop this into your CBA?

Safety is a major issue for all air travellers. Although it is not expressed as a CBA, it is common knowledge that Qantas has an excellent record of air safety, and in all likelihood this has influenced many people to travel with the Flying Kangaroo rather than one of its overseas competitors. This would seem to represent a golden opportunity for Australia's national carrier to use the safety niche to create a devastating security meme, and in the process significantly increase its share of business on the world market.

Is safety an issue as far as your customers are concerned? What does your research show in this regard? Is it possible that by focusing on safety rather than your product, you might have a greater impact on your customers' sense of well-being? Do any of your competitors already own the 'safety' niche?

28   SIMPLICITY

Is your product easier to operate than your competitors'? Does it operate with less or no moving parts? Because it is simple, is it easy to clean, or easy to repair, thus eliminating downtime? Is it the quality of simplicity that gives your product its classic appeal? Is the word 'simplicity' itself something that might catch the attention of your target audience?

Rather than a product, does the term 'simplicity' refer to a system or process with a consumer benefit attached to it? Does simplicity relate directly to your customers' emotional needs? Is there a possibility that simplicity might hold the key to identifying your CBA? What does your research say about this? Do any of your competitors already own the 'simplicity' niche?

29   FLEXIBILITY

In a world where so many businesses go 'by the book' and treat customers as though they were the enemy, does your business provide a breath of fresh air by the simple expedient of being flexible? Do your people have the authority to do whatever it takes, on their own initiative, to solve customer problems? Do you bend the rules a little if it will help a customer out of a difficult situation? Do you have the kinds of people who are prepared to deliver something important to a customer after hours on the way home from the office?

Is flexibility, or the lack of it, an issue for your customers? In your research, have people expressed frustration or concern about people in your industry being too unbending or rigid in their interpretation or execution of company policy? Would the word 'flexible' as it relates to your industry convey a positive meaning to your customers? If this is the case, it may be that the flexibility route may lead you to your CBA. Do any of your competitors already own the 'flexibility' niche?

3 0   R E V E R S I N G   A   F R U S T R A T I O N

This is arguably one of the most profitable ways of arriving at your CBA with a minimum of effort. Think about your own experience. Imagine for a moment you're seriously disappointed with some kind of product or service.

How would you then feel if you saw an advertisement from another supplier who specifically guaranteed that the source of your disappointment would not happen if you bought from it? Where would you go next time?

Take a look through your research, particularly the part about consumer frustrations and irritations. Is there any way you could reverse one or more of them without creating too many problems within your organisation? Could your system be modified to accommodate this new idea? Do any of these things hold enough promise to become your principal area of focus? Understand that in effect, a CBA is *a frustration in reverse*. Do any of your competitors already own the 'frustration reversal' niche?

C R E A T I N G   Y O U R   O W N
E X P A N D E D   L I S T
O F   N I C H E   O P T I O N S

Now that you have the above list of possibilities and thought-starter questions, you will need to go through your research findings and isolate any possible market niches that may have emerged but do not appear in our thirty alternatives. From this, you should then create your own expanded list. Try to come up with some new thought-starter questions for any items you may have added.

When you have all your research collated, analysed, interpreted and summarised, and you have answers to all the issues relating to both you and your main competitors, you are ready to get down to the exciting task of developing your CBA.

You will need to have at your fingertips things like your customers' and prospects' major frustrations, and the real reasons why they either buy or do not buy from both you and your competitors. You will also need to be able to quickly put your hands on information which identifies the exact market niche that each of your competitors occupies, and whether or not they already own that position in the marketplace.

Keep in mind that your CBA is a dynamic marketing tool which is painstakingly arrived at by taking into account all of the following:

1   What your customers think, and what they want most of all.
2   What your competitors are doing, and exactly which market niches they occupy and own. It is not worth even considering a market niche which is obviously dominated by a competitor. Two companies cannot own the same niche in the mind of the consumer.
3   What you are comfortable in adopting. It has to be something that fits into your existing business structure as easily as possible. Anything that requires an overnight change in attitudes or corporate culture is probably not going to work. Ideally, you will be able to use the collective focus of the group to identify some existing facet of your business which can be lifted out, cleaned up, polished, expanded and dramatised in a way that does not upset the corporate applecart.

Your CBA is going to be based on a synthesis of all these things. As a result of this process, you will be adopting a stance which is in harmony with your customers' needs and desires, you will be separated from your competitors by the dynamics of market segmentation, and you will be doing something which feels comfortable to you, and, we hope, something you were basically doing anyway.

YOUR CBA WORKSHOP

The day has come, and you are now with your people at the venue. It's time to get the show on the road. You'll need a whiteboard, a board containing loose sheets for capturing ideas you want to keep (or a whiteboard that produces photocopies), and a volunteer to write down information and ideas as things develop. You might also want to consider using an overhead projector when you're discussing your research findings. Each person will need a pad and pencil.

Although your people have all been briefed in advance, you should begin by restating the reason you are all here. Everybody must have a clear understanding of the outcome you're looking for and, even more importantly, what it will do both for themselves and the company.

Each person present must understand that it is quite possible that he or she may be the one who will happen to say just the right thing at the right time. Quite often, the person who has just uttered these words is not aware of their profound implications right then and there. Usually it is another person who picks it up, and there it is.

RULES

Before you begin, it is important you lay down some ground rules in order to get the best out of your workshop.

1 **No negativity**

You must stress that no negativity of any kind is allowed during the workshop. It takes only one person with a negative disposition to bring the whole thing undone. Anybody can judge or criticise, but it can instantly deflate the other person and mean sudden death to what may have been the basis for a great creative idea. Encourage the members of the group to respond instantly to any inadvertent negativity and immediately nip it in the bud.

We recommend you consider adopting the procedures outlined in Edward de Bono's book *The Six Thinking Hats*. The Six Hats concept is an excellent way to keep things on track, to avoid negativity, to get your team thinking creatively, to express their feelings in a way that avoids conflict, and most of all, to all pull in the one direction.

Also recommended for this purpose is de Bono's book *Parallel Thinking*. It gives the reader many fascinating insights as to why we in western society think as we do, and how we can alter our style of thinking to generate new ideas and stimulate the creative process. Parallel thinking removes judgement and criticism from the discussion and focuses on alternatives and possibilities.

2 **Nothing is too outrageous**

A creative group workshop such as this derives much of its effectiveness from the power of synergy. Something which may sound like nonsense on first hearing may spark another idea in another person, an idea which makes profound sense. This second idea would never have happened but for the first 'impractical' remark. If your people are confident they can say anything at all without fear of criticism, they're much more likely to open up.

Imagine your company is a bank, and you're conducting a CBA workshop. Somebody says: 'Let's have ballet dancers dancing on the counters'. Just as you're about to open your mouth to harpoon the idea, somebody says: 'Maybe not dancing on the counters, but how about if we were to sponsor the ballet?' It is this type of interplay that makes the sparks fly, and gets you where you want to go. Sometimes a crazy idea flipped around the other way turns out to be something quite brilliant. Encourage your people to say it before it disappears, or at least write it down. Ideas which seem to come from nowhere are often not just impulsive, but are the result of the subconscious working on the problem and bringing some aspect of the solution to the surface. When one of these intuitive ideas disappears, it is often lost forever. Sometimes an outrageous idea turns out not to be so outrageous at all when you take off your blinkers, and begin to think laterally and question the status quo.

IDENTITY AND POSITIONING

Begin by asking everybody in the room to write down on their pads the answer to the question 'Who are you?', as it relates to your company, product or brand. It must be expressed as a short, lucid, defining statement which accurately captures the way they believe the marketplace perceives your company or brand at this point in time.

This exercise establishes a point of comparison between the way you and your people see your business operation as it now stands, and the way this perception may change as you get further into the process.

There is a strong likelihood of a wide range of opinion as to who your people think you are as a company or brand. This invariably comes as a surprise to them, and points to the need for consensus if you are to project a congruent identity into the marketplace.

Your positioning statement should reflect your area of specialisation. For this reason, we suggest you take your CBA into account before you actually commit yourself to a positioning statement. If you can relate the two, you put yourself ahead of the game.

EMOTION

Have the group discuss and answer the question 'Do you have any idea of what I *really* want?', expressed from your customer's point of view. You are looking for their impressions of the *real* reasons why people buy from you, the meaning behind the meaning. What do they feel is the emotional pay-off for the customer as a direct result of buying from you? If there are several possibilities, which one do they believe is the strongest? If your people are not aware of the *real* reason customers buy from you, that hidden emotional pay-off, how can they even begin to create the kind of feeling that comes from understanding and empathy?

These answers are best expressed as simply as possible. You are looking for words like 'security', 'fun', 'pride', or 'peace of mind'. This discussion will allow you to compare their responses with your customers' responses to your third-level questions. The comparison will reveal any disparity between what your people think and what your customers think, and can only serve to improve rapport and create better 'buying facilitators'.

When you know for certain what your *real* product is (the emotion), you have the opportunity either to weave it into your CBA, or to feature it as a meme in your ongoing advertising. Find a way to express the emotion as a self-explanatory symbol. It may appear as words, a picture, a sound of some kind, an action, or it may be some kind of background imagery. It doesn't matter a great deal how you do it, as long as it works.

CUSTOMER IRRITATIONS AND FRUSTRATIONS

Now have the group discuss the question 'What do you believe is the biggest source of irritation or frustration customers experience when dealing with your *industry*?' This includes both your company and your competitors.

This part of the process is designed to get your people in tune with what is actually going on in your typical customer's mind. If there is any major disparity between what your customers think, and what your people think, there is really no contest. The customer is always right.

There is a great deal of value in discussing these customer frustrations at a time when your people are together as a group. They are more likely to realise, perhaps for the first time, the significance of these frustrations in terms of the way they impact upon your business on a daily basis. They are then in the frame of mind to resolve to do something about it.

IDENTIFYING YOUR PRESENT LEVEL OF INFLUENCE

Ask your people to answer the question 'Why should people buy from us rather than one of our competitors? Invariably people have a great amount of difficulty with this question, which is not surprising, considering the number of companies and brands that find themselves negatively affected by the curse of market parity.

Go through their list of possible options one by one, and ask them which ones your competitors would be likely to claim, even if it were not entirely true. Usually at this point, virtually everything on the list is eliminated. If there are any items still left standing, it means there are at least some areas of uniqueness to play with. Keep a record of them and see if any have the potential to be developed into a CBA.

If your group follows the normal pattern, you will get people talking about either promotional offers, or things like quality, service and those other basic attributes that constitute 'ground zero' for the customer. But with any luck, you will also get a few gems, and these are what you are looking for. One or more of their answers may be right on track. If this is the case, as it sometimes is, it can save you time and effort down the track in developing your CBA. When these ideas come from employees rather than management, they become a source of pride, and are more likely to be adopted and implemented.

HOW YOUR PEOPLE SEE YOUR IDEAL NICHE

Distribute a copy of your expanded version of 'Thirty ways to create a CBA' to each of your people, then discuss and seriously consider each of these niche possibilities. This process will enable you to identify the niche areas you and your people feel are the most viable for your company.

Using both your research information and input from the group, debate, discuss and gradually eliminate your alternatives until you are left with just one. Try to define this market niche as a single word, like 'expertise', 'exclusivity' or 'convenience'. Understand the power of owning a word in the minds of your prospects, and try to use this concept to your advantage. What is the operative word which defines your selected market niche?

At the time when Federal Express was setting up its operation in the United States, there were many market niche options it could have addressed. Federal Express chief Fred Smith had the foresight and vision to zero in on the one niche option which was most sorely needed by the marketplace, but which none of his competitors either saw as viable, or were set up to exploit. In identifying and adopting this one alternative, to the exclusion of all others, he found the gap – fast, reliable, overnight delivery of small items right across the United States. The word which defined their market niche was 'overnight'. From this simple idea came that now famous attraction meme which got FedEx off the ground, and helped it to become the first American company to achieve one billion dollars turnover in ten years:

Absolutely, positively overnight.

In retrospect, you can see how this 'overnight' idea could have been spun off any of several niche options from our thirty alternatives, such as 'on time', 'exclusivity', 'security', or 'the system'. Incidentally, from your new knowledge of memes, you may now notice that 'Absolutely, positively overnight' is actually a sophisticated compound meme created by stacking three individual memes:

1   'Absolutely, positively overnight' is an identity meme, and functions perfectly as a positioning statement.

2   'Absolutely, positively overnight' is an emotion meme, pushing the 'security' and 'trust' buttons in a big way.

3   'Absolutely, positively overnight' is an influence meme, giving both customers and prospects a compelling answer to the question 'Why should I buy from you rather than one of your competitors?' Interestingly, it sidesteps the price issue completely.

Its one weakness is that it fails to engage Activator Four, which drives brand recall. 'Absolutely, positively overnight' is a powerful mnemonic recall trigger, but does not contain the brand name. From our discussion on the dramatic effect of mnemonics, you can see how much stronger this idea would have been had it locked the brand name into the proposition. Consequently, there is no doubt that it cost the company considerably more in hard dollar terms to generate a high level of brand recall than would otherwise have been necessary.

Even so, with such a devastating compound meme working for it, it's little wonder the then fledgling freight company was able to surge ahead of its competition and gain its pre-eminent position in the American freight industry.

Interestingly, Federal Express has since made a move which is unlikely to be in its best interest. It has now dropped the 'Absolutely, positively overnight' positioning statement in favour of 'The world on time'. While this may make sense in the boardroom, as a meme it loses a lot in the translation. The words 'Federal Express' will mean 'Absolutely, positively overnight' to people all over the world for many years to come, and no amount of advertising is going to alter that fact.

'The world on time' is not a positioning statement. It's a slogan. In widening rather than narrowing its focus, for whatever reason, FedEx has blurred its profile, and as a result is less distinguishable from its many global competitors.

THE FINAL PHASE

You are now within reach of your objective. With the information and groundwork you now have, you are in a position to:

1   identify your preferred niche
2   create and articulate your positioning statement, based upon your area of specialisation, your niche
3   understand, perhaps for the first time, the *real* reasons people buy from you (emotions)
4   identify and develop the device, the idea which will underpin your CBA
5   articulate your CBA.

CREATING AND ARTICULATING YOUR POSITIONING STATEMENT

This statement should indicate not just what your name means in a literal sense, but how you want people to relate to you, and where you fit into their world. In Chapter 3, we mentioned the idea of a literal versus a perceptual identity.

When you see your business operation as an aggregation of complementary niche areas of service, you're laying the groundwork for your positioning. To stand out from the pack, you need to take on the persona of a specialist. Your positioning statement should then reflect that area of specialisation, rather than simply describe you in a way that makes you appear to be just like your competition.

For example, your positioning statement could be articulated as a literal description of your company or brand:

Aristocrat
The pickle people

However, it is far more effective to describe your area of specialisation, your point of focus as a company:

Fisher & Paykel
The innovators

When you also align the focus of your positioning statement with the focus of your CBA, you have the opportunity to create a stacked compound meme. This provides people with two levels of meaning simultaneously, making the communication process much more efficient.

Using the information from your research and input from the group, discuss, debate and gradually eliminate the possible positioning options available to you until you are left with just one. When you have identified it, articulate it in a simple clear statement.

IDENTIFYING YOUR CBA DEVICE

Now that you have established your ultimate niche, and your positioning statement is taking shape, things should appear greatly simplified. You can now direct your attention to one clearly defined area of focus.

Look at your organisation with new eyes. You need to find the mainspring to drive your CBA. Try to identify some kind of mechanism, some process within your business operation which relates to your chosen niche – something which is already up and running or something you can develop and dramatise. The opportunity you are looking for *is there* in one form or another. As a group, you need to cooperatively sift it through until somebody identifies it and recognises it for what it is. Just remember:

-
>> **There is *always* an angle.**
-

To get everybody thinking in the right direction, have your people look through our CBA examples and then go back one step. In each case, try to look *behind* the CBA until you recognise the device which underpins it. Invariably, the device is something quite simple or mundane, something that has gone unnoticed, until somebody has the imagination to lift it out and make it larger than life by transposing it into a more spectacular setting, and articulating it as a CBA.

The key to identifying a device is imagination; the ability to see something familiar in a different way, to alter your perception until you see a 'crocodile'. Experience has shown that the best creativity and imagination often come from the most unlikely people. When you take a spark of an idea and bounce it around a group of enthusiastic people, you create an environment capable of producing quite extraordinary results.

Encourage the group to think outside the square, and consider some new, even outrageous possibilities. But most importantly, just lay these possibilities out in parallel, without judging or criticising them. Everything will sort itself out at a later stage.

Edward de Bono has a useful idea which may help your people to think in different ways. He calls it the 'random word technique'. Take a dictionary, and open it up at any page. Choose some arbitrary number, say fourteen, count down fourteen words from the top of the page. If the word you stop at is not a noun, then go to the next noun. Now have the group come up with as many ideas as they can, relating their random word to your chosen CBA niche.

The idea behind this brilliant technique is to 'derail' your habitual line of thinking and kick it over onto a different track. It forces you to look at the problem from a perspective you would otherwise never have considered.

For example, if your random word was 'bottle', and your CBA niche was 'service', you are looking for as many ways as possible to relate these two normally unrelated things: A bottle has a label. Like Pureau, could you feature your competitive advantage right there on the label or packaging of your product to boost sales? A bottle is made of glass. Could glass somehow be related to customer service? Could you provide some unique kind of viewing area with circular glass walls so that your customers can see their product being prepared or serviced in some way? A bottle often has a barcode. Is there any way you could radically speed up the system by introducing the latest barcode technology, or maybe some other kind of technology, into whatever it is you do? A bottle can be used to hold water. Is there some way you could use water that relates to customer service? We heard about a restaurant where the customers' cars are washed free of charge while they dine.

Do you see the potential in this simple idea? When you relate things which are not normally related, the creative juices begin to flow. The random word technique provokes creativity, even in people who do not consider themselves to be creative. If you don't have any luck with your first word, you can always try another. It's a very powerful idea.

Set your group to work, each with a random word they are to relate to your selected niche, and give them a time limit to put some pressure on them. There is every possibility that this will produce at least one idea with the potential to hold up as a device to support your CBA.

If your niche is 'service', what could you do to elevate your service to the level of the extreme? What could you do that your competitors would never even consider doing; something which would excite and delight your customers and prospects, something guaranteed to make people talk? What could you do to not only 'dress it up', but to develop something quite innovative, and unique to your industry? What could you do to give your service such an overt presence that the public could not fail to pick up on it, and make it a topic of discussion because of its extreme nature? How far over the top could you go? How high is high? Case studies abound of companies which have become legendary through their innovative approach to customer service.

If customer service as a CBA appeals to you, we suggest you read Ken Blanchard's insightful book *Raving Fans*. It approaches the whole issue of customer service in a fresh and exciting way, and is quite inspirational. For some time now, we at WAM have been gifting the cassette tape version of *Raving Fans* to particular clients who have expressed a strong desire to develop their level of customer service.

If your niche happens to be 'on time', what kind of foolproof system could you devise that would ensure that whatever it is you do happens on time, every time? What kind of guarantee might you be able to apply to this? Whatever it is, it should be something your competitors would never do for fear of losing money by having to honour such a guarantee.

There are at least three hidden advantages in having a heavily self-punitive guarantee. Your competitors would be afraid to adopt it, it keeps you on your toes, and you attract a level of market share out of all proportion to the minimal number of claims against the guarantee. It becomes a self-regulating mechanism which ensures that you never forget your promise to the marketplace. All you have to do is to consistently deliver, or preferably over-deliver on that promise.

Record the high points of this process, and work it through until you have identified a device you all feel has CBA potential. When you have isolated and identified your device, your angle, all that remains is to articulate it. Your CBA is now just a short step away.

The final articulation of your CBA as a meme may or may not be accomplished during the course of your workshop, but you should get something very close. Invariably it comes out 'lumpy', and needs to be put through the process we outlined earlier. A meme needs to be refined, distilled, stripped down to its bare essentials, and then polished until it sparkles with clarity. It must take the form of a self-explanatory symbol representing a complete idea. At some point, the magic happens and the meme suddenly appears out of the blue, as clear as crystal.

ARTICULATING YOUR CUSTOMER BUYING ADVANTAGE

Take another look at the CBA examples we have given you, and try to emulate the thought process which might have produced them. Notice how the articulation springs directly from the device, but in a way that is quite radical, and is calculated to grab people's attention. This will give you a feel for the process, and how the idea can be refined and simplified.

Remember the first of our eight CBA qualifiers? It must be a big idea, capable of supporting a major advertising campaign. This means that right now, you're not looking for just another promotional idea. You're looking for something well beyond that. Something that transcends 'dime a dozen' promotional offers.

GOING OVER THE TOP

Go for something that sounds outrageous, even risky. Don't let fear get in your way. The idea should strike you as awesome when you first see it. However, the more breathtaking the idea, the more likely it will be that certain members of your group will insist that it won't work. When this happens, set them to work figuring out possible ways that it *can* be made to work. Often things seem unworkable only because of the way things are presently being done. What roadblocks could you remove? What could you do to change the system in order to make the impossible possible?

Another of our eight CBA qualifiers was that it must lock your name permanently and indelibly into the concept. Your product or brand name should be woven into the final statement. When you do this, you take ownership of the idea. Pre-empting a concept in this way effectively blocks any competitor from moving in and stealing it, provided you have acted decisively and driven the idea into the public mind. When you execute this correctly, you come across as the original, and anybody trying to copy you will be seen as an imitator.

Edward de Bono has a lateral thinking technique which may be useful here. When we think in our customary linear fashion, we think in terms of logical steps. A leads to B, which leads to C, which leads to D, until ultimately we arrive at a logical destination. De Bono's idea in essence is to begin by taking a quantum leap to some place you would like to be, without concerning yourself with how you got there. You then ask yourself: 'How did I get here? What steps would I have had to take in order to get to this place?' You then begin to build a bridge *backwards* until you arrive at where you are now. In this way, you can generate quite extraordinary ideas which would not normally occur to you as a linear thinker.

Can you use this idea to articulate your CBA? However you go about it, keep at it until you come up with something that feels right –

something that would fit quite comfortably into our list of examples. Hopefully, during this final process, the line you have been looking for will emerge. Often somebody has it nearly right, but not quite. From this point, it is usually not too difficult to knock it into shape.

When you have established your CBA, or at least have it basically under control, you should then take another look at your positioning statement to see if it still makes sense. Your very best outcome is to link the two as a compound meme. When you do this, you kill two birds with the one stone.

The final thing you should consider is the issue of a strapline. If brand recall is important to you, then a mnemonic recall trigger in the form of a well-crafted strapline will do wonders for you. Keep in mind, however, that you need to make an important decision. Your strapline is something you should keep intact for many years to come. The more you hardwire your brand name into people's minds in this way, the greater the brand awareness and brand recall you generate, and the more brand equity you build. Consistency over time is the key.

Consider whether your strapline is likely to outlast your CBA. Imagine for a moment you had the best CBA in the world, and some new technology suddenly rendered it obsolete. If that CBA happened to be incorporated into your strapline, you would be forced to abandon it. You can always create another CBA, but the 'real estate' you acquire in people's minds over time is priceless. For this reason, it is often wise to keep your strapline separate from your CBA.

Your strapline may, however, still link up with your positioning statement. At the end of the day, your outcome is to make the best possible use of meme technology to bring your advertising to life.

Creating an effective strapline is something of an art form. When you get it right, it can produce quite extraordinary levels of brand awareness and brand recall in a surprisingly short amount of time, depending upon the amount of media frequency you are able to establish. Take a good look at our examples and model them. Reread the chapter on recall, and you'll find everything you need to know to develop a powerful strapline that will burn your brand name into people's minds forever.

If you don't manage to get the final articulation of your CBA during your workshop, that's okay. Just keep working on it. As long as you have your basic concept, your device, it's only a matter of time before it will come to you in a flash of inspiration, probably at four in the morning. In that moment, you'll realise that it has all been worth it.

READING LIST

ADVERTISING AND MARKETING

Bottom-Up Marketing • Al Ries & Jack Trout • McGraw Hill • 1989

Communicating or Just Making Pretty Shapes • Colin Wheildon •
    Newspaper Advertising Bureau of Australia • 1995

Focus • Al Ries • Harper Business • 1996

Great Australian Advertising Campaigns • Neil Shoebridge • McGraw Hill • 1992

Horse Sense • Al Ries & Jack Trout • Plume Books • 1992

My Life in Advertising • Claude C. Hopkins • NTC • 1987

Ogilvy on Advertising • David Ogilvy • Prion • 1983

Positioning: The Battle for Your Mind • Al Ries & Jack Trout • Warner Books • 1986

Raving Fans • Ken Blanchard • Business Library • 1993

Tested Advertising Methods • John Caples • Reward Books • 1974

The Art of Writing Advertising • Interviews by Dennis Higgins •
    NTC Business Books • 1995

The 22 Immutable Laws of Marketing • Al Ries & Jack Trout • HarperCollins • 1994

The E-Myth Revisited • Michael Gerber • HarperCollins • 1995

The New Positioning • Jack Trout • McGraw Hill • 1996

CREATIVITY

How to Get Ideas • Jack Foster • Berrett-Koehler • 1996
Lateral Thinking • Edward de Bono • Pelican Books • 1985
Parallel Thinking • Edward de Bono • Penguin • 1995
Serious Creativity • Edward de Bono • HarperCollins • 1995
Textbook of Wisdom • Edward de Bono • Viking Books • 1996
The Six Thinking Hats • Edward de Bono • Penguin • 1987

MEMES

Consciousness Explained • Daniel Dennett • Penguin Books • 1991
Spiral Dynamics • Don Beck & Christopher Cowan • Blackwell • 1996
The Selfish Gene • Richard Dawkins • Oxford University Press • 1978
Virus of the Mind • Richard Brodie • Integral Press • 1996

PSYCHOLOGY

Awaken the Giant Within • Anthony Robbins • Simon & Schuster • 1992
Influence: The Psychology of Persuasion • Robert Cialdini •
    The Business Library • 1984
The Seven Habits of Highly Effective People • Stephen Covey •
    The Business Library • 1993
Perception • Irvin Rock • Scientific American Library • 1995
Emotional Intelligence • Daniel Goleman • Bloomsbury Publishing • 1996

The WAM Communications Group
is based in Sydney Australia, and conducts
specialised CBA Clinics for companies and brands.
For information call WAM on:
61 2 9869 8066 or fax: 61 2 9869 1124
or visit the WAM website at:
www.wam.net.au